HEARNES

D1110021

DATE DUE

AUG 7			

DEMCO 38-297

The Beauty of Men

Also by Andrew Holleran

Dancer from the Dance
Nights in Aruba
Ground Zero

A   N   O   V   E   L   B   Y

William Morrow and Company, Inc.   New York

PS
3558
.O3496
B43
1996

THE BEAUTY OF MEN

A N D R E W   H O L L E R A N

Missouri Western State College
Hearnes Learning Resources Center
4525 Downs Drive
St. Joseph, Missouri 64507

This is a work of fiction. The events and characters portrayed are imaginary. Their resemblance to real-life counterparts, if any, is entirely coincidental.

Copyright © 1996 by Andrew Holleran

All rights reserved. No part of this book may be reproduced or utilized in any form or by any means, electronic or mechanical, including photocopying, recording, or by any information storage or retrieval system, without permission in writing from the Publisher. Inquiries should be addressed to Permissions Department, William Morrow and Company, Inc., 1350 Avenue of the Americas, New York, N.Y. 10019.

It is the policy of William Morrow and Company, Inc., and its imprints and affiliates, recognizing the importance of preserving what has been written, to print the books we publish on acid-free paper, and we exert our best efforts to that end.

LIBRARY OF CONGRESS CATALOGING-IN-PUBLICATION DATA

Holleran, Andrew.
The beauty of men : a novel / Andrew Holleran.—1st ed.
p.   cm.
ISBN 0-688-04857-9
1. Gay men—Psychology—Fiction.   2. Aging—Fiction.   I. Title.
PS3558.03496B63   1996
813'.54—dc20   96-2035 CIP

Printed in the United States of America

First Edition

1   2   3   4   5   6   7   8   9   10

BOOK DESIGN BY FRITZ METSCH

Bodily decrepitude is wisdom; young
We loved each other and were ignorant.
    —W. B. YEATS, *After Long Silence*

The Beauty of Men

The Boat Ramp

~~~~~~

The boat ramp looks quite different depending on the time you
go there—night or day—but because it's just a sandy clearing
in the woods, it's always clean and beautiful; and because the
lake it serves is in a remote part of Florida, far from both coasts,
the place is seldom very crowded. The river that creates the
lake winds its way south through some of the last big tracts of
forest left in the northern part of the state, and the rest of the
countryside consists mostly of small towns and farms.

During the day visitors come to launch their boats, eat lunch,
or just sit; at night they come for other reasons. Teen-agers who
have no other place to go, fishermen who set out on the lake at
all hours, and men looking for each other gather there. Lately,
the latter have started coming in the afternoon. The next morning there is no trace of anyone's presence except some litter,
usually spilling out of a full garbage can, and the fact that once
every two weeks a young man drives in with his small son, opens
the utility closet behind the rest room, and erases the graffiti
on the walls. Then, after mopping the floor and washing the
urinals and washbasins, he drives off and leaves the walls to
the people who write messages on them, until, by the time he
returns, the walls are like something in ancient Pompeii: ob-
scene and lurid.

Everything else is gentle and bucolic. The live oaks on the
oval of grass, the owls that live in them, the carpet of dead
leaves, the slanting shafts of sunlight, the still, gray water of the

canal that leads, between two walls of golden weeds, to the lake through a skein of cypress trees crowned with enormous osprey nests, all give the place a secret, quiet air that is out of proportion to its size. In the far parking lot you can hear the sound of traffic on the highway; but once you have rounded the bend and reached the boat ramp itself, the only sound is the intermittent barking of some distant dog, or the wind in the trees. No matter what you think of the boat ramp, or the reason you've come here, the peace and beauty of the place steal into your soul.

Most people are not even aware it's here—the small brown sign on the two-lane highway announcing its presence is something they drive by for years without ever bothering to read. It's rare that a car or a truck slows down to turn off the highway at that point. Usually there is a motorboat on a trailer following the vehicle that turns in, but sometimes it's just a car or truck with nothing attached, like the dark-blue Buick Skylark with mud splattered on its fenders making the turn shortly after one o'clock on an April afternoon in 1995. Its driver, Mr. Lark, passed this turnoff for years without ever going down the narrow asphalt road that winds through the woods in such a fashion that the boat ramp is invisible till you come around the final curve. Nor has he ever brought a boat in here; even now, making the turn in broad daylight, Lark assumes everyone in the cars behind him is wondering why anyone should go there without one. That's why he has a few crusts of sandwich bread, an empty yogurt cup, and an apple core arranged on a paper napkin on the front seat—so that, if a policeman should ask what he's doing here, he can say, "Why, I just stopped to eat lunch."

That's what Ernie told me to do, he thinks, as he pulls up twenty feet from the red Chevrolet parked beneath the trees and shuts off his engine. How strange the way lives end up, he thinks as he twists around and removes a copy of *Men's Health* from the stack on the backseat. After waving at Ernie, he starts to read an article on six ways to get bigger biceps; then he puts that down, reaches for *Vanity Fair,* and opens it to an article on Princess Diana, as yellow flies begin to swarm through the open window. This is ridiculous, Lark thinks. There is no other word for it. I sit here reading an article about Princess Di, while Ernie, twenty feet away, reads a book about Russia, waiting for a potato chip salesman he met here two weeks ago, who may or may not come here today on his lunch hour. Ernie shaved, showered, dressed, and came over expressly to be here when the salesman drives in. I at least am on my way to Gainesville. A crucial difference. Stopping by on your way to, or from, Gainesville is acceptable—but coming here during the day to sit and wait for someone is pathetic.

Yet here I am, Lark thinks, as he folds the magazine into a cylinder, smacks a fly on the dashboard, and looks at the guts smeared across Princess Di's tiara, pretending to care about the potato chip salesman while really waiting for someone else entirely: Becker. Since he met Becker, the boat ramp has changed for Lark. He has to *pretend* he cares about the potato chip salesman.

"So why don't you ever ask him back to your house?" he says now to Ernie in the next car.

"Oh, I would never ask a stranger back to my house," Ernie says in his calm, toneless voice, turning to look at him. "First of all, I live alone; I could be robbed and murdered and no one would know. Second, my neighbor, bless her heart, notices absolutely everything that goes on in the neighborhood, and if I were to be so foolish as to start having gentlemen callers, for whatever length of time, you bet she'd see every one of them. No, I would never ask anyone back to the house. Why should I? I can get with them here."

Here, thinks Lark, on the tiled floor of a public rest room. Here, in a simple decor of classic porcelain urinals. Here, where Love has pitched his mansion in the place of excrement—the only place to meet people for miles around, those who drop in on their way to other places or come here like Ernie to sit. Harry, the prison guard, spends his vacation here, partly because he can't afford to go anywhere else, but mostly because he doesn't want to, because you never know when the man who sells potato chips is going to stop by. Ernie gets impatient when asked for descriptions—especially of clothes—but, on the other hand, he never exaggerates; so when Ernie said, "I think you'd find him attractive," Lark had to take it seriously. Though at this point it's more an irritation than a joy to have to drive over and check out the new beauty, especially since the police have started driving in and asking people for identification.

The only people who are not asked for identification are the ones like the occupants of a Jeep Cherokee with a white motorboat attached that slowly comes around the curve now, and drives down to the boat ramp itself, and backs up so that the boat and the trailer descend into the water. Three young men in baggy shorts get out and detach the boat, while he gets out of his car, quietly closing the door, and crosses the picnic area to the latrine—through the first door, which admits him to a narrow lobby, then a second, which puts him in the men's room. (The first door's squeak provides a warning to those inside.) There's no one here now, but his heart still accelerates, and his stomach still tenses, and he has to take a quick deep breath. It is the moment of adjustment upon first entering a church.

He's happiest coming here on his way back from Gainesville late at night and finding not a soul; that means he can go home at a decent hour and get to bed. Now, at one o'clock in the afternoon, the wire mesh that runs beneath the eaves lets a soft, gentle light suffuse the room; a faucet on one of the metal washbasins is quietly dripping; outside, through the mesh he can see the leaves of the oak trees. He loves it in all seasons. Late in November, on a cold, wet night, dead leaves pasted with mud to the floor, there's nothing more thrilling than sinking to your knees here; it's the essence of autumn. Now, the rest room has a different feeling. It's shadowy and cool on this sunny spring day, and the perfect silence is deepened by the drip of the faucet. The graffiti on the wall is meager. HERE 4/6/95, 3:30 P.M., one reads. HERE 4/8/95, 7:30 A.M., reads another. JESUS LOVES YOU, reads a third, the work of a minister who lives across the highway and runs a Christian preschool: a handsome man who chats up men and then asks them back to his "father's house," which, when they finally get there, turns out to be a church on County Road 305. Otherwise, the graffiti is a sort of shrine to missed connections. Sometimes all Lark has to do is read these messages to alleviate his loneliness—his favorite newspaper, until it spins out of control, as it did last spring when someone claiming to be a hung black man married to a white woman was proposing threesomes of a humiliating nature in huge block letters. That's the graffiti that embarrasses everyone. Today's is modest.

The metal partition between the toilet and the urinals, in which someone carved a hole, has been gone for some time, replaced—after a metal plate was bolted over the aperture and even that was dislodged—by a wall of brown cement blocks too dark to write anything on, which sometimes however conceals someone sitting quietly on the toilet, waiting. Today, there's only empty space when Lark walks around the wall and climbs up on the bowl to look out through the wire mesh at the scene outside. He feels as if he is looking at his life from a distance. Ernie in his red Chevrolet, reading, while, down by the narrow canal that leads eventually to the invisible lake, the trio of shirt-less teen-agers are guiding their boat as it floats free from the trailer, while the wind stirs the lowest branches of the trees around them. It's like a print by Currier & Ives, or a painting by Thomas Eakins: *The Swimming Hole.*

Americans are so beautiful: healthy bodies, good teeth, sa-lubrious childhoods, each generation taller than the last, he thinks as he climbs down off the toilet seat, goes to the dripping faucet, and tries to turn it off. I can't stand waste, he thinks, no doubt because I'm wasting my life. ("*This* is a sin!" Ernie told the minister one afternoon when they came inside and found a faucet running. "How could *any*one leave water on, when we're in the middle of a drought? And who do they think they are, leaving trash around?" he said, retrieving a plastic cup. "Do they think there are maids walking around after them, picking up? Were they all raised in châteaus?")

Lark can't quite get the drip to stop, though he reduces its frequency, and then looks around the room to see if there's any litter. A few cigarette butts in the urinals, but nothing more; he's been here when people have left turds in them. Leaving a turd in a urinal seems to Lark an act of aggression; Ernie says it's more likely an act of desperation when the only toilet is occupied. Which explanation you prefer depends on your view of human nature. Lark's is paranoid and bleak; a turd in a urinal means vandalism. Today, however, the place is almost spotless, and he stands there motionless for a few seconds, lingering as long as he can in the soft shadows of the room, which seems— devoid of the fear, the tension, the awfulness of sex—profoundly peaceful now. He could stay right here forever; it's as warm and quiet as a nursery; he's as far from his life as it is possible to be; he feels safe. Monks used to live in caves in Cappadocia— I could just as well live here, he thinks, and have elegant stationery made up, bisque linen stock with simple crimson letters saying, "The Boat Ramp."

Alas, life has its demands. Soon it's going to be two o'clock, and he has to be in Gainesville at two-thirty. So he goes outside and gets back into the car, thinking, as he brushes yellow flies away and opens up his magazine to an article on Arianna Huffington, The boat ramp is pathetic.

It's taken him more than ten years to arrive at this point— twelve years since leaving New York in 1983. He left New York when his friend Eddie was dying of a rare new cancer afflicting gay men; and the idea that you could contract a fatal illness from a single sexual encounter seemed just as preposterous as the news, over the telephone, that while visiting her goddaughter in Chicago, his mother had arisen in darkness to go to the bathroom, tripped on a rug, and broken her neck. Eddie has been dead twelve years—he died the autumn Lark's mother fell; Lark got the news one night after coming back from the rehabilitation center where his mother was living at the time. Eddie died listening to Mozart—a composer he had only just discovered—at home, completely blind, in his apartment building on Fifth Avenue, while snow fell outside. That's how a mutual friend described it, at any rate, when Lark went back for the funeral.

The year 1983 marked a deep change in his world. Lark is still waiting for someone to step forward and say, "This has all been a mistake. Let's go back to the second scene on page eight and start all over from there." But no one has. It's all stood as is. The deaths, accident, dying. The last time he saw Eddie remains the last time. He was at Eddie's apartment to have lunch; Eddie, gaunt, ill, still liked to cook for his friends; they'd had some wedding soup, even as Lark wondered with each spoonful that he swallowed, Can I get sick from this? Then they went to a video store downtown. They went at a very slow pace. Eddie could only shuffle, like an old man. They shuffled right down Fifth Avenue while Eddie told Lark about the Kaposi's sarcoma his dentist had discovered on his gums, and then came to a full stop and said, "Do you want to see them?" And before Lark could reply, Eddie pulled back his upper lip like a naughty girl lifting her skirt, so that Lark could see, hanging down like dark-purple grapes above his teeth, the tumors. Then they resumed their walk down Fifth Avenue, Eddie in a big black Perry Ellis overcoat on a warm day. When they got to the video store, it took Eddie several minutes to cross the threshold; by the time they left with a porn tape in his shopping bag, people were standing back with subdued expressions of horror, repulsion, and fear on their faces, to let him pass. They said good-bye on the sidewalk outside. Lark turned one more time, after the good-bye kiss, to look back at him in his black overcoat, moving north as slowly as one of the old men who took the sun opposite Grace Church on the arm of a nurse's aide from Martinique. He looked ninety-two.

That's all AIDS is, thinks Lark now as he sits in the Buick Skylark on a spring afternoon at the boat ramp in north Florida, accelerated aging. *Very* accelerated aging, illness, and death. Eddie went from forty to ninety-two in less than a year. The first to go. "Always a trend setter!" Sutcliffe said. And now Lark sits here at the boat ramp, wondering if Becker would ever come here during the day. He doesn't think so. Becker doesn't even come here at night, so far as he knows—at least Lark hasn't seen him here since the night they met last April, a year ago.

It has been a year; incredible as that seems, he's sure of that, though time has sort of flattened out the past decade. (Or contained such dreadful events he hasn't wanted to remember any of their dates.) That's characteristic of middle age, he's heard: Life turns into a vast flat ocean, like the sea at the equator, on which the two points of departure and arrival—Birth and Death—are, for a while, invisible. He no longer makes any effort to measure Time. He no longer schedules or plans. One year seems like another. He dates the beginning of this epoch of timelessness from his mother's fall and Eddie's death; but from then on, it is all a seamless, odorless, featureless continuum, like the drab landscape of pine and oak around here—a sort of limbo. He can't remember when anything else happened.

He suspects it was about two years after his mother's return home from the rehabilitation center up north—though "return home" is not quite the phrase; she went straight from the airport to the nursing home—that he was lying in his room reading one afternoon, when he heard a voice calling his name, a voice so indistinct he got up and went out onto the porch out of curiosity more than anything else. His father sat facing him at his favorite table on the porch, holding his limp right arm, saying in a calm voice, "I think I've had a stroke." That is the next thing he remembers—that and his father's death a month later. But he still can't say what year it happened, partly because so little changed: Lark continued to see his mother in the nursing home, her bills paid by the income from the savings his father left behind, the good provider even after his death. Everything now simply belonged to his mother. The rest was the same; they had established their routine. "I'm holding you back, aren't I?" she said one day out of the blue. And then another afternoon, "You'll never leave me; your conscience won't let you."

She was right—on both counts—though every six months or so, he went back to New York for a brief visit to the life he had abandoned there, of which she knew so little; back to the apartment he had left behind, and Joshua, his roommate, who seemed to resent his having left. Those visits have blurred too. All he knows is that each time he returned to New York, it was different, and so was he; the plague, which seems in 1995 routine, normal, was still altering people's moods then with each new blow. But he can't date those subtle, incremental changes. He can't recall which year his roommate committed suicide. He does remember walking downstairs a few days after Joshua was carried out of the building in a body bag and meeting the superintendent, mopping the floor by the mailboxes.

"Was it AIDS?" the superintendent said.

"No," said Lark, thinking at the time: It was the fear of AIDS. It was his failure to find the affection he craved. But he can't say what year it was. He does remember visiting Joshua in Bellevue after his first attempt. But when was that—1985? He remembers taking his first sublet—a handsome Argentinean architect—so that there would be someone in the apartment while he remained in Florida. He remembers beginning to feel more like a ghost himself each time he returned, walking the streets with the realization that his own friends, his youth, his visibility were gone—that you can become a ghost before you die sometimes, not after. He remembers going to an Act Up meeting for the first time. ("That's where all the hot men are," Sutcliffe said.) He remembers going out with Sutcliffe to restaurants. ("Eating in restaurants is safe sex! *If* they wash their hands before making the salad.") He remembers Eddie's memorial service; he remembers many others besides; but if he had to say exactly when Joshua killed himself, or when his father died, or when Sutcliffe checked out—mercifully, at a distance—he couldn't supply the year with any confidence. Because on some stubborn level he's refused the whole twelve years, all the data—everything that's happened. On some level he has reduced everything to those trips to the nursing home, to the blessed tunnel vision that comes with caring for someone else, and finally to the oval in the woods he sits in now, this county park, this haunt of whoever drives in next, this swatch of forest set in a patchwork of pecan farms and fields, this demi-Eden, this row of urinals, this boat ramp.

Even the boat ramp has had its own history the past twelve years, but he can't assign specific years to its events either; they've run parallel, in their own universe, to everything else. To the initial epoch belong the first five years he drove right past it, not knowing of its existence—and then the night he first heard about it in a bar in Gainesville ("Oh, you live out there in never-never land, by the boat ramp!"), afraid even to stop when he drove in the first time and saw the men, at one end of the parking lot, giving Lark a piercing look as he drove by that reduced him to one thing: fresh meat. He remembers the first night he stopped and the cast of characters that summer, a third of whom are now in jail, including the handsome plumber on the motorcycle who used to fart on cue and ended up murdering a court reporter who lived alone in the woods. The rest of the summers are a blur. Till he met Becker. Which brings him to the present, a year later, on this sunny, soft April afternoon. And the reason he's parked here, like Ernie.

For Ernie, he thinks, it makes sense to be here: He's retired, he's seventy, he's haunted rest rooms all his life; on the days he isn't experimenting with his hydroponic tomatoes, he comes here the way straight retired men play golf. For me, it is still an embarrassment. I'm not ready for the boat ramp as a just reward for a lifetime's work—for one thing, I haven't done a lifetime's work. That's the odd part. A year after Lark finished his thesis on William Blake at Columbia, he quit teaching prep school because he met someone in *A Chorus Line*. Love replaced career goals. Or rather, the work he did was always related to the man he was in love with—and that took him from teaching to producing plays to fund raising to cleaning apartments and walking dogs. He became one of those people whose lives were not visible on a résumé—so that even now his mother would occasionally say, as he rewrapped the bandage guarding a skin tear on her emaciated arm, "You should have been a doctor." I should have been many things, he thinks, but I wasn't, and I've ended up here instead.

"Tell me," he says now, turning to Ernie, "do you ever come here hoping you'll meet someone and fall in love?"

Ernie puts his book down. "I think you can fall in love in your twenties or thirties," he says, "but after that, I think it's much less likely that will happen. *I* certainly don't come here to fall in love," he says with a laugh. "And if you do, that's because you're still in transition! I'm not. I know I'm old. I come here just to get with someone. I'd get with him if I could," he says, stroking his beard and nodding at a young man across the parking lot who has just graduated from the junior college in Gainesville. "But he looks right through me," he says in a softer southern accent, "as if I were invisible. Which I am. To him," he says, with a laugh.

I wish I could find that funny, thinks Lark, but I can't. Even his mother said, years before her accident, after returning from a day spent shopping in Jacksonville, "The worst thing about getting old is being invisible." He was startled when she said this—it had never occurred to him that his mother cared about such things—then he thought, She wants to be looked at too. The trouble was, he couldn't tell who was looking down here, or even what he was looking at. The town in which he and Ernie lived—hedges trimmed, garden hoses coiled—looked like a painting of some army post in peacetime, and it was just as lifeless.

It's like that story by Chekhov called "The Steppes," he thinks. A young woman arrives in a muddy little town in the sticks from Moscow, where she has attended the conservatory; she intends to give piano lessons, and bring Culture and Light to the provinces; instead the mud, the dust, the long hot summers, the provincial torpor, the nothingness of the hideous little town defeat and drag her down, and she ends up as muddy, dusty, and dull as the place itself. These are the Steppes, thinks Lark. The same nothingness. Nothing in the air, on the horizon; no change of seasons, the way they change up north; no scents, no odors, no hills or valleys; just a vast sand bar raised above the sea centuries ago, covered now with pinewoods, turkey oaks, and pecan groves—like the Amazon in summer—nothing really but sky, the vast, overarching sky with its thunderheads turning plum-purple just before a storm. A perfect place to hide. That's what he's been accused of by his friends—the few remaining. Though he's not here because of that; he's here because his mother tripped on a rolled-up rug. She's paralyzed. He's paralyzed. They're all paralyzed, in these little towns on the Steppes.

Of course, you could argue that such a place is just where men past their prime should be, he thinks. Here in the woods it's easier to disintegrate, the way animals die alone in the forest; no sidewalk cafés, no plate-glass windows, no queens making a point not to cruise you as you walk by; the gauntlet of averted eyes. No feeling, as you pause in the doorway of a restaurant filled with young men, that you mar the landscape. The boat ramp is, like the woods themselves, a place to vanish. Like the animals that try to reach it but end up smeared on the road just outside the entrance every morning, blood and guts and fur, people need shelter too. The boat ramp may not be the baths, but at least it's a place to go. And Lark turns to Ernie now and says, "Why don't you ever drive into Jacksonville and go to the tubs?"

Ernie lifts his head from *Lenin's Tomb* and says, "Because I do better dressed than undressed. Undressed," he says, glancing down at the belly straining the buttons of his shirt, "all this would show. Dressed, I'm just a mouth."

What extraordinary resignation, thinks Lark. Like the Cheshire Cat, reduced to just . . . a mouth. Once on Fire Island, he met a man reduced to just a mouth, an older man who had no interest in accompanying others to Tea Dance or the Sandpiper at night, or even the beach during the day. He was cheerful, good-natured, spent the day in the house reading books and magazines, like Ernie, and then at night went into the dunes and extracted men's seed—a nocturnal hunter with a very specific ecological niche: a dune creature. He'd found his function; he was content. His only regret, he told Lark on the boat back to the mainland one afternoon, was that he had to do all this with false teeth; and when sometimes the man evidently liked him and wished to talk, or kiss, or in some way build upon the climax they'd just shared, he would have to refuse and walk away into the night, so that he could put his dentures back into his mouth in private. "It broke my heart last night," he said, "but I couldn't let him know." Poor Cyrano! It depressed Lark at the time, and it depresses him still, sitting next to Ernie: the patience, the humility, the resignation.

"Do you let them ejaculate in your mouth?" he says now to Ernie.

"Of course," Ernie says. "I don't feel it's complete unless I do."

"You know you're taking a risk," says Lark.

"We all are," says Ernie in a calm voice. "But, unless I've a cut in my mouth, I think the risk is relatively low. And I'm at an age now when I don't have too many years left on earth anyway," he laughs. "In fact," he says, "I had to ask that nice man who drives the potato chip truck to help me stand up after we'd got together the last time—because my knees had locked." He turns to Lark and says, "Don't get old, if you can possibly avoid it."

But there doesn't seem to be a possibility, thinks Lark. His roommate in New York, Joshua, loved to say, "I can't wait till I'm old! I'm going to be such a wonderful old man!" But then Joshua also used to say, every year when they set out to the West Village for the Gay Pride March, "I'm so happy I'm gay; the only thing I'd rather be is a lesbian!" Joshua ended up neither a lesbian nor an old man. He killed himself before either transformation could oc-cur. Poor Joshua. The depth of despair, of loneliness, he must have been in, to do that; unless it was some long-held aim, some ultimate direction he had been moving toward all his life, like Anne Sexton, whose poems Joshua had loved to read aloud in that apartment before they set off to their gyms.

With suicides, one never knew; that was why they haunted the people left behind—a murder mystery that could never be solved, as to motive, at least—though still Lark chalks Joshua's death up to AIDS, a psychic casualty of the plague.

Here there is no plague, thinks Lark. Save what from heaven is with the breezes blown/Through verdurous glooms and wind-ing mossy ways. Most of the time. At the moment, Ocala Joe is parked outside the men's room, so altered by the disease that when he reappeared a few days ago, after almost a year's ab-sence, neither Lark nor Ernie recognized him; weight loss, and the fact that he had bought a new truck, confused them, al-though they both agreed that whoever it was, was extremely handsome. Until Ocala Joe got sick, thinks Lark, he was handsome in a different way: a roly-poly pretty southern boy who used to look like Elvis. Now he's a more austere knockout. He looks serious, mature, masculine. When he was well, he was a chatty queen who used to talk about nothing but the size of people's dicks, and lie. Like Joshua, he lied constantly. And for the same reason: to amuse, to entertain, to boast. Occasionally Life outstripped Invention. Lark still remembers the afternoon Ocala Joe drove straight here from his mother's deathbed in Tampa; now he's here on his own deathwatch, a year later. Though he told Lark he informs everyone he attracts that he has AIDS, given his past history, there is no way of knowing if he's telling the truth. It doesn't matter—*Caveat emptor* is the rule— and as he watches, Ocala Joe starts his engine and slowly drives out of the parking lot, glancing at the rest room—another handsome man in a pickup truck; the reason they all come here.

"That was Ocala Joe," says Lark.

"I always get his truck confused with Palatka Bill's," says Ernie.

"He used to drive a big one," says Lark, "that's why. A blue Dodge Ram. Now he's got a smaller one, a Nissan," he says, watching it disappear around the bend. One more Japanese product, he thinks. The wind rustles the leaves of the live oaks, and a profound peace settles upon the boat ramp, just the way he likes it. Time to sit and think of Eddie, Sutcliffe, Joshua, the whole history that seems far away from this place—events that Sutcliffe called The Avalanche. What's that? he asked Sutcliffe. "When everyone starts to go," Sutcliffe explained, "with or without AIDS. Everyone you care for just starts to fall down," he said. Still, it seemed wrong for Joshua to take himself out by his own hand—no matter how badly things were going in 1986. It haunts Lark still. Everything haunts him, he thinks as a battered beige Mazda comes around the corner and both he and

Ernie look in their rearview mirrors. In their mirrors is the face of a handsome young man with acne scars and curly blond hair, smoking a cigarette. "Who's that?" says Ernie.

"That's Vern," says Lark, as the car slows down to make the curve. "He lives with his parents on their ranch near Williston and trains horses. The man who owns the Ambush asked him to enter the Miss Gainesville contest last month because he said he needed more white boys in the lineup."

"And did he?" says Ernie.

"Yes," says Lark. "He wore a blue sequined dress, he told me. He mixed cake batter in a bowl while he sang 'I'm Gonna Bake Me a Man.' But he lost to a queen who lip-synced a song called 'Vision of Love.' Anyone would lose to 'Vision of Love,' " says Lark as they watch the beige Mazda continue around the bend and out of the park. "And who's this?" he says as a small gray Honda comes in.

"My age," Ernie says, "with a belly about as big as mine. And one of those small peters I'm afraid are really more work than they're worth. It took for*ever* to get him off."

"And the man in the bread delivery truck?"

"It's not really worth your time," Ernie says. "I used to think he was the handsomest man here, till he smiled one day after we got together. Teeth are so important to me. His are very disappointing."

Like Life itself, thinks Lark. Or at least, certain aspects of it. No matter how I try to rationalize this, he tells himself now— as a small red Toyota, with tinted windows that make it impossible to see who's inside, drives in and parks on the opposite side of the picnic green—I am sitting next to a retired chemical engineer at a boat ramp on a spring afternoon, waiting for a potato chip salesman who may or may not have work in this area today, and hoping Becker will appear instead.

The Toyota parks on the other side of the picnic green. Both Lark and Ernie stare at the tinted windows, waiting for someone to get out. Tinted windows, thinks Lark, create expectations. Are all that's left of Mystery in modern life. Of course they work only as long as someone is behind them: Eventually he has to open the door.

Eventually everyone has to open the door, he thinks, which is the cruel part of the boat ramp—the moment of truth—and of Life. The boat ramp is a terrible place to lose your looks. Men come here—those who've survived, that is—looking for a second youth. They come here after living in cities up north, and think that just because it's a boat ramp in north central Florida, they can start all over again. Sorry. They're new only as long as they stay in the car; when they do get out and walk into the men's room in full view, Reality intervenes. Once inside the john, as the engine of the only other car parked outside starts up and the young man in it drives off, they're left all by themselves at the urinal with a terrible truth: the sound of a disappearing car. And then silence. *The silence of oblivion.* The silence of that single dripping faucet, and the wind moving through the trees outside, and the knowledge of their approaching death.

A death no one escapes with or without AIDS, Lark thinks as the door of the Toyota opens and a pudgy young person with shoulder-length hair, glasses, skintight white spandex shorts, sandals, and a loose brown top gets out and walks into the latrine. "What is that?" says Lark. "I can't tell if it's a man or a woman."

"It's a man," says Ernie, "from Gainesville. He has a very nice one. He's fatter than he was the last time I saw him, though. He used to be pear-shaped, and now he looks pregnant. I'll pass," he says, and returns to his book.

And so will I, Lark thinks, as he lifts his sweaty buttocks from the seat. In fact, I'll get out of here. "Well," he says, as he starts his car, "happy hunting! Maybe I'll see you tonight!" And he drives off, knowing he will be back here on his way home from Gainesville in the evening.

I Am Just a Mouth

Leaving the boat ramp feels like leaving church—outside, the flat two-lane highway stretches into the bright sunlight between the pale scar of an old phosphate mine and a pecan grove in which a cluster of white farm houses sits—and he has to adjust to reality. There's nothing to look forward to now, except a hitchhiker. But Lark hasn't seen one of those in years. The roads are almost empty at two in the afternoon.

They're state roads that used to be dirt—even now you still see their precursors intersecting with the highway: bands of reddish earth leading to some lost lake deep in the pinewoods. Before the Second World War, Florida's chief industries were cattle and timber; the town Lark lives in had a fence around it to keep out cows. Now the number one moneymaker is tourism, and Disney World is the world's number one tourist destination, and the open range is gone. The last time Lark flew back to Florida, via Orlando, the plane was filled with women in saris with caste marks on their foreheads, taking their grandchildren to the Magic Kingdom. Nothing surprises Lark in this regard anymore. The night he ran out of heat five years ago, because the alcoholic who was supposed to fill the gas tank hadn't, he had to take himself and his mother to Starke to spend Christmas Eve in a motel, it was so cold that night; the woman who came out to the motel desk to check them in was from Lahore. The motel business in the American South has become a lodestar for immigrants from the Punjab. And the ones who aren't running motels in places like Starke—a town that always reminds Lark of *The Last Picture Show*—are going to Disney World on Delta.

When Lark comes to a stop at the red light in Orange Heights, he watches the station wagons go flying past on Highway 301 with their luggage strapped to the roof and tarps flapping in the wind, hell-bent for the Magic Kingdom, and he thinks, *That's right! Keep going!* How nice of Disney to build a park with artificial rivers, man-made lakes, trucked-in beaches; it drains off the hordes who might otherwise visit the real thing. Leaving untouched for at least a few more years the rural patchwork of farm, field, pecan grove, Baptist church that makes up the journey between his town and Gainesville, though he cannot predict how many more years this will still be true. South Florida is backing up like a septic tank, sending people up north to places they had never even heard of two decades ago: Kissimmee, Ocala, High Springs, Lake City—the heart of the heart of the country. He wants to send away for a T-shirt he saw advertised in *Out* magazine: CAN'T FEED 'EM, DON'T BREED 'EM. Even if his mother has said on more than one occasion, "Without children, life is pretty pointless." She is still hoping, on some deep, crazy level only mothers are tuned in to, that he'll have one. Meanwhile, everyone else is. And that's why people from all over the world are running the motels in Starke and settling in Kissimmee. The small gilded fly does lecher in my sight, he thinks. Let copulation thrive. I have spilled my seed on stony ground. When he crosses 301 and passes the Baptist church in Orange Heights, he's grateful for the woods that remain: the pine trees and palmettos. Homosexuals should be the heroes of the world: We're not overpopulating.

A few miles out of Gainesville, just over a stream, there is a road sign that says, GAINESVILLE 10 MILES. He has called the Department of Transportation six times and told it Gainesville cannot possibly be ten miles from that sign—it's three, at most—but the sign is still there. Your government at work. Past the sign are two miles of dense woods that turn slightly yellow and red in the fall and remind him of New England; then the ranch houses and satellite dishes of the black middle class begin, and the school buses he often has to stop behind, while children descend with their books and lunch bags and then walk off down a dirt road into the woods. Then there is a trailer park from which people come onto the highway in cars so decrepit they seem to sit there, rather than accelerate, and he has to come to a stop for them. Then the institutions begin, the temples of hormonal imbalance and character defect—the juvenile detention center, the drug rehabilitation headquarters, the home for unwed teen-age mothers, the prison for the crews that work outdoors cutting grass along the highways.

(Once Lark stopped to pick up a hitchhiker here: a young man in an orange tank top, carrying a brown paper bag. He very politely told Lark he had just been let out of prison, where he'd been confined on a charge of shoplifting a chainsaw at Kmart; a chainsaw, he told Lark, that someone had sold him on the street and that he had tried to return for a refund. Now he was hitching home to Alabama. What was it like in prison, Lark asked; were you with serious criminals? Murderers, the young man replied. Lark let him out at Sixth Street, where he always makes his turn, but driving away he wished he had given the young man money, or asked him home to spend the night. Those were the kinds of fantasies one drove with through the hot, stuporous afternoon down here.)

Past the juvenile detention center and the prison is the airport, and then the county fairgrounds, and, south on Waldo Road, a large village for the handicapped. Institutional Gainesville is all on the east side, the northeast. The southeast is almost entirely residential, black. And where the northeast and southeast converge, Eighth Avenue, is the institution that Lark is visiting today, before he goes to the gym and the nursing home.

He swore he'd never come back to this place, but several years since making that vow, he is walking toward it again in the humid sunlight of an April afternoon. All the people on the benches outside, on the walk, in the little breezeway connecting the two buildings, are young and black. He wonders what they think he, a middle-aged white man, is doing here. He's too old to be coming to these places, he thinks as he walks in and tells the receptionist he's here for a two-thirty appointment. These places are for the sexually active, he thinks; the sexually active are young. I'm too old, too white, too gray, too brittle; I'm the Aging Queen I see every now and then in airports—still in jeans and polo shirt, carrying a gym bag, the same outfit he wore when he was twenty-five, the costume of the only role he feels he can play: Young Man—a piece of coral that would crack if you touched it.

Five minutes later, five minutes of wondering what the receptionist thinks of him, another woman appears—a short woman in her twenties with short brown hair, a print blouse of red orchids, and glasses whose plastic frames have a lavender tinge—and asks him if he is her appointment. They exit the room and cross the breezeway to the adjacent building.

"The AIDS test used to be here," he says, meaning the building they just left.

"It all got bigger," she says, opening the door to the building where they also test for hepatitis and TB, and do dental work.

Like everything about AIDS, he thinks.

She takes him to her office, he sits down, then she excuses herself to get some forms.

Her bulletin board is covered with a Clinton/Gore sticker, a quote from Ann Landers about being comfortable with our sexuality, a photograph of a female baseball team. He examines them and concludes: This woman is a dyke. Her little bulletin board is her way of coming out. He is glad. It will make it all easier, he thinks. When she returns with the questionnaires and begins asking questions, he feels entirely uninhibited.

So uninhibited, he gets up and walks around the room, sits down in another chair, then returns to the first, stands up again, backs himself into a corner, sags against the wall, and wrings his hands. He says—pointing to the book on her shelf—he has finally just read *And the Band Played On,* and become depressed, after visiting in Gainesville a blind friend covered with Kaposi's sarcoma. He tells her he thought, on leaving the friend's room: He got this for having sex? This? The wasting, the blindness, the lesions, the oncoming death? For having sex? He goes on to say that even without AIDS gay men have terrible problems: loneliness; lack of companionship, shelter, love. He says AIDS proves how intractable these structural problems are—that even *it* hasn't changed gay males' behavior. We still look for each other in toilets, he says. Nothing has come of all the deaths. No change, no redemption, no justification for their suffering. "I've lost all my friends, and still I go out, to the baths, the boat ramp. Everyone I knew has died. Outrageous, ugly deaths they did not deserve. And still I go out." She listens calmly, looking at him through her round glasses as her two white hands cradle the questionnaire she is waiting to fill out. Then she says, "May I ask you some questions?"

"Of course," he sighs, sitting down in the chair by her desk, bent forward, like a woman keening or a man with gas.

"How many partners would you say you've had in the last year?"

He frowns and begins to compute, an unpleasant chill coming over him under the cool white gaze of Science, the shift to the clinical mode. He says, "Twenty-four." This seems to take the lean months with the fat ones, the periods of drought with the sudden binges. (Man lives, said Erik Erikson, by the Carnival-Atonement cycle.)

"What sexual practices?" she asks next. "Rimming?"

"One time at the baths," he says. How neurotic these answers seem when voiced in an office, he thinks: the lunacy of sexual desire, withering under the scientific gaze. *But he was so good-looking,* he wants to say, *I had to.* (It had done him no good: When, after licking his rectum, Lark got up to obtain a condom, the man stood up frowning, wrapped a towel around his chiseled torso, said, "I don't think so!" and stormed out of the room.)

"About how many partners have you had in the past six months?" she says.

He computes a figure of ten.

"Any steady sexual partners?" she asks.

He bends forward. "No," he says, looking down at the floor. (This is my whole failure, he thinks, the reason I'm here at all, at this advanced age: I've not been able to find a steady sexual partner. I've been a flop as a homosexual. Some final loathing of the condition, some inability to accept my fate, has led me, like so many of my kind, to dissociate sex from everything else in my life, from every other aspect of my character. I've devoted my whole life to being homosexual, he thinks, I've majored in Gay, and what has it got me? Not even a steady sexual partner. How embarrassing. I've failed.)

"Tell me," he says, looking up, "do you have a relationship?"

"Yes," she says.

"For how long?"

"Eleven years."

"Eleven years!" he says. "Is it monogamous?"

"For the last three," she says.

"And what do *you* do about safe sex?" he says. "Do you use dental dams?"

"I prefer Saran Wrap," she says. He doesn't know what to say. She returns her gaze to the questionnaire. "What effect would testing negative have on you?" she asks.

"I'd get very close to Jesus," he says.

"And what effect would testing positive have?"

He stands bolt upright and wrings his hands. "I'd be a wreck," he says, "because I'd have only myself to blame. Because I have been operating on the basis that oral sex is safe, and that would mean it isn't." He sits down. "You know," he says, "most gay men *are* having oral sex. I mean, much of the sex that's going on right now in the cities, New York, San Francisco, Los Angeles, is oral sex. And they're *not* using rubbers. Believe me. It's *very* rare for gay men to use rubbers for oral sex. Almost never! It's much easier to expect someone to use a rubber for intercourse. You don't even have to ask. Whereas for oral sex, the opposite is true. All the sex that's going on now is oral, and it's without condoms."

She sits back and puts her pencil down on the blotter. "Gay men are just having a temper tantrum right now," she says.

"A temper tantrum?"

"Yes. Because AIDS has gone on for so long and there is no cure in sight."

A temper tantrum, he thinks. A temper tantrum. He divides his friends into two groups: Those who do, and those who don't. He thinks of the ones who have stopped having sex altogether— the Amazing Celibates, exemplars of a steel will, a discipline that baffles him. Then he thinks of John, who, when he was dying, said, "Think of being negative as like having ten million dollars." ("Ten million dollars you can't spend," Sutcliffe said as they went downstairs afterward.) "*I* wouldn't be out there, risking it," said John. Lark thinks now of friends who still are. Indeed, there is nothing more ironic than the fact that one would expect the people who carry the virus to stop having sex— whereas, in fact, exactly the opposite has happened. The negatives have stopped having sex—to preserve their capital, their ten million bucks. The positives have gone on having sex—to forget the deadline that has been placed in their lives. But then why should it be otherwise? About sex and death none of us is rational.

John burst into tears the first time these questions were put to him—burst into tears in the doctor's office. Now Lark sees why: How humiliating the hallowed expressions of love, of desire, look under the dispassionate gaze of a clinician. You were in denial. You had a temper tantrum. You lifted your wet mouth from the source of life, slimy with saliva, to find a counselor in a relationship of eleven years with a pencil and questionnaire looking across the desk at you. A woman who prefers Saran Wrap to dental dams. Who actually uses Saran Wrap for something other than leftovers. Who gets up and says to you now, "I have some dry condoms. Would you like those? They have no taste."

"No," Lark says, "I'd never use them." He sighs. There seems nothing left to say—it's all come down to an offer of condoms—but he wants to ask her a perhaps more spiritual question. He wants to ask her, Why? And will she absolve him? And does she have some solution to his loneliness? But the offer of dry condoms, the filling out of the questionnaire, have brought the interview to an end. She stands up. He rises and follows her out the door to the nurse's aide, who administers his blood test in another room. Then he leaves, arm folded, pressing the cotton ball between his bicep and forearm to stanch the blood, passing doctors younger than himself (the most astonishing fact of aging: Your doctor is younger than you), on his way out through a small, crowded lobby filled with men and women holding babies: the whole effluvia of heterosexuality, all young. He exits the lobby, walks past the dental office, out into the humid sunlight to his car. He opens the door, pushes aside the mound of tape cassettes—Mozart, Schubert, Beethoven, Jerome Kern—and drives out of the parking lot, wondering why all the guilt, fear, remorse, depression, and shattering clarity he has experienced just now are never present when he finds himself, at eleven-thirty on a wet autumn night, kneeling on the dirty tiles of the boat ramp men's room, one inch away from the appetizing head of a naked penis engorged with blood. Sad but true, he thinks: Oral sex is, at this point, my main connection to the human race—the part currently living, that is.

The Forge of Vulcan

~~~~~~

It's a curious thing about the dead, Lark thinks, as he drives down Eighth Avenue past the Army Reserve headquarters, the forlorn doughnut shop, on this stretch of Eighth that is still black, just before it hits Fifth Avenue and it turns into a white manicured neighborhood called the Duck Pond—it's a curious thing about the dead that we keep talking to people even after they die. In fact, that may be when we *really* start talking to them: when they're no longer able to talk. I talk to Sutcliffe, he thinks, even though he isn't there to pick up the phone. To answer a letter. To open the door when I go back to New York. He isn't there, but I keep talking to him. Just the way I keep talking to Eddie, to Joshua, to Michael, to John. Curious. These one-way conversations, like the spasms the brain causes in my mother's legs, brain impulses that shoot out from the cortex to the tips of her paralyzed toes, and then, finding no response there, cramp the muscles and die. A dead end. *Nobody home.* You keep talking anyway, however, even though they're not talking back. You want to talk to them as you drive in your car through Gainesville, because frankly you're by yourself so much you might as well talk to someone, even the dead, and because you got used to talking to them all the years you were alive together, and because the reason you talked to them was that you were, somehow, kindred spirits.

He talks to Sutcliffe because Sutcliffe was, no doubt, his best friend—something he realized only after Sutcliffe died. In New

York, who was assigning categories? You had so many friends. You all had so many friends, you understood that each of your friends had other friends with whom he did things he didn't do with you. But somehow, out of this whirl, a few relationships precipitated; the most important friend was the person with whom you spent Sunday—the person you called, late that morning, to ask if he wanted to take a walk in the park. And all that led to. Marriage, said Nietzsche, or Shaw or Chekhov, is one long conversation. So is friendship, thinks Lark as he drives down Eighth Avenue. And Sutcliffe's was the conversation that mattered most, even toward the end—when, of course, their lives, like those of everyone else they knew, grew drab. What else could have happened? Though it wasn't just disease; it was some inevitable sclerosis.

Toward the end, he and Sutcliffe found themselves on the PATH train going to Newark one Sunday afternoon to bury the ashes of one of Sutcliffe's friends—a friend so furious at his family in Bryn Mawr for having disowned him after learning he was gay, he made Sutcliffe promise to inter him in a pet cemetery. "Put me someplace they can never find me," he told Sutcliffe before he died. "Put me in a Bide-A-Wee in Newark." So they got on the train one Sunday in November and rode out to New Jersey with a small white jar of ashes, and had them interred between a parakeet and a collie beneath the words MY BELOVED JACK.

Then they stopped in Newark on the way back to have lunch in a restaurant Sutcliffe said served wonderful *feijoada*. But the *feijoada* wasn't wonderful, and the restaurant wasn't either, and afterward when they walked to the PATH train they couldn't find any of the beautiful Portuguese men they were sure would be out there.

Newark was forlorn that day. They stopped to sit while Sutcliffe smoked a cigarette, wondering what to do, loath to return just yet. They sat there watching children who were not theirs play kickball, postponing the moment when they would get on the PATH train and go back to a Manhattan that now seemed intensely sinister and tired. Or rather, Lark reminded himself, *they* were sinister and tired. And completely out of it.

They were being moved aside, thought Lark as he sat there, staring out at the dusk gathering to the west; reduced and moved aside. That was why they went to Queens these days, to see if they'd find in the discos out there some gorgeous Italian, some remnant of their own youth, when discos had been thrilling. All they found in Jackson Heights was an elevated subway track, a bar in its shadow, and five Colombian queens sitting morosely in the gloom inside; the creature they had come to find had gone into Manhattan years ago, of course. And died. He wasn't out there. He wasn't in Coney Island either, the Russian neighborhood, or in Bensonhurst, or even Newark. They were already leaving Manhattan, he thought that day in New Jersey, as he sat on a park bench watching children walk by with their parents and grandparents. He and Sutcliffe were attending their own wake in Newark that day, when a man and a girl about eight stopped before their bench, completely ignoring them, as if he and Sutcliffe really were what they felt like—ghosts.

"Where's your glove?" said the man to the girl, who looked down at the ground and said nothing.

"You mean I have to take you to your mother's now, missing a glove? What's she going to say? Where's your other glove?"

The girl, biting her lower lip, started to cry. Then they walked on, and Sutcliffe, removing the cigarette from his mouth, looked at Lark and said, "Nobody asks me where *my* glove is. They ask me if I've come yet, or if I'm into scat, but nobody ever asks me where I lost my glove."

"You see?" said Lark. "That's why gay romances don't last."

"Speak for yourself," said Sutcliffe. "I'm still in love with all my boyfriends. In fact," he said, standing up, "I'll call Silvio!" And he went off to call the Brazilian professor of Romance languages he had met two winters ago. He won't be home, thought Lark. In the seventies he would have been, but not now. Nobody was anymore. They were either sick, or taking care of someone who was, or attending macrobiotic cooking school, or getting in touch with their inner child, or attending classes at Silva Mind Control. Sutcliffe blamed AIDS on est. The city changed, despite one's best efforts to keep the town the way you wanted it; people moved on to different obsessions, different amusements, and the party could not be kept going past its natural span of life. There was nothing he or Sutcliffe could do. Nothing but sit here on a park bench in a Portuguese neighborhood of Newark while Sutcliffe phoned a handsome young language professor he had met in Rio two winters before while getting a pedicure in Ipanema, the Land of Purple Dick. And Lark watched the children play kickball, watched the winter dusk deepen in the bare branches of the oak trees, watched evening gather, like some old man parked there to supervise the kids. Only I have no grandkids, he thought. I have only Sutcliffe—dear Sutcliffe— the party-giver in the phone booth who could no longer find the party, the tour guide whose trips dead-ended, the magician who could not pull the rabbit out of the hat anymore. Even without AIDS their world would have come to an end, thought Lark; their nightclubs would have filled up with another generation. On the sidewalk on St. Marks Place someone—a group called Fags Against Facial Hair—had been stenciling the words CLONES GO HOME. In other words: We need the space; turn the city over to us. You guys are tired.

"The trouble with Sutcliffe," someone had said to Lark one evening a week before, as they left a memorial service in a funeral home on Second Avenue, "is that the seventies are over, and he doesn't know it. He sits there at home waiting for the phone to ring, with a cocktail and a cigarette, and the phone doesn't ring—because the seventies are over. They're over." They were indeed. That was why they were in Newark that afternoon. People died. The phone stopped ringing anyway, at a certain age; nobody asked you to play; and that was that. When you did try to party, you ended up sitting on a park bench in New Jersey on a winter afternoon watching children kick a red ball to one another while Sutcliffe tried to get a Brazilian professor to ask you over for a drink. Only Lark was sure the professor wasn't there, and he wasn't sure, even if he was there, whether they should mention they'd just come from a pet cemetery where the man in charge had said, "A bit large for a dog," when handed the container of ashes, and then interred them under the words MY BELOVED JACK, which could of course apply to a parakeet, dog, or cat, as well as Zoli's most popular male model for most of the seventies.

How many Brooks Brothers bathrobes, how many Armani suits, how many Ralph Lauren polo shirts, how many houndstooth sports coats and Burberry raincoats had been sold because of this man, all of them in closets and wardrobes all across the country, while he, the inspiration, had found a resting place among the dogs and cockatoos where his own well-dressed family could not find him? Tell me—do you wish to be buried as a pet or a person? Two other friends were buried over here in New Jersey, as human beings, on a bluff overlooking the Hudson River; but Lark hadn't the heart, or the desire, to go look them up. He wasn't handling AIDS well. In some peculiar sense both he and Sutcliffe refused to accept it. It was too stupid; beneath contempt. It played into every puritanical conviction, every suppressed suspicion that life would punish you if you lay with another man. We're like two brokers in the twenties, he thought, who lost everything in the stock market crash. The business in which they had invested everything had collapsed. It was so sad he could hardly watch Sutcliffe coming back from the pay phone, still handsome in his slim black overcoat, black wavy hair, and black moustache, only two small creases like parentheses around his mouth to betray his age. He looked distinguished. Distinguished but alone. As alone as Lark was—the two of them relics of the same period. Lark was even disappointed, though not surprised, when Sutcliffe said nobody had answered the phone. "No answering machine?" said Lark.

"No, thank God," said Sutcliffe.

"I must tell you," said Lark, "how much I respect *you,* for not having one. I hate the things."

"Why should I?" said Sutcliffe. "Nobody calls."

And they got the PATH train and went back to Manhattan, seated next to a young Italian American all done up for an afternoon on Christopher Street, Lark suspected, so handsome he went home and wrote down a description of him in a notebook, the way a bird watcher would record a sighting.

It was hard now to know what to do with the allure of men; every one was under a cloud of suspicion. A certain trust, a certain innocence, had vanished. And still men were beautiful. One winter afternoon after Lark had returned to Florida, Sutcliffe was walking home from Central Park, just before Christmas, across from the brand-new Givenchy showroom whose windows, lighted at night, gave the same feeling of warmth *luminarias* did in a small town, when he came abreast of a young man walking in the opposite direction. For a moment their eyes locked. (That was one of the first things to go: the eyes. Not simply their appearance, but rather the knowledge of how to use them on the street—that sense, that intuition, left you when you began to feel like someone who had stayed outdoors too long to play. When you began to look like a puppy who would go home with anyone.) Sutcliffe looked at the young man, the young man looked at Sutcliffe, and then—instead of the pause, the "Hello," the "Would you like to come up for a drink?," the handshake, the usual conclusion of eyes that linger on other eyes—the man shot out his right leg like someone in a kung fu movie playing on Times Square, hit Sutcliffe square in the chest, knocked him onto the ground, and then began screaming *"Maricón!"* at him.

The ladies with whom Sutcliffe went to mass in the neighborhood, emerging from Gristede's at that moment with their bags of cat food, together shooed the young man away, while Sutcliffe, in his Perry Ellis overcoat, his Brooks Brothers shoes, struggled to sit up, clutching his Mark Cross briefcase, too stunned to do anything but say, "Thank you, thank you, I'm quite all right, oh, Mrs. Moriarty, don't worry, please, I'm really okay," and, smiling and laughing, wave good night to them and walk back to the apartment; where, upstairs, he locked the door, poured himself a glass of vodka, and sat down, shaking all over and thinking, My eyes, my eyes, I've got to discipline my eyes, like a Jesuit in the nineteenth century. Then he called Lark and said, "This is not my city anymore."

It wasn't, actually. That summer Sutcliffe got smacked again—by a friend Lark called The Playmate. Sutcliffe always had a Playmate. Not necessarily a best friend, The Playmate was someone younger who would go out with him to nightclubs, bars, parties, openings, restaurants, places Lark and other friends no longer had much desire to visit. Restaurants seemed to have replaced sex in the eighties; as for the music people were dancing to now, Lark thought it nasty.

"I'm waiting for rap to go away," he said to Sutcliffe.

"Oh, darling, you're going to be waiting a very long time," said Sutcliffe, and went out anyway with his Playmate—an art dealer named Prescott, who rented a room each summer in Sutcliffe's house on Fire Island, and got into the water taxi with him at midnight, and went down to the Pines to drink and dance. One night, on the dance floor of the Pavilion, very late, when the sleazy music was being played, Sutcliffe pressed his lips to Prescott's, and Prescott pulled back his arm and socked him in the jaw. This blow hurt much more than the kick from the young man outside Givenchy, because this scene would have never happened in the seventies. But that was just it. Lark wasn't sure what law Sutcliffe had tried to flout—the one that says our friends cannot be lovers, the one that says a playmate is just a playmate, the one that says middle-aged drunks cannot be expected to have their desire for other people returned, or the one that says once one's youth is gone, one has to accept a diminished status. Whatever the law, it was obdurate, and, listening to Sutcliffe describe the incident, Lark remembered a woman whose Christmas party Sutcliffe had taken him to in 1972 on Madison Avenue—a famous art collector who, in her mid-fifties, kept Kotex in the medicine cabinet of her bathroom so that guests who used the bathroom and peeked in would think she was still menstruating. Sutcliffe had told the story as they walked home, laughing, through a gently falling snow.

Now he was far from that snow, from Sutcliffe, and from the youth that had made her vanity funny. In fact that woman had been one of the ladies who knelt down to help Sutcliffe up after he was knocked to the ground by the Puerto Rican. ("Ah," said Sutcliffe to her, "I didn't expect to see you till it was time for madrigals.") Now when Lark spoke to Sutcliffe on the telephone, he sensed Sutcliffe was as alone in his room as Lark was in his— both of them stranded in a way they never thought they'd be, confined for the same reason to separate cells, in two places that may have been distinct physically but not, he realized, psychologically. They were both waiting for a call that never came.

"The phone never rings," Sutcliffe said, the first time Lark visited him in his new apartment in the Wordsworth. "I swear, the phone never rings."

"Stop it!" laughed Lark, when he heard this. "The phone always rings at your place! I don't believe it!"

"It has not rung *once* all day," said Sutcliffe, sitting there with a cigarette dangling from his lower lip, which looked a bit swollen and red, a cocktail on the table, and the expression of a woman in a B-movie who is not being invited to have a drink with anyone at the bar. The truth was, the phone did not ring. It left the two of them quite unmolested, sitting there in the new apartment Sutcliffe had been forced to find when the old one—the one in which they had first met the model now buried in the pet cemetery, the one where all the parties, all the romances, all the adventures had begun—had been acquired by the museum next door because it needed additional space for administrative offices. "I blame everything on the Whitney," said Sutcliffe as they sat in his new apartment, a set of cubelike rooms in a tower of cubelike rooms, with the same windows, balconies, and a view of the tram to Roosevelt Island, the gray river, the flat roofs of Long Island City, "including the eighties." It was a New York Lark never thought Sutcliffe would inhabit: high-rise, odd-smells-in-the-corridor New York, strangers in the elevator, bad lighting, plastic flowers in the lobby, the only funny part of it the name on the canopy: THE WORDSWORTH—something out of a Ruth Draper monologue. But Ruth Draper was dead. So were their friends. And now they met, in Sutcliffe's new cube, as he smoked a cigarette, nursed a glass of white wine, and waited for the phone that did not ring to ring.

The phone did not ring because they were middle-aged now, and men who do things together at twenty-eight tend to evolve their own routines, their own solitary hunting patterns, more than a decade later—and because there was a plague about.

It was hard to distinguish sometimes between the psychological effects of the two—age and AIDS. Both tended to produce withdrawal. Lark's phone in Florida didn't ring either—he had already received so much bad news through the one in the dining room, he refused even to pick it up when it did, regarding that particular extension the way a primitive man might an object with a malevolent deity inside it. One night Sutcliffe called and asked Lark—on the other, less evil extension—what he had been doing. "Oh!" said Lark, excited to have his friend on the line, "I just watched a marvelous documentary on the Polynesians, their migrations across the Pacific, and then a program on *bees*, and then a wonderful movie I'd never seen before, *The King and I!*"

"My, my," said Sutcliffe, "we've been busy."

It took Lark a moment to laugh—he had forgotten that watching television was not doing anything. Of course Sutcliffe took a dim view of his having left New York at all, even to care for his parents, and he began calling him "the good Catholic daughter." Lark even suspected Sutcliffe was right, but he couldn't help it. And then he reflected that if he hadn't left New York for that reason he'd be spending the same sort of evening anyway—watching the same program on Polynesians in his apartment, while people had their noses pierced downstairs on St. Marks Place.

Instead they stayed home and for two or three years talked on the telephone about their fear, horror, and dread. "It's like living in Beirut," said Sutcliffe, "you never know when the next car bomb is going off." Diagnoses were exploding like Semtex around the city. Sutcliffe's reclusiveness deepened—as if, like the Jews on the first Passover, you could stay at home and hope the Angel of Death would not stop at your house. "You're blessed," said Sutcliffe when Lark told him the test that he took in 1985 had found none of the antibodies to the virus in his blood. Lark could not ask Sutcliffe his own status. Some things were too personal. Sutcliffe had had hepatitis, and had kept drinking through the seventies and eighties continuously, so when Sutcliffe did talk about his visits to the doctor, the subject was his liver. One day friends put him into Payne Whitney to sober up. After that he attended meetings of Alcoholics Anonymous, at which, he told Lark, he finally discovered where the seventies had gone, when he walked into a room in a seminary in Chelsea and found what remained of the men he and Lark had admired on the floor of the Sandpiper, the ones who'd vanished, like the seventies themselves, but had not died. But aside from re-locating a group of people he thought he'd never see again, and the lunches and dinners he asked them to, Sutcliffe made no more use of AA. He was too proud to consider himself an alcoholic. He continued to drink, at a diminished level; in January he went to Hawaii for a month. Hawaii itself was a sign of middle age, or some chastened approach to life. Rio was now off limits; Hawaii, with its midwestern whites and Japanese, was more reassuring. Sutcliffe was nut-brown when Lark saw him that March at the Wordsworth and Sutcliffe told him he was taking him to lunch.

"I can't," said Lark. "I can't be seen in public—especially not at a restaurant, unless it's very dark."

"Why?" said Sutcliffe.

"Because *you* still look great, you always will, but I'm starting to look old."

"And you think they'll refuse you admittance to a restaurant?"

"Yes," said Lark.

"Dear God! Is this what you're going to be like in your golden years?" said Sutcliffe. "Unable to leave your room because you can't stand daylight? Darling, I would hate to see you say no to the pleasures of maturity, which are considerable! It's not a crime to be an old man, you know. You are still allowed to use the sidewalks! Mortimer's would be out of business if the old were not allowed to eat out! We had it written into law. They can't refuse to serve old cows like us." And Sutcliffe began to moo as they went out the door.

So it was a shock the next time he saw Sutcliffe—tall, distinguished, handsome Sutcliffe, with his thick, wavy black hair and moustache—on the steps of the Metropolitan Museum, an hour after Lark had returned to the city that winter. He said not a word after he dashed up the broad stone steps and saw Sutcliffe at the top of them—wasted, gaunt, skinny as a stick, in his neat khaki pants and navy cardigan. His face was ashen and collapsed, the flesh between his eyes and chin drooping.

Lark embraced him. Then he accompanied Sutcliffe as he shuffled, in his scuffed Top-Siders, into the Velázquez exhibition. "I want to find a painting I first saw here years ago," Sutcliffe whispered as he took the arm Lark offered him, "called *The Forge of Vulcan.* I saw it first in the seventies, and I remember thinking how beautiful the men's arms and backs were, and how Vulcan reminded me of Julio Perez—the hairdresser I used to chase around the Everard. He was so beautiful. Then the painting disappeared, and I found it in the Prado a few years ago when I went to Spain. And here it is again," he said, coming to a stop as he squeezed Lark's forearm. They stood there and looked at the painting; the men in it were still beautiful, Lark thought, their faces awestruck in the presence of the glowing god—as he himself had once been, those first years in New York, stepping into the hallways of the Everard—but everything else outside the painting had crumbled, including his friend, whose face was haggard when he turned to Lark and said, "Can we go now? I'm tired."

Then they walked down the steps of the museum in the cold December air, got into a cab, and went back to the Wordsworth, where they sat in the room with a view of smokestacks along the river, the plumes of white smoke frozen like a thick impasto against the sky.

A week later when they spoke—on the telephone again, now that he was back in Florida—Sutcliffe sounded so slurred, so sloppy, Lark thought he was drunk; and he hung up in anger. In fact, Sutcliffe was dying. Later that night when his liver started to fail, Sutcliffe began to swell. He called a man who lived three floors beneath him, an old friend from high school, and this man, whom Lark had never even met, found Sutcliffe vomiting blood and took him to Lenox Hill Hospital, where he died three hours later. That was it: the end of the seventies, for real. Except one thing.

That winter, the winter he died, the winter he no longer felt up to the plane ride to Hawaii, Sutcliffe had asked if he could come and visit Lark. He thought he'd fly to Jacksonville, rent a car, and drive around. Lark panicked. He was ashamed of the town and his life there, which consisted of trips back and forth to the nursing home in which his mother was confined. "It's like the Steppes of Russia!" he said over the long-distance wire. "It's completely flat, people sell boiled peanuts by the side of the road, there are no distinguishing features, no beauty, nothing! Next year, maybe if I go to the bars I'll have a few friends; give me some more time to find out what there is to *do* down here, so that when you do come, I can introduce you to friends, take you places. At the moment it would be like coming to see me at—a fishing camp, on the Amazon! It's like living in Ecuador!"

But the more he tried to explain his reluctance to play host, the more Sutcliffe got angry. He told Lark he was selfish and cold—even when Lark repeated his invitation to visit the following year. A month later Sutcliffe was dead, and now Lark drove around talking to him in the front seat, as if Sutcliffe were seated beside him, showing him the little towns, the campus of the university, the gay bars. One afternoon he saw a woman in the car beside his at a stoplight staring at him—and he realized he had become that oddity: a man talking to himself out loud in his car. No matter. Sutcliffe was dead, and Lark was not, and no one knew why, really.

As he drives through Gainesville toward the nursing home— wondering if it would make any difference if he didn't visit his mother later this evening—he thinks, The problem with my mother is the same problem as with Sutcliffe. I didn't know when he was going to die. I don't know when she is going to die. It makes a difference, knowing that. If we knew exactly when all of us were going to die, he thinks as he comes to Main Street and stops at the light, it would make it so much easier to be hospitable—to others and oneself. But we don't.

What he did know was that he seemed to have become angry with all those he cared for before they died, like the man across the hall from his apartment in New York, who, when he realized his dog was failing, started to beat it.

Youth and Beauty

~~~~~~

At the corner of Eighth Avenue and Main Street, stopped at the
red light, he rolls the window down—sitting in the sun, you feel
how hot it is, how hot it's going to be—and decides to take a
detour to Goering's. It's always cool at Goering's, browsing
books—cool and quiet—so when he gets to Sixth Street, he
turns left, drives south along the railroad tracks, and then turns
right onto University Avenue. On University Avenue—once
shaded by oak trees, cut down so that it could be widened for,
what else, cars—he goes past the bank, bookstore, athletic
goods store, vegetarian restaurant, rooming house, nightclub,
Taco Bell, pizza parlor, students in line at the ATM machine,
and finally the Holiday Inn; and then turns right on Thirteenth,
left at the next street, and finds, to his great relief, a parking
place behind Goering's. A fat man in mirrored sunglasses,
whose job it is to see that only patrons of the bookstore use this
parking lot, watches Lark walk across the asphalt to the back
door; once inside, Lark feels safe in the world of books. The
meanness of humanity—from chicken queens to Bosnian
Serbs—seems banished from this room. The magazines are on
a rack that stretches the length of the store, the general interest
periodicals closest to the street—at the rear, on the top shelf,
all the porn.

Lark enters an aisle of paperback books (Theater/Drama),
opens a collection of plays by Aeschylus, and gazes over the
top of it at the men cruising. A professor of physics he has seen

around is standing directly in front of Lark, as still and patient as an egret stalking fish at the margin of a lake—pretending to read a *New York Review of Books* (talk about meanness!) while waiting for the handsome student beside him to reach for a magazine on the top shelf. The question is simple: *Playboy* or *Inches*? A clear-cut choice, Lark thinks, that obviates the cloudy protestations of adolescence when people are alleged to be confused. He was confused himself in that respect for years and years, a confusion he now thinks was mere reluctance to face the fact that one day ages hence he would be standing here pretending to read the *Oresteia* while watching out of the corner of his eye the handsome student reaching up for an issue of *Playboy* or *Inches*. Whatever the cause, genetic or cultural or some combination of the two, the result is simple: One takes down the photographs of naked men or naked women. Simple, yes, but what torture, on the other hand, to the youth of nineteen who senses the consequences of his preference: the withdrawal from family, customs, ceremonies, expectations, dreams, the life cycle itself! That was why Lark denied it until he was twenty-five, so lonely one summer night at graduate school, his peers all married by now, that he got up from his desk, left his room at the university, and walked downtown like a man crossing the desert in search of water. Water he found. Now he watches a young man with a dark crew cut, thick eyelashes, and a serious, morose expression, tinged with the slightest blush on the cheeks, take down an issue of *Honcho* from the shelf.

The entire culture is so pornographic at this point, Lark does not even pause to marvel that at nineteen this young man can do something that was beyond his ken thirty years ago. And why should he? TV commercials for Zest and Diet Pepsi, not to mention Soloflex and Irish Spring soap, make it unnecessary to buy the VCR friends in cities are always recommending to him so he can watch porn tapes. The young man does not even look at the physics professor, now frankly staring at him as he reaches up and takes down another magazine, *The American Spectator*, puts the *Honcho* under it, and walks toward the cash register, while Lark follows with the *Oresteia*.

"Will that be all?" says the young blond woman ringing up both magazines at the register, in a breezy, pleasant voice, determined, in these nonjudgmental times, to ignore the fact that her classmate is buying a magazine whose cover story deals with penis piercing.

"Yes," he mumbles.

Lark buys his Aeschylus and follows the man outside, past the parking lot in which a sextet of bare-chested Methodists are playing volleyball in the small backyard of their church, and then across University Avenue to the campus.

The young man, Lark thinks, is evidently a conservative, or he would not be reading *The American Spectator*. Conservatives, he thinks, being strict and puritanical, are always better sex; he follows him across the dusty Plaza of the Americas, deserted now, filled with the arcadian peace that campus towns all have when the students are on semester break, all the way to Little Hall—the building whose rest rooms are so famous as the haunt of homosexuals, they were the subject of a radio call-in talk show Lark listened to one night, during which a Phi Kappa Delta man telephoned to say, "If I were gay, I'd put a gun in my mouth and pull the trigger." Reactionary attitudes die hard. At the Student Union, the doors are open, and he can hear the distinctive sound track of a Fellini movie being shown inside. The young man turns right and enters one of the red-brick Gothic dormitories encrusted with bicycle racks; Lark stops and sits on the bench outside, like the Little Mermaid after she returns the prince to land but must hang back in the waves herself. Like her, he sits there staring at the dormitory, hoping for a glimpse of his fellow customer at one of the window screens, imagining him now upstairs in some stuffy room whose door he has just locked, expending on the pages of the magazine—as Lark did his sophomore year, using a swimsuit ad for Paar of Arizona in the back of *Esquire*—the spermatozoa that have been building in his scrotal sac. How clean his come must be, thinks Lark as he stares up at the row of windows.

How clean, how fresh, at the beginning! Whereas the blood of me and most of my friends is as polluted as an open sewer! If only I could tell him all I know, thinks Lark, if only we could bridge the years that lie between us.

But we can't. Why would such a youth be interested in me? Treasures of the soul notwithstanding, I loathed older men when I was young, he thinks as a pair of legs crosses his field of vision and he looks up to see a man with dirty blond hair in a buzz cut looking down at him. Lark sits up. The student looks back at him, continues walking, glances back again; till Lark, like some creature in a ballet brought to life by a swan, rises and follows him down the path. They are near Little Hall after all: the Zona Rosa, the Sacred Stone. The young man with the buzz cut and perfect features looks like a budding air force pilot; hundreds do at this school. He walks onto the side porch of the Student Union, turns, and waits for Lark. Lark's heart is not even pounding; the sequence of events, of signals, has been too clear; they have just spoken the international language of cruising.

"Hello, how are you?" he says to the youth.

"How's it going?" the young man says—and then they converse. The young man replies to all his queries—where he is from (Fort Lauderdale), what he is studying (marketing)—for almost fifteen minutes in a pleasant tone, as they discuss school, politics, sports, life, and finally the weather; then suddenly, after a discussion of the coming cold front, his voice darkens and a sneer deforms his lips as he says, reality dawning on him, "Why are you asking me this stuff? Are you a faggot?"

"No, no!" says Lark, smiling. "I was just curious! Well, have a good day! Nice talking to you!" And he turns and walks away—having denied his homosexuality more quickly, he thinks as he crosses University Avenue and finds himself in front of the Catholic church frequented by students, than Peter denied Christ. So much for ten years of Gay Pride, he thinks as he goes inside the church to hide and collect his thoughts; so much for maturity, he thinks as he walks to the front and sits down in a pew before a statue of Saint Joseph and the Blessed Virgin; so much for *Oprah* and Queer Nation.

Oh, Sutcliffe, he thinks as he stares at the plaster images of the Holy Family, no wonder the Puerto Rican knocked you on your ass outside of Givenchy! This is what happens when we get to middle age: this is what happens when we leave New York and our friends all die. We lose our bearings! We end up on the Lido in Venice with mascara running down our cheeks! All you're missing, Sutcliffe, he thinks as he looks up at the face of Joseph, is the last act of a dreadful farce. I'm sorry I never let you come visit. You could have shared this with me; we would have been appalled together. You, who looked forward to old age, lost it. I, who get to have it, am horrified. And with that he feels himself collapse ever so slightly, slump back against the seat, and sigh.

The Japanese have a saying: To think of someone is to pray for him. If only it were that simple, he thinks. But he hopes they're right. Because praying, really praying, is such hard work. He's read somewhere that patients who are prayed for do better in hospitals, as if some mental energy is actually transferred. He half believes this, and half considers it New Age shit. He prays anyway, for what it's worth, even though he no longer thinks it likely that God will act on any of his requests, if God is even there. That's the problem. To grow up basing your values and conduct on the existence of a being your adult self decides is purely imaginary—what a great preparation for reality! God simply isn't taking calls. He's an absentee father, in another universe somewhere. Or so it seems. Unless—the Catholic view—all this suffering is to some end, part of His design. What that could be, Lark can't imagine. So he prays for people, just in case. And stops in churches sometimes just to rest. In Madrid or New York, wherever he's gone the last few years, he's been surprised, in fact, at how often he enters a church when he stumbles on it and sits there as if there is no point in going farther.

Today there is, however. He has to be somewhere. So he stands up, genuflects, crosses himself, walks back to the parking lot of Goering's, gets into his car, and drives to Eighth Avenue, where he turns left and hits his first red light at the corner of Thirty-fourth Street opposite a municipal park with tennis courts, a baseball field, a swimming pool, and picnic tables.

On the weekends this park is crowded with families and their children. Now, a pod of high school runners comes around the corner, their pale faces shocked, sweat streaming down their necks, eyes wide, as if they cannot believe they are still running. He loves seeing them. They're so skinny and young—but an age he does not envy. He sits there at the intersection, watching the crossing guard blow his whistle and wave the school kids across the street. He watches the teens jog around the park, where one night he stopped on his way home and walked into the trees because he'd heard the place was cruisy; met a middle-aged, pudgy man, no doubt a professor, beneath a pine tree; when the man put his hand on Lark's stomach, Lark flinched and walked away. We are so unkind to one another, he thinks.

The light seems to take forever. He turns down the volume on the radio—the *Spring* Sonata of Beethoven—in deference to the cars around him, even though he thinks people could use a little Beethoven. The light changes and he turns left onto Thirty-fourth Street, a block of brick ranch houses racially mixed a few years ago, although last month a household of renters hung a Confederate flag outside their garage; turns right at Mott's Tire and Brake, where he has his oil changed by young men in navy slacks and red polo shirts, so handsome he believes one should research the relationship between the desire to work on car engines and good looks; stops at the Suwannee Swifty to buy a copy of *The New York Times* from the chatty lesbian at the register; then, glancing at the beautiful student snoozing in the Laundromat next door while his wash dries—so blissfully far from adult troubles and heartbreak, thinks Lark—he gets back into the car and crosses University Avenue to the strip mall where his health club is housed.

Sutcliffe never went to a gym. Or rather he went, but he went socially, casually, without the religious fervor that characterizes certain New Yorkers. Lark still remembers the first night they ran into each other in the locker room of the West Side Y—Sutcliffe, just showered and dressed, was buying a V8 juice from the vending machine; together they walked across the park beneath a starry November sky to his apartment to have a drink and talk. It remains, years later, one of the those chance encounters New York is full of when you are young, because people do not spend their time enclosed in metal boxes on wheels, thinks Lark, they actually run into each other on foot, a revolutionary concept, considering the car culture he is part of now. That was when he was happiest, perhaps: that night they met by accident after their workouts and walked across Central Park.

Now the gym culture, like the whole country, is a little more intense. Where on earth did people get the idea that all that counted was their bodies? Their appearance? "A very important stomach," Eddie used to say as they watched the beach parade on Fire Island. Joshua would not even take a vacation to San Francisco without making arrangements first to use a gym there, as if he were afraid he would—by the time he got off the plane—deflate. Joshua, who built up a chest so enormous he claimed people "decapitated" him when they passed on the beach—stared, that is, at his chest, not his face. Joshua, who spent three hours every day in the gym on Sheridan Square and then complained that men were interested only in his "blorts."

He, Lark, is not as fanatical as that. He enters the gym with a feeling of despair. The pert young woman at the desk in the lobby types the number on his membership card into the computer, and then, when a blank comes up on the screen where his face should be, she hands his card to him and says, "Could we get your photograph?"

"*Now?*" he says, in so loud, alarmed, and appalled a voice it startles him and the people standing in line behind him. It's a policy they recently initiated: You stand next to the desk against a white screen on the wall, floodlights blaze, and the picture is taken. He's seen them all, pinned like crime suspects to the wall, in all their youth and beauty. "I'm late today," he says. "Next time, okay?" She nods and takes the next customer's card; Lark enters the gym. He cannot bear the idea of being photographed. The results have been so hideous the past few years. Nor will he look at mirrors. Alas, this gym is full of mirrors. Up north he chose run-down YMCAs because they had a track and swimming pool and weight rooms with no pretensions to glamour. What you got instead was an atmosphere of decay and a suggestion of sex. He loved going to the McBurney Y late on a Saturday afternoon, staying till there were only a few men left in the locker room, then walking home. This gym in a Florida strip mall is all glitz, mirrored walls, neon tubing, recorded music, spandex, leotards, aerobics, and StairMasters. It induces in him a feeling of Death. It makes him recall, each time he enters the locker room, the fallen, and ask if their deaths don't obligate him to do something with his life. What he does with it is go to the gym.

The gym is popular with students. *Look but do not touch* is the caption. They work out in artfully color-coordinated layers of Lycra and cotton shorts and tank tops. They emerge onto the floor like dancers auditioning for *Star Search*. When he mounts the StairMaster and looks out over the sea of bodies, he sees one thing and one thing only: Time. Slabs of Time. Oodles and oodles of Time. Time they still have on earth: years and years left of smooth skin, thick hair, and sex appeal, solid chunks of unchipped Time. It makes them stupid, and it makes them gods. They are beautiful and young, and because they are young they cannot know how beautiful they are—though they might suspect intellectually that other people envy their youth, that it must therefore, for some reason they cannot see, be valuable.

They are so young he feels sordid trying to maintain the shape of a body that is, Sutcliffe once said, settling, like a house, on its foundations. And yet my ass, he thinks, has never been firmer, harder, more muscular; but I can no longer use it. The rectum *is* a grave. The mind, of course, is just a little bit above the rectum in the scheme of things, but the mind tells us that the rectum at the moment is off limits. The mind tells us that homosexual congress makes no sense, is pointless, sterile, insane, against all reason, a case of bad wiring; the mind deduces there is absolutely no point in loving other men. But the rectum has reasons the mind knows not of. The rectum and, of course, the heart. We need to touch one another and be touched—to ground ourselves like Antaeus against the earth—and that is that. It isn't homosexuality that mystifies him; it's heterosexuality. Men and women are so different. Men looking at one another can easily admire superior versions of themselves; he does so every time he comes here.

How little, he thinks, do these young men realize the full extent to which they supply images the older, decrepit gentlemen will carry with them the rest of the day. Like the blonde looking at himself now in the mirrors behind the StairMasters as he walks by. It is shocking to see. Only youth can stand beneath those bright ceiling lights, its smooth white skin irradiated; the old would be covered with warts, body hair, wens, sagging folds, spots. Youth's envelope is new. It says, Open Me.

Whereas I walk around the gym from machine to machine with eyes averted, or like a Jesuit novice with eyes on the ground, head down, shoulders slumped—the posture, he thinks, of someone ashamed. Ashamed of what? Of being old. Treasures of the soul notwithstanding.

The woman on the bicycle in front of him is reading a magazine whose cover lists these articles: "I Was a Prisoner of Love." (Me too, he thinks.) "How to Get a Man to Call Back." (Tell me.) "What Men Really Want." (I wish I knew.) "Ten Ways to Lose Weight Without Dieting." (Take speed.)

A man and a woman mount the StairMasters on either side of him, talking to each other over his head. "Aerobics class is fabulous!" she says.

"That's because you're a woman," he says. "Aerobics are genetically programmed in females."

"Then swim!" she says.

"I don't get enough of a workout," he says. "My stroke is too efficient."

"Then golf!" she says.

"I've let my game slide," he says. "Were you at Contracts Wednesday?"

"God, yes!" she says. "I was totally confused! He's too old to be teaching! He forgets things, he should be retired!"

Lark wants to slap both of them across the face, but stares instead at the glowing green dashboard of his StairMaster, watching the level of stress increase and subside in little peaks and valleys. How much of the earth's resources are we using for this little electronic display? he wonders. He looks around at the people with plastic bottles of water they sip at intervals while riding the stationary bicycles, the others running on the treadmills facing a plate-glass window overlooking the parking lot, the beautiful, thin students who look so melancholy, the happy young husbands, the jocks, the black staffer who flirts only with white women, the dark, curly-haired, middle-aged men who stand there talking to blondes half their age on the StairMasters, the pale, gray-haired biology professor whose T-shirt bears a diagram of the molecular structure of aspirin, the young father who comes on Saturday morning with three children draped on his hip. Lark never speaks to anybody. A man he knew, a Cuban professor, after a year's friendship with a trainer here, told the youth one evening how good-looking he was; the trainer never spoke to him again. Nevertheless, all is vanity, especially when you stand before the mirrors in the shower room shaving, or toweling yourself dry in the nude, which two men are doing as he exits the shower afterward. That's all he needs to get through the day: one glimpse of the measure of all things.

Outside his car is broiling in the sun, warping his tape cassettes of the Beethoven sonatas. He has lost decades of German music this way: the Mozart C minor Mass was the latest to go. The button is hot when he turns on the radio to get *All Things Considered*—a news program he loved when he first moved down here, desperate to stay in touch with the real world, but which now seems another version of the White Man's Burden; in traffic at five o'clock, on University Avenue, the world-weary tone of the anchorman sounds like that of a bored waiter in a fancy restaurant handing you a plate of that morning's shit, fresh from Somalia, North Korea, Bosnia, the Gaza Strip. The world seems to be decaying—overpopulation, or just the fact that in every generation there will always be the same percentage of assholes. He changes to the Christian radio station and listens to Alexander Scourby read from the Book of Numbers—at least it has grandeur—till he turns off to the nursing home opposite the mall. Malls, gymnasiums, nursing homes—the institutions of modern life, he thinks; the Culture of Death, the pope calls it, the late Pax Americana: quadriplegia, AIDS, and television. Then he parks, buttons his shirt, takes a deep breath, and gets out of the car.

Age and Decrepitude

~~~~~~

He enters the nursing home with the feeling of entering a jail, a tomb, or the boarding school he used to return to after Christmas vacations with a heart so heavy he could barely drag the suitcase down the frozen snow of Main Street to his dormitory, unable to understand why his parents were making him do this. Nursing homes, the joke goes, are the Jews' revenge for summer camp. This one is revenge for boarding school. Living with a roommate, on a hall of other rooms, according to a fixed schedule: There's no difference. No wonder his father refused to give Lark the name of his doctor, the day he had his stroke; his father knew that once the doctor was called, the Medical Industrial Complex had you on its conveyor belt, and that conveyor belt ran straight from your own bed in your house to the nursing home to the ovens. ("Don't! Don't!" his mother cried out in pain one evening, when he tried gently to straighten out the right hand crippled into the shape of a claw. "I'm going to be cremated! What difference does it make?") His mother too wants to be in her own bed. At home. That is all she wants, really, besides the use of her arms and legs; but he can't give it to her, because one night she got up in the darkness to pee, tripped on a rug, fell, broke her neck, and that was that. "Whatever you do," an old friend wrote to him, "don't bring her home!" He brings her home weekends and holidays. The only way she could come home for good, he thinks, would be if she was dying. Yes, you can go home for good—*if* you are dying.

She has every right to be home. His father had every right to be home, but they took him from the hospital to the nursing home; where, his mother firmly believes, he bribed a nurse to give him poison so he could get out the only way open to him— by dying. You know you're in a bad way, he thinks, when the only door out is marked Death.

It's odd that this should have happened almost simultaneously with the onslaught of AIDS—two parallel disasters occurring in the separate compartments of his life; his friends dying in New York, his mother paralyzed down here. There are various theories to explain it—his cousin said, weeping, that his mother's accident had taken him out of New York and saved him from the plague; Sutcliffe told him he was there only to hide from the horror; another friend, in therapy in San Francisco, told him his mother had fallen in order to keep him by her side, out of the world of men. The fact is, two things happened for quite different reasons—Eddie, and all who followed, acquired a virus; his mother tripped on a rug.

In the meantime, he has come to realize that, whether or not he ever sees the connection between these two forms of suffering—these two disasters—life will not wait till he achieves his understanding; and that while he may feel Time has stopped, it hasn't. In fact, it's only when he walks through the door here and sees the faces of the octogenarians in the wheelchairs all turn, like men in a gay bar, to see who's come in that he feels what he used to when he walked into the Melody Club: young.

Sometimes there is real youth and beauty in the nursing home—a grandson visiting, a paramedic come to transfer someone to the hospital, a grounds keeper mowing the lawn outside, a nurse's aide, another employee. The best looking works in the kitchen, comes out after dinner with a plastic cap on his blond head, and pushes his cart through the hallways, offering the patients ice cream and cookies before bedtime from a red-and-white-striped wooden chest. Each time Lark sees him he thinks,

In Los Angeles you could be making porn films. Here you're delivering ice cream to incontinents. The women sometimes take the ice cream, sometimes do not. His mother's roommate—a gracious, dignified lunatic who eats a tin of Danish butter cookies every single day—always takes the ice cream. She eats nothing but sweets; he does not know how she can still be alive. His mother has gone through nine roommates—most of them have died. She is a veteran of the place; the eleventh customer, after it opened, in 1983. His mother has surprised everyone by lasting this long.

The other nursing home in town rejected his mother when he applied by mail from Chicago, while she was still in the rehabilitation center. The head nurse at the other nursing home explained they had one quadriplegic already and the staff didn't feel they could handle a second. He was horrified—so when this nursing home, brand-new, accepted his mother a week later, he danced around the kitchen, as if his daughter had just been accepted by Harvard and Yale. That evening, to celebrate, he took his mother down to the lounge of the rehabilitation center to hear a dance band; she burst into tears after hearing five bars of "I Get Ideas." It was the only time ever she did that, and as he wheeled her back to her room, he thought, I should have realized it would only remind her of the fact that she can't dance.

The day she entered the nursing home, he did something equally insensitive out on the patio after checking in: Under an umbrella in the bright sunshine, still optimistic, cheerful, humorous, he insisted his mother move across the tabletop—with what little power she had in her shoulder muscles—a dollar bill he had put beneath her lifeless hand. Then he saw, in the expression on her face, that this was painful to her too; she didn't, at this stage in her life, want to perform like a trained seal. She didn't want to learn to use the electric wheelchair; it frightened her—she knew the jig was up. Youth accepts tragedy more lightly than old age, and Lark was still young at the time. Twelve years later he is not. Yet all the years he's been coming to this door, he's felt that some sort of optimism, some sort of cheerfulness, are essential on his part.

Fortunately, once past his initial revulsion, he feels as if he's entering a cloister of contented nuns the minute the door of the nursing home closes behind him—a place as apart, as removed from the world outside, as a twelfth-century convent. Once he opens the side entrance door and walks past the woman who sits there for hours—staring through a glass panel into the parking lot, in hopes the son who does not come as often as she wishes will appear—a magic change takes place: Even he is young here—an infant among octogenarians. And there are no AIDS patients in the place; there never have been. They go to the other nursing home, he's learned; he's not sure why. When news of AIDS comes through the television, he and his mother never discuss it, even though he sometimes thinks of turning to her and saying, You know, by all rights, I shouldn't be here at all—it's inexplicable that I'm alive. But he doesn't. He doesn't know why he's not got AIDS and is able to come to this nursing home to help her; but not knowing makes it impossible for him to accept the fact, much less enjoy or discuss it. He merely wants to outlive his mother. He doesn't want the roles to be reversed. He's like a man full of superstitions, hiding in a cave in the Ice Age, when life was brutish and short.

One day he and Sutcliffe were walking down Madison Avenue when a man they knew came up and told them a mutual friend had just died in San Francisco. "Of It?" they gasped. "No," the man said, "he was run over by a taxicab." "Oh, thank *God!*" they both said in unison. That was where AIDS stood in the hierarchy of misfortune, somehow; in a class by itself—so grim its aura extended to the fact, he thinks as he enters the nursing home, that people who don't have AIDS imagine somehow they're not going to die.

But they are—and they'll probably end up here first, he thinks. Pleasant thought. My mother has me to help her out, but I'm going to have nobody. The homosexual nightmare: No child to wipe your fevered brow. Even if children live thousands of miles away these days, and come back, if at all, only for brief visits. He's seen a lot of people die here without kin. After twelve years, he walks past room after room, doorway after doorway, associated with someone he and his mother came to like. Eventually you stop making new friends—as in life—because you just can't care anymore; your supply of love and devotion has been depleted. And yet the moment he enters the nursing home, he can still feel from the nurses' demeanor when someone else has died—after all their years in places like this, it still affects them—and on those nights he will look up and see, passing in the doorway, someone on a stretcher being wheeled down to the exit by two handsome young paramedics in blue pants and short-sleeved white shirts, one of them with a walkie-talkie. The First Law of the Medical Industrial Complex is: Paramedics are always good-looking. Like firemen. Or is it just the uniform? Living down here, Lark has become a fan of the men who deliver parcels, fill the gas tank, check the electric meter, install the washing machine, fix the toilet, trim the trees: all in uniform.

Very few people return to the nursing home once they have left—patients or employees. Even this home's other quadriplegic—a young man of thirty, shot accidentally by his best friend while hunting—went to live with a nurse who fell in love with him, and he never came back. Occasionally family members who visit make a vow that, when their loved one gets out—through death or recovered health—they will come back and see the friends they made among the other patients. They seldom do. They send flowers instead, and a thank-you note to the nurses. Even the Sullivan sisters, who came every day at nine in the morning and stayed till five, for three years, until the death of their mother. Even the parents of a young man bed-bound in the final stages of multiple sclerosis, who came every day of the week and sat beside the bed in which he lay speechless and paralyzed, staring at the mirror on the ceiling put there so he might have something to look at. His father came and read the Bible to a few patients with whom he had become friendly. But then he stopped. The only man who reads the Bible to patients now is a man who works there, vacuuming and shampooing the carpet; in the evening after work he has a Bible reading in the dining room, while his wife plays the piano, and he delivers homilies. Lark considers him a saint, not because he does this, but because he is kind to all the patients.

Of course, there are those who are not kind to the patients. Sometimes he arrives for dinner and finds his mother seething over the rudeness of a nurse's aide; but when he asks the aide's name so he can report her, his mother refuses—fearing retaliation. It's like a prison. She is, after all, helpless and knows it. Sometimes he finds her lying on urine-soaked pads. Sometimes he finds a fly on her forehead. Other times he walks in and there is no one in the hall, and the long beige corridors look like the interior of an expensive passenger ship. The nurses' desk is crowded with enormous flower arrangements grateful sons and daughters have sent after their parents' funerals; behind the gladiolas and tulips, the nurses are all quietly filling out forms, eating pizza, or talking on the telephone to a child at home. ("I don't care what Billy says, you stay there and *do* your homework!") In the Activities Room, a table is lined with patients playing bingo or cutting pictures out of magazines to make a collage, and there are family groups on the patio lingering over dinner with their father or mother at one of the umbrella-shaded tables, and everything looks like the brochure. The next time it is clearly an insane asylum, something from the nineteenth century. He never knows what to expect and always braces himself when he opens the door, even after coming here for twelve years.

Today the nurses are all clustered at the desk, on the telephone, trying to get a doctor to accept a patient, so that she can be transferred to the hospital. Mrs. Caldwell, just out of Shands Hospital after having 80 percent of her bowels cut out because they were full of cancer, is not breathing; the feeding tube they inserted into her small colon has backed up and feces are coming through it. "Feces were coming out everywhere," he hears the nurse saying calmly into the phone. "She isn't breathing and doesn't have much of a pulse." The nurse has called 911; the paramedics have injected Mrs. Caldwell with sodium pentothal to bring her back, while the doctor, on the telephone, is telling the nurse to let her go. The nurse tells the paramedics the doctor wants to speak to them. The paramedics refuse, knowing he wants them to stop. "We're going to do our job!" they call. "We need to get her to the hospital."

"But she can't go to North Florida," the nurse calls. "She came from Shands!"

"She'll never make it to Shands," says the paramedic. "We're talking her to North Florida!"

Hearing this, the doctor, on the telephone, begins to curse. The paramedics wheel Mrs. Caldwell into the hallway and begin doing CPR. "This is gross," says the nurse, hanging up the phone.

Up to the desk walks a man whose father has just been transferred to VISTA—the nut house—without his dentures. "No one can find the dentures. Where are they?"

Lark goes to his mother's room two doors down from the desk. Her face lights up the moment he appears. She is in bed, a bib at her neck, food on her lips, as the aide holds a spoonful of pureed peas. "You see, I told you he was coming," says the aide, standing up, "I got you an extra tray," as he bends down and places his face next to his mother's.

His mother cannot embrace him as either a greeting or good-bye; her arms lie limp at her sides. (Limp, not rigid. When you hear someone is paralyzed, you imagine solidity, stiffness, as in "paralyzed with fear"; but in fact, paralyzed people, he's come to realize, are just the opposite—utterly, hopelessly limp: rag dolls, when you pick them up. If he lifted his mother's arms now, they would instantly flop to the bed, the minute he let them go.) She cannot voluntarily touch anyone. She cannot prevent herself from being touched either. Sometimes at home, as she lies on the foam rubber mattress watching television, or simply looking out of the window, or even counting the number of panels in the ceiling, he will lie down on the mattress beside her or even throw an arm across her chest and hug her as best he can; but she cannot respond. She is completely limp. Others touch her; she does not touch them. She simply lies there, while the well meaning take her hand (which hurts), or even pat her on the head, or, worse, bend down and kiss her. She has no protection against kisses. Anyone, anything, even a fly, can land on her; she cannot deter the contact. It's one of those aspects of her situation that he never allows himself to think about. All he knows is his mother cannot embrace him; she can only lie there as he comes up to the bed and bends down and puts his face beside hers—a custom that started as an air-kiss on either side of the face, though now he merely puts his head next to hers and keeps it there a minute as she says, "Thank God you're here, I was waiting for you, the nurse said it was five o'clock"; and keeping it there for a long minute manages to be the equivalent, somehow, of a good strong hug. Then he sits down and takes the aide's place at her bedside, while the aide watches all this with a smile.

"I thought we were going to the mall," his mother says in a faint voice. "I wanted to have a hot dog!"

"Well," Lark says, "we can still go if you like, but since you've started eating this, why not finish?"

"I'm so glad you're here, so glad you're here, I can't tell you," she says.

"You must be unmarried," says the aide with a smile.

"Yes," he says, thinking, and a homosexual child. Racked with guilt for my failure to have children, my failure to pass on the love, encouragement, support, and advantages in life that were given me.

"Well, she was callin' for you," says the aide, as she pauses in the doorway.

"No!" says Lark.

"Yes," says the aide, laughing. "She be callin' your name long before you get here."

He waits for the aide to leave and then says to his mother, "Do you call my name when I'm not here?"

"Yes," she says, an innocent expression on her face.

"Why?" he says.

"Because I miss you," she says.

"You mustn't do that," he says, now placing a spoonful of mashed potatoes before her mouth. "It sounds pathetic."

"I can't help it," she says. "I was going nuts before you got here. The aide left both TVs on all afternoon, tuned to different stations. I thought I was going out of my mind."

"That is so awful," he says, but his anger is countered by the fact that both TVs are now tuned to the same local news program: pert Deborah Gianoulis and Tom Wills, on Channel 4, are broadcasting a news program recently expanded to an hour and a half that is about an hour too long. He turns away from her and pretends to watch the news, but it's really to hide his smile—his feeling of joy at being with her, here in the familiar room, for this regular visit; knowing he can rescue her from the long, dull day, the televisions tuned to different stations, the aides and nurses, the mad roommate. The feeling of joy he gets from helping her is so intense at times, so rich, he's sure it has ruined his sex life. The love, the intimacy, the affection men search for—whether they'll admit it or not—at places like the baths and the boat ramp, he receives three times a week in a broth so nutritious, so concentrated, anything else seems insipid. The only problem: It's his mother. A woman he thought he had detached himself from, in a "normal" way, till her accident. A woman he now finds himself rejoined with, reattached to, in a way that only complete helplessness and utter dependency could bring about. "She lives for one thing," her doctor told him, "the sight of you coming around that corner. That's it." Oh God, he thinks, no one should have this power. No one. His mother—once beautiful, charismatic, stylish, witty, athletic, often the center of attention—has now been reduced to only one thing: him. It isn't right, he thinks, it isn't right.

"What good am I?" his mother has asked on more than one occasion. "I'm paralyzed. I can't do anything for myself. I wonder why the Lord doesn't take me. What good am I?"

The question always stumps him. He says, "You don't have to be anything. You're you. I love you. That's all." And he thinks of Saint Augustine's definition: *Love means I want you to be.* What good are any of us, he always wonders when she asks this question. All five billion, or whatever the number is now, increasing daily. Surely it must be obvious to everyone at this point, he thinks, that the species is in no danger of dying out, that we have enough, that we can stop now, thank you.

They could all ask the question his mother asks, and he would have just as much trouble coming up with an answer. When his mother asks it again—and she does, every now and then, when she gets discouraged and depressed—he tells her that she doesn't have to be good for anything, she only has to exist, and that he loves her, which he does. Which makes him turn back toward her now and raise a spoonful of peas to her lips.

"What do you feel like being fed?" Lark asks her now, out of curiosity.

"A dog," his mother replies.

Dinner done, he dresses her, gets her up in the wheelchair—that transfer that can be done so many ways, with gentleness and tenderness or, conversely, when he is tired or angry with her, as if her she were a sack of flour—and, tipping it back to compensate for the curvature of her spine, he pushes her out into the corridor and heads toward the wing that contains most of the dementia cases. He has just received an engraved invitation from the nursing home administrator to attend the grand opening of "the new Dementia Unit," which made him laugh out loud, since the entire place, so far as he can tell, is a dementia unit. The televisions in the rooms they pass are all tuned to the news. As he walks down the hall, he glances into 156 and sees a woman sitting all alone in front of her set, yelling at Deborah Gianoulis, "Go to hell! Go to hell! You're not worth anything, anyway!" in a sharp, vituperative voice. In 158 an old man is offering the news anchor the food on a tray he holds out to the screen. The sets are all tuned to the same segment: the return of a navy ship to Mayport—a young father holding a baby born while he was at sea. "What can I say? I'm speechless," the sailor says, but the camera stays on him, refusing to accept speechlessness, demanding a tear. Tears on TV are like the come shot in a porn film, he thinks, as he wheels his mother past a medicine cart. In both cases, the fluid must be seen. "Go to hell! Go to hell! You're lousy yourself!" the woman yells in a voice that carries down the hall. Extraordinary, the sounds that carry down an entire hall: the moans, the shrieks. One woman crying "Mama, take me home!" can fill the whole place, with an effect that Callas would have envied at her peak.

The only way to shut out the cries, and the loud TVs, is to close your door. His mother never wants her door closed, not even when he is visiting her. She wants to see what's going on outside, in the hall. As he pushes his mother's wheelchair around the four corridors, which surround a central open patio, his mother is finally content. She loves people. Tours of the rose garden up the hill, the flower beds planted in front of the numerous doctors' offices, she has no interest in. She wants people.

Tonight he even takes her out the door, through the parking lot, and across University Avenue to the mall, and wheels her down its long, cool, air-conditioned esplanades, parting the shoppers coming toward them the way Moses parted the Red Sea—so extraordinary is the sight of his mother, tiny and gnarled, tilted in her wheelchair. He can see her presence register on the faces of the oncoming pedestrians: the quick, panicky moment of debate—to look at or away from her—and then the outcome. Only children stare, over the shoulders of their mommies. He wheels her first through JCPenney, past the computer, shoe, and sportswear stores, to the fountain in the atrium where the railroad that kids ride at Christmas is put up. Then he has a hot dog and a root beer and frozen yogurt. His mother is content. She likes to shop in Penney's on the way, with the garments on the rack at eye level. He likes to look at the teens walking in flocks to the movie theater. There is a men's room here that used to be popular with homosexuals, but its popularity created problems, and the management has since removed the partition that enclosed the toilet, which now sits, naked, cold, and gleaming, on the tiled floor, like a primitive throne in the palace of Knossos, a monument to that unalterable law: Popularity Kills.

Today it's slow at the mall, however—even if it's air-conditioned—and he's relieved thirty minutes later that his mother agrees to return to the nursing home, where he resumes wheeling her around the halls, past the woman who has cancer and an incomprehensible southern accent, and who sits outside her room in a wheelchair reading *Jackie* in large type. ("You'll know more about her than anyone here!" he says, pausing a moment beside her. "More than I want to know!" she growls.) Past the vacant room of a friend who left to live with her daughter and son-in-law. Around the corner of Station One, and into the corridor of mostly mad people—a woman who was a professor of geography at the university, strapped into her wheelchair, clawing the air with her hands, as if sorting cards in the drawer of a card catalog; a young woman paralyzed in an automobile accident who hennas her hair, wears dark glasses, and talks for hours on the pay phone to someone about what she ate that day; a short Frenchwoman in faux pearls and a polka-dot dress, carrying both her purse and a framed photograph of her daughter ("Madame Char*beau*") and son-in-law, asking whomever she meets where they are; a woman who clutches a plastic baby on her lap; a woman who circles the corridors on foot, grasping the wooden rail as she pulls herself along; a former dean of students at a college in Pittsburgh, who wears a hat with a feather in its brim and sits in his chair whistling "Begin the Beguine" with perfect pitch; a woman who stops when Lark and his mother approach and always says something desperately urgent to them that they cannot understand; a former mathematics teacher who lives in his pajamas, confined to the nursing home for no reason Lark can see; a gaunt man dying of cancer who sits in his doorway staring at his bare feet; a tall woman who hugs herself as she walks around, gasping with emphysema every few steps; a woman who used to be his mother's roommate till the woman threatened to hit her one afternoon; the Cuban couple who walk everywhere together, the wife so jealous she walks one step behind her husband and beats him up when she thinks he has been looking at another woman, so that sometimes his handsome face is bruised; and next a cluster of three women who sit at the main intersection commenting on what goes by in sympathetic tones ("Poor thing! Isn't that sad!")—since in a nursing home, as in life, there is a snobbery of grief, a hierarchy of pity, in which nearly all the residents can, and do, find someone else to feel sorry for, worse off in their view than themselves—then past the TV lounge, the pantry, Station One, back to his mother's room, where her current roommate lies, watching a TV she cannot comprehend as she eats from her tin of Danish cookies, and back to bed beside the window through which he sees a handsome, red-haired grounds keeper trimming the grass at the edge of the building, beaded with sweat, oblivious to Lark's admiration.

The first year his mother was paralyzed, she would often say, "I want to die," but, horrified by the words, he would tell her there was no reason to think this way; then one day she amended it to "When you quit, I quit," which meant they were bound together, the two of them, in this peculiar endeavor to nullify as much as possible the results of her accident; to bring her back to where she had been, before she left on that trip to Chicago and fell. Someone in Miami is doing research on the spinal cord, funded by the father of a football player injured in a game; though Lark does not hold out much hope for a breakthrough there, he tries to imagine a discovery that would restore communication through the spinal jelly from brain to muscles, tries to imagine the injection that would restore her power to walk and move her arms, tries to imagine her getting up like Lazarus one day, dressing herself, and walking out of the nursing home. He likes to imagine the quips. The revenge! On all the aides who were lazy, ignored her, talked back, put cartoons on the TV and walked out of the room. But he does not expect it to happen; it's like the final scene in *Longtime Companion* where all the gay men dead of AIDS come back to life on the beach. A fantasy. As if heaven *were* just a disco in the sky. Instead, a therapist told him one day in the parking lot, "What she needs is another body." His is her other body: He scratches her nose when it itches; he rubs her forehead, feeds her dinner, clothes and pushes her around the hall, takes her home each weekend to sleep in her own bed. And then brings her back to this building they cannot entirely leave behind, the nursing home he sometimes feels is a gas oven he is pushing his mother into when he takes her back and sometimes thinks is salvation itself, the nursing home they have been in longer than anyone here except the nurse on Station One, the nursing home that makes every weekend away a sentimental gesture at best. As Sutcliffe once said, it's not easy being a single parent.

But he is—even if the role reversal is cruel. No one should have the power over his parent I do, he thinks, as he puts her into her bed and turns on *Murder, She Wrote*. It is very important she see Angela Lansbury. The year Angela got tired of doing the show, she merely introduced episodes in which other people acted. "I'm out of luck," his mother says now, when one of these is rerun. "I've waited all day for this show, and she's not in it. I'm paralyzed, have only one good eye, my skin itches and burns, and she's not in *Murder, She Wrote*." Even he misses her; Angela soothes them both. Her cheerfulness, her acting skill, her outfits, the cozy interior of her house, the comfortable stereotypes of the little town—so obviously the northern coast of California, not Maine—the actors brought out of retirement for cameo roles, the sprightly music of the theme. Even his mother's roommate turns her face toward their set when Angela comes on, like a flower turning toward light.

After they watch *Murder, She Wrote*, he gets her up in the wheelchair again and takes her out to Station One to get her sleeping pill and Tylenol; then they take a turn around the corridors, mostly empty now, while she says in a dull disappointed voice, "Everybody's gone to bed," the way he says "It's slow tonight" to the only other patron of a bathhouse. Then he takes her back to her room, puts her to bed, brushes and flosses her teeth, washes her face, and undresses her. She always claims he missed food particles between her teeth. He says, "I floss your teeth more thoroughly than I floss my own!"

Now *Larry King Live* comes on. Though he used to become impatient at this time, eager to get out of the building, he has learned that an act of kindness that lasted four hours can be completely ruined by five seconds of last-minute anger; and his chief goal is to leave the place without guilt, since he carries so much with him already. So he becomes even more patient toward the end, while Victoria Principal talks about a TV movie she has just made. He does everything his mother asks, as he arranges her bed for the night. Even then, she hates to let him go. "My right arm is throbbing," she says, after he has placed it on a pillow. "Could you move it toward the window?" And: "My left arm is throbbing now. Move the pillow up." And: "I'm not vertical. I should be in line with the picture of Jesus on the wall." And: "Shouldn't I be higher up in bed?" And: "Could you lower the bed?" And: "Are my legs on the pillow?" And: "Scratch my eye! My right eye! Now the left one, it's leaking. Why does my skin burn and itch? Do my eye again! Between the eyebrows!" And: "One more kiss!" And: "I want to thank you for all you do for me, you're so patient. Just wait till I see how my right arm feels, it's so important you can't imagine." He can imagine; that's the trouble. It's inconceivable, on the other hand.

He waits till she decides her arm feels right, then says good night, crosses to the door, as she calls, "One more kiss! One more kiss!" And he goes back, bends down, and gives her a symbolic buss. Her skin has broken out; her eyes are swollen; she is so emaciated that, when he saw her once in the front seat of the car he'd parked outside a convenience store, as he came back with his newspaper, he thought, My God, how can I be keeping that alive?

She says, "Move my right arm once more." He does this. "Drive carefully," she says, "drive *very* carefully." Meaning: You're all I have; if I lose you, I'm stuck. There's no one to scratch my nose. By the time he has arranged her right arm, kissed her good night, and left the nursing home, he is so depressed, the exhilaration of being free of the place is null. There is a basic unfairness here, he thinks as he walks out. Sutcliffe died, I'm alive. She stays behind, I leave.

At times he has to remind himself, She fell, I didn't. But it doesn't matter. She fell on him. All accidents on a certain scale, he noticed early on, sitting in the waiting rooms of intensive care units, affect not only the person who had the accident, they affect the person's family as well. "She'd be better off dead!" his cousin said the evening she visited his mother for the first time after the fall; he wanted to slap her, for saying precisely what they could not allow themselves to think. "Would you rather have died the night you fell?" he recently asked his mother. "Oh God, yes!" she said in a loud croak. So much for the twelve years: They were victims, all of them, of Technology—she'd been on her way out of Life, in a revolving door, and been caught when the door stopped—she'd been stepping into Charon's boat to cross the river Styx when she was pulled back, one foot in the boat, one foot on the bank. Death had been devouring her and dropped her to the floor, like a dog distracted by other prey, mangled and crippled and sore.

Sometimes he tries to understand her situation as he drives off from the nursing home, by refusing to scratch his face when it begins to itch; but he never makes it very far, a few blocks at most, before giving in and reaching up to rub the irritated skin. Mostly he does not even try. Tonight he does not even make it to the stop sign at the top of the hill before stifling a dry itch with the blunt tip of his right forefinger. The death she could have had, he thinks as he drives past the new surgical pavilion, the drugstore, the hospital parking lot, where a few figures are walking to their cars—workers getting off or families grieving for someone inside—was an easy one; she would have died without ever knowing what had happened. That death had been denied her, however. By the misfortune of falling in a big North American city with the latest in hospital technology. Her life was saved, her neck fused, and then the doctor walked out of the room on to the next assignment. There is a Chinese prov-erb: He who saves a life is responsible for it. Ha! he thinks. In modern America, he sends you a bill. What if, he wonders as he waits at the stop light on University Avenue, doctors *were* responsible for the lives they saved? What if Americans had to pick their own fruit and vegetables? Someday, he thinks, they may be able to restore movement to quads—but now we are caught between two eras, when people who broke their necks died, and the yet-to-arrive moment when quads get movement back. A way station. A sacrifice for Science. That's Mum, he thinks, as the light turns green and he accelerates onto Univer-sity Avenue. The parking lot of the Oaks Mall is empty—an evening's spending spent. A pleasant air of exhaustion hangs over Burger King, Pic 'N Save, McDonald's. He puts a tape into the machine, presses the button, listens to the adagio swell, and thinks as he drives on, I've exchanged my mother for a Mozart piano concerto; I've turned her, like Peneus turning Daphne into a tree, into music. And now I need something very gay. And he drives straight to Gaytalk.

Talking About It

He parks at the far end of Nineteenth Street and hurries down the dark leafy sidewalk. He can hear Roger's voice delivering a report on the Outwrite conference in San Francisco he has just returned from, as he turns in on the narrow walk of the Quaker meeting house. On Tuesday nights the Nicaraguan family that lives there—five refugees sheltered by the church—is out bowling. The white frame building is a sort of time-share. America itself is a sort of time-share, he thinks, different groups using it at different times. When he slips into the building, he is too self-conscious to scan the group already seated on folding chairs. He takes a seat near the door and stares intensely at Roger, to make up for his lateness by presenting the tableau of a man drinking in every syllable that's uttered. Becker does not come to these meetings. (Why should Becker talk about the issues of gay life? Lark wonders. He lives them.)

The speakers who address the group are solicited by the middle-aged psychiatrist who runs the group; a man who, after raising two children, left his wife for a middle-aged dentist even plumper than himself. It is hard coming up with a new topic every week. What is there to say about being gay? Coming out is the central story, told over and over again, like people describing how they found Christ. The group is mostly middle-aged men; the students, loath to attend a group with older people, have formed a club of their own at the university. When he was twenty years old, Lark did not want to have anything to do with older men either: trolls, lurking beneath the bridges over the River of Life he was floating down. So, cut off from the rich possibilities of intergenerational exchange—the real function this meeting might have served, the old and young infusing one another with their different perceptions—they are herded into a little corral of age before slaughter.

If there is no new book to be described or video to be shown, the psychiatrist imports a speaker—an instructor from the university conducts psychological tests; one week someone tries to explain Foucault; the next week a woman is brought from a department store in the Oaks Mall to lecture on cosmetics. Or someone who has a project of his own going on at the graduate school will use the men as guinea pigs. It doesn't matter. Lark knows the real reason for this meeting is not the topic, the information exchanged; it's to meet other guys. Most nights the talk is a drone, and the eyes glaze over. Occasionally someone who has been to one of the gay conferences convening at a different university each year will return from San Francisco or Boston or New Haven or Chicago to report on his experience there. (Indeed, there are suddenly so many conferences at universities now, such a flood of gay studies, gay symposia, gay books, gay banquets, Lark thinks; yet most of us still can't get laid.) He sits beneath the whirring ceiling fan, on a metal folding chair, in the pale radiance of the ceiling light bulb, in this house owned by the Quakers, most peaceful of all religious groups, their peace, their friendliness, extending to him, and watches young men drift by on bicycles in the street outside, their black Lycra butts high in the air, like lovebugs floating through the dusk, and feels a great peace stealing over him, the feeling he used to get at church, at evening mass. The words of the speaker are not important. Mostly he is conscious of the room, the physical gathering of men in the evening together—not in a sexual sense, but in a deeper, more spiritual bond. Men coming together in what is—for homosexuals—a neutral environment.

On the edge of the group, the core of which consists of six people—the psychiatrist, a professor, a pediatrician, an attorney, Roger, and a gigantic postman who collects gay books—there are always the newcomers; the men no one has seen before, the ones who never speak during the discussion afterward, who, when the meeting is brought to a close by the psychiatrist and everyone stands, hesitate for a moment like deer on the edge of a highway and then bolt, as quickly as they can, overcome by the horrible realization that what they came for is not the lecture but the relief of their awful loneliness. Even he, his first few times, would slip away and drive off immediately, choked with shyness. Now he has his eye on the silent, somber, balding man in the third row with a big moustache and glasses: Who is that?

The man is losing his hair just the way Lark is losing his—a plus in Lark's eyes: He refuses to sleep with anyone his age who has more hair than he does. He's furious that his hair is thinning. In fact, when he saw Sutcliffe lying in the coffin, all he could think was, He still has that gorgeous hair. Indeed, he has had to admit that his mother's paralysis, his friends' death and suffering from AIDS, do not really horrify him on an immediate, daily basis the way his rapidly receding hairline does. So I'm shallow, he thinks. If only I'd known it sooner, I would have been a lot nicer to people.

This is the second edition of Gaytalk; the first disbanded after its founder, a well-known psychology professor at the university, slept with everyone in it. Lark sits here now with his usual feeling of unreality, brooding about his hair as he listens to Roger report on the Outwrite conference, and thinks, Life is like a movie that runs forever—only some people have to leave the theater early and don't get to see the next part, while others do. Sutcliffe isn't here anymore. Or Shannon. Or Eddie. I am. Seeing what happens next. For no reason I can discern. Which leaves one with the deep impression, as if my mother's situation wasn't enough, that life is unfair, accidental, and completely without any regard for the little system of truth and justice we have set up in our hearts. How quickly that little system collapses when one is faced with the fact that one's body is deserting—turning traitor, bringing this road show to a close, much sooner than one expected. I'm sitting here worried about my receding hairline, the gray hair on my chest, and they watched KS cover their arms and feet, their ribs outline themselves against their skin, their faces turn into those of ninety-year-old men. What a sadistic disease for homosexuals—who *are* their looks, who *are* their bodies. How the Fundamentalists love it! he thinks. Finally, Jehovah acting the way He's supposed to. An example of divine eugenics—eliminating fags, drug users, the gene pool of the inner cities, the blacks and Puerto Ricans nobody wants in this country anyway. And what really happened? A large mass of people in the world's most prosperous nation, toward the end of the twentieth century, in the great flush of material abundance—the reward, you might say, for winning a large world war—see no reason to cleave to long-held standards of sexual and social conduct. In other words, penicillin is discovered; everyone gets rich and screws everyone else. In the meantime, jet planes are ferrying peoples formerly separated by miles of mountains, deserts, oceans, and throwing them together willy-nilly in large cities. The fecundity of the tropics, with its myriad forms of microscopic life, flows north. And *voilà*, like the ancient Romans poisoned by the lead in their drinking water, society begins to succumb to tiny viruses, stupid microscopic parasites, and falls down, demented, delirious, dead. The dick of death, thinks Lark as the ceiling fan blows warm air down onto the top of his balding head, has become indeed the dick of death. And everyone has caught the fatal flu. And Eddie and Sutcliffe and Shannon and Michael and John and Robert and Joshua and Clovis and Vito and Charles and Ocsi and Metro are all gone. Gone, gone, gone. Leaving the rest of us—for no reason we can see—to carry on.

Which leads him to the overwhelming question: Why, he wonders, isn't having been spared sufficient to make one happy? Why isn't that enough? Why aren't the ones who were left behind beaming with joy? Why does life still sting with envy and frustration, loneliness and desire? One would think that not having AIDS—or not being paralyzed—would be enough to make you awaken every day in a state of bliss. But no, it's not. You still want a ten-inch dick, a full head of hair, two more decades of unblemished youth, and everyone to want you when you walk into the bar.

Disgusting species. He sighs, and shifts his weight on the folding chair to relieve the pressure on his buttocks. At least I *have* a butt, he thinks. A butt I do several exercises for, three times a week. Sutcliffe had no butt when he died. My butt is as hard as marble, and I have no sex at all. What brave men, he thinks, looking at his companions on the folding chairs. How decent, how good they are. To keep trying, within this context, to connect with another human being. Because the context is not that easy. Because, he thinks, being a homosexual is like trying to climb Niagara Falls. Eventually you have to admit: The water is going the other way. If you would only go in its direction, Life would take you right along downstream. Heterosexuality is like having a room ready for you at a hotel: The staff is expecting you—everyone knows his role. The homosexual shows up and has no reservation; he ends up outside, quite literally in the bushes.

But still we go on, he thinks with a sigh as he crosses his legs, boats against the current, borne back ceaselessly into the police station and doctor's office. This part of my life—this hour here, this room, these men, this calm deliberation—I cannot relate in any way to my four hours at the nursing home. Two fates, entirely separate.

Yes, everyone's tragedy is quite his own. When Lark's mother was still in the rehabilitation center, he went to the mall one evening to get her a Christmas present and suddenly realized there was nothing in the whole vast place she could use. Not perfume, not a new dress, not jewelry or books. He wandered and wandered until he chose scented body-powder and a few pairs of socks: the things you might purchase for a baby. And he thought, as he wandered through the crowds of shoppers that night, There is an invisible department store in Life, a department store of Tragedy; everyone has to get something. There are different tragedies on different floors, on all the counters, in various departments, but you can't buy nothing; you have to leave with one. Or two. Or more. That was how he felt that Christmas.

Now all he thinks about is sex, he realizes as another young man on a bicycle floats down the street outside toward the leafy glade of the student ghetto. The man seated in front of him turns too, to follow the disappearing Lycra butt, the sinews of distended triceps; Lark wonders why—given all this—people have not been able to stop having sex, even after learning it can be lethal, or at least provides no permanent shelter or rest for the weary. It is his anodyne. The more friends dead, the more he wishes to have sex; to do what he imagines they wish they could do. What was the most horrifying thing the day he learned that Eddie had KS? That he could not have sex anymore. So they thought in 1983. Now everyone he knows with HIV is tricking like mad. Still, sex seems like the only escape from the general horror, the ticking clock. I don't care about politics, he thinks. I don't care if the military ever accepts gays or America accepts homosexuals, but I do want to get laid. I want to be ravished, he thinks, as he sits there listening to the drone of voices, the whir of the ceiling fan; I want to be taken, fainting with pleasure, as Leda was taken by the swan; I want a golden, smooth-skinned, fine-limbed man with a big moustache, gaunt cheeks, and large, soulful, Scotch-Irish eyes to pound his member into my helpless flesh; I want to be raped, he thinks, raising his hand to the corner of his mouth where a bit of spit, of drool, has escaped his lower lip. Who cares about politics and interest groups?—I'm not getting laid. And he glares for a moment at the handsome stranger in the folding chair one row ahead of him, wondering what his type could be.

He never finds out—the stranger, like all strangers, bolts when the meeting comes to a close; dashes off rather than admit he knows no one in the room, and is as alienated as if he were in a bar. Lark drives to the bar, to see if he might be there. In the old days a group used to repair to the Ambush together—including an assistant professor of Chinese history fresh from Berkeley who excited them all, until they learned he was interested only in young Asians. A chicken-*and*-rice queen, thought Lark. None of them goes anymore. The professor has since taken a job at the University of Kansas and moved away. That's Gainesville for you. That's American life: The average American, he read somewhere, moves twelve times in his life. This seems high to Lark, but Americans *are* nervous. At the stoplight on Thirteenth Street, he watches a man in a Volvo talking on a car phone. He wants to roll down the window and yell, Who's on the line? Henry Kissinger? He turns on *Adventures in Good Music* instead and listens to Karl Haas discuss Beethoven as he drives north on Thirteenth Street. The slow movement of the *Pathétique* Sonata is playing when he pulls into the parking lot of the Ambush; he parks, turns off the engine, flips the key one more notch to maintain electrical power, and stays in his car till the music finishes. Other cars pull up and disgorge their passengers. He sits there through the slow movement of the *Pathétique* and a late string quartet—until he realizes he is sitting in a parking lot not because he wants to, or even because the string quartet is beautiful, but because he cannot enter the bar. He can't imagine opening that door and receiving, on his person, the sudden, simultaneous gaze of twenty other homosexual men turning with undying hope to see Who Walked In. He can't imagine ordering a drink, or standing against the wall, or perching on a ledge in the pool room, on the pretense that he has come to find Love. Or even Sex. After twenty years of going to places like this, one has to face certain statistical facts. After all the bars I've walked into, Lark thinks, every time with a little thrill, I am sitting in a Buick Skylark in a parking lot in Gainesville, Florida, wondering what is the point.

He watches two men leave the bar together, get into separate cars, and drive off—to another bar? The University Club? Or home to an apartment to have sex? Is it possible that they have actually met each other in the bar and are now going home to do it? Of course it's possible: They're young. The blond had that gorgeous haircut that looks like the helmet the guards at Buckingham Palace wear—the Roman helmet, with the plume. All done in human hair. He watches two other men get out of their cars and walk to the bar, passing under the light in the colonnade at the entrance, one of them hitching his belt up, the other patting his dark cloud of hair, the last nervous gesture before—Making an Entrance. For them the bar *is* exciting. The rewards are Sex and Pleasure. No wonder Youth has fun—it has so much time to reproduce. Or not reproduce, as the case may be.

With this thought he backs out. A man in a white tank top standing under the colonnade follows him with his eyes—a kindred spirit, Lark thinks, a man who also finds the bar beside the point, or the parking lot easier to cruise—but he does nothing about that either. He drives home through a light rain, listening now to the *Organ* Symphony of Saint-Saëns. That's middle age, he thinks: I'm going home with the *Organ* Symphony. Ten years ago I'd be going home with an organ. Ten years ago, men used to follow me in their cars when I drove away from the bar; now that my hair has gone entirely gray, I am allowed to disappear unchased. I don't feel there's any point in even going inside.

Which is why he's so grateful for the boat ramp. It's the boat ramp that has got him through the last years. His next stop.

Watering the Flowers

Twelve years ago, driving this stretch of Thirty-ninth Avenue, he always felt Bar Regret (I should have talked to the man standing there as I drove away; I should have talked to the guy playing pool; next time I'll make the effort), but now he feels none. Instead, he thinks as he comes to a stop at Waldo Road and he hears the strange whirring sound that someone told him is caused by the air-conditioner, I've got to get the air-conditioner fixed. He never uses it. That's why it's broken. It has to be used once a week, the man told him, to keep the rings lubricated. Like the *Challenger*, the space shuttle that blew up. You have to use your air-conditioner or lose it. (A man can spend his whole life in America taking care of appliances.) But he prefers the warm rush of wind in the front seat, he hates having the windows closed; and as he drives out of town, past the Honda dealer, the juvenile detention center, the jail, the airport, the trailer park, and finally the stop sign at Highway 26, he begins to feel almost happy and, for the moment, free.

His mother has been put to bed—he hopes she's sleeping by now—and he can hope that Becker will be at the boat ramp, though he knows that's unlikely. Earlier that evening, as he stood in the middle of her room, wondering if he had changed her pad or not, his mother—shrewd as ever—said, "Is there something wrong with you?" He turned to her and wanted to say, Yes, I'm in love with a man who doesn't want to see me. But he didn't. He can't confess something so embarrassing to his mother. So humiliating. So not-what-she-had-in-mind-for-me as a part of life. He said, "No." He didn't say that when he called Becker the previous day, Becker said he had taken so long to answer because he and his boyfriend had been out in the backyard "watering the flowers."

Watering the flowers—the phrase ran through Lark's mind over and over as he went about his business, getting more diapers and pads from the linen closet, making sure he'd taken the dirty clothes out of her plastic laundry bin—her name stenciled on it in black letters—and smoothing the ointment on her face so that the itching and the redness would go away for a day. *Watering the flowers.* It summed up everything he dreamed of, and what Becker actually had. "We were out back, watering the flowers." That's all. No AIDS, or even fear of AIDS when taking the test (Becker had said). No friends dead of It (that Becker mentioned); no years in New York City—the miles of bathhouse hallways trudged, the endless hours of patient waiting, in parks, corridors, bars; on beaches, sidewalks, dance floors, subway platforms; the sense, sitting in the park at three A.M., that you were wasting your life—no weights lifted, laps swum, haircuts labored over, clothes selected, disappointments absorbed, telephones stared at, heartbreaks, crushes, rejections, courtships, deaths of friends, hospital rooms, trips to Vieques or Fire Island or California or Berlin; no panic staring at oneself in the mirror, thinking, You're too old now to get anyone; you're already invisible, over the hill; you'll be spending the rest of *your* life alone, thinking of dead friends. No, none of that. No inability to sleep at night, conscious of the empty darkness of the house, the absence of a body beside one's own. Just watering the flowers in the backyard, on a hot summer afternoon, with the daughter he was raising on his own and his lover, because the flowers were parched and needed moisture. Oh, that you would water me, thinks Lark as he drives past pecan groves, and fields where that afternoon people on their knees had been planting strawberries. Oh, that your beautiful huge hands would hold the hose and let the stream of water fall into my mouth as I knelt before you, parched and hot. (Is that what I want, he thinks, his piss?) Or just him standing beside me, watering the flowers. Watering the flowers. That's all he wants to do at this point in life: water the flowers with someone he loves, or at least has regular sex with—that would be enough—while friends who telephone have to be dealt with politely, so that one can get back to the flower bed. "Who was that?" the lover must have inquired. "Some old fart who won't take no for an answer." Forget Love; that was much too dicey, quite possibly a myth. Just affection shown his body by another body. Becker's.

It's not likely that Becker will be at the boat ramp this evening. So far as he knows, Becker has only gone once; the night Lark met him there and took him home. But the thought that Becker might be at the boat ramp makes the ride across the dark, sleeping countryside more exciting than usual. Usually it's enough to be putting more distance between him and the nursing home with each passing mile, but now he's so preoccupied with getting to the boat ramp that when, past the failed pecan nursery east of Waldo, he notices four automobiles abandoned on the side of the road, they look to him like cars whose occupants stopped there and ran into the woods because they were suddenly overcome by lust. Strange thoughts one has driving these roads after dark; the most nondescript car, sitting in a puddle of light near a convenience store, in an otherwise empty parking lot, assumes an erotic significance it does not have during the day. Two police cars, pulled up beside each other, in a pool of lamplight near a liquor store, look like they're mating. Houses in the countryside, their windows lighted, with nothing for miles around; people walking by the side of the road; or even the glow of a distant town over the horizon—all suggest sexual emotions as he drives along, because he's going to the boat ramp.

There's finally something furtive about slowing down to turn off the highway at ten-thirty at night, at a spot in the road where only someone who knows the boat ramp would be able to pick out of the darkness the dull-brown sign announcing it, or perceive that in the wall of black forest on the left there is an opening in the trees. Tonight, he's even embarrassed when the cars coming the other way make him come to a full stop before making the turn—even though the people he's holding up behind him can't possibly understand why he's turning in to the boat ramp now.

Once past the embarrassment of turning off at the boat ramp, however—once past the spectral playground near the highway, its play equipment standing out on the white sand as if on a beach—the road comes around a curve, the darkness and the forest open up, and there's the rest room itself—floating, in a golden cloud of light shining through the wire mesh under the eaves, like some temple in Arcadia. Ah, he thinks the moment he catches sight of it, the glory that was Greece, the grandeur that was Rome! It looks so lovely in the darkness; it has a chaste and radiant air—unless some queen who prefers the dark has turned off the light inside, and then it looks sinister and Gothic, the shadows of the tree limbs traced across its oleaginous beige facade. Glowing or dark, the sight always relieves him when he finally sees it.

Tonight he breathes a sigh of relief: The parking lot is vacant save for an empty truck in the far corner—Ernie has finally gone home—he can unwind by himself, and contemplate the spot where Becker stood that wet April evening a year ago, leaning against his car, in blue jeans, black T-shirt, and bulging crotch, his arms folded across his chest, the very image of a porn star in the movie Eddie had rented that warm spring day on University Place to watch while he lay dying. A fantasy. A member of the cast of *Teen Marine*. At the boat ramp! Lark had been so undone by the juxtaposition of that image and the place, he'd cowered in his car, telling himself he had to finish listening to the Beethoven Seventh Symphony on the radio, knowing deep down, That man is trouble. Finally he got out; now, driving in a year later, he isn't sure if he should mark the spot where Becker stood with a small religious statue, like a roadside shrine in Mexico, or one of those white crosses people here put along the highways where someone died in an auto accident. In fact he doesn't know if he wants Becker to be there or doesn't want him to be there; part of the spell he's cast is that Becker doesn't go to the boat ramp. What he does instead Lark isn't sure, and wondering drives him crazy.

Becker's not here now, for instance—but Lark parks his car anyway underneath the single lamppost on the broad, empty patch of asphalt that looks now like the piazza of an Italian hill town in some opera, waiting for the soprano to enter. An owl is sitting in the middle of the pavement, and flies up into the largest oak tree when Lark gets out of his car. The air is moist and cool. Down by the water frogs are croaking. Everything is trying to reproduce but me, he thinks as he walks onto the dock, where two figures at the very end suddenly become visible—two regulars standing on the edge of the dock, where one pees into the canal and the other runs back and forth beneath the stream of urine, like a child avoiding a garden hose; they're drunk, and ask Lark if he wants to run under too. Lark says, "No," and lies down on the other side of the dark dock. Then the two reverse their roles. This must be, thinks Lark, what Marx meant by the idiocy of rural life. For this I went to Columbia. Then, moments later, the two men decide they need more beer and drive off to the convenience store, leaving the boat ramp to the owl, the frogs, the darkness, and the stars.

He's staring at the stars—thinking they're dead friends, transferred to points of light in the vastness of outer space—when a beige pickup truck painted with leopard spots drives in with a pile of chairs and tables underneath a sheet in the back.

It's Rick. Who went to school with Becker, thinks Lark. Since Becker never comes, he takes what scraps he can—from, say, this young man who knows Becker not only from high school but also through his boyfriend, with whom Rick plays volleyball every year at a ranch near Jasper owned by a retired neurosurgeon. Lark may be reduced to lying on a boat ramp dock, looking up at the Milky Way, on one more night when Becker is elsewhere, but it's some small thrill to get up now, walk over to Rick's truck, and talk to someone who at least went to school with the man.

Rick's also the friend of Susan, a beautiful woman who appeared at the nursing home one evening a few years ago—a former actress from New York, who had come down to Waldo to care for *her* mother, and nursed her through a year of bone cancer till she died; two years of heavy drinking, and one attempted suicide on her part, followed. Then she took a course in how to be a nurse's aide, and when Lark came for dinner one Tuesday, she was sitting at his mother's bedside, scratching his mother's forehead and feeding her the supper that had arrived. "I've a friend you must meet!" Susan said, after she and Lark had talked: a man who lived in Waldo and had helped her mother plan her garden when she was alive, a man with a degree in art history from Michigan who had returned home after working in Los Angeles. "But he's really an artist," she said—meaning, thought Lark, he's gay. "He's a sculptor, who does amazing things. He travels around to estate sales, finds odd pieces, welds them together, and *faux marbres* them. You'll see!"

Listening to these facts, Lark pictured a battered, jaded object-queen in his late forties, come back to lick his wounds after years of running around L.A.; cranky but bright, with the coldness of those whose dreams of interior decoration have been shattered. Instead, the night Susan and Rick arrived at Lark's house, a man of thirty in blue jeans, Doc Martens, and white T-shirt, with a tattoo on his right forearm—the uniform of the young—walked in. Lark was thrilled. He talked until they parted. Not only was Rick young, intelligent, sardonic, and handsome—he knew Becker. Or rather, after discussing the isolation of lives in these small towns, Rick asked Lark if *he* knew Becker. And Lark, choking back his unrequited love, said, "No, I've only heard about him." (And gone to heaven in his arms, he thought.) That was his only instance of discretion, however, and the next day he was crushed to learn from Susan that Rick had been "overwhelmed" by Lark's personality.

That's because I'm needy, he thought. I touched him too much while talking; gave him too strong, too long a hug when saying good-bye; insisted he call me. That's the reason. I'm needy. He could smell it. He could see it. And there's nothing more frightening than someone who's needy—someone who's drowning and may pull you under—which meant he refrained from calling the thirty-year old. I *won't* be the older man courting the young artist, he decided; and he waited till he saw him months later in a bar in Gainesville. Now he's here—no doubt on his way to, or from, that bar—though when Lark approaches the truck, both windows are rolled up, and he has to speak to Rick—who sits behind the wheel perusing a magazine devoted to antiques—through the opening in the sunroof, like a man confessing to a priest through the grille of a confessional. This aloofness, this *noli me tangere*, does not surprise him. I bore Rick, thinks Lark as he says hello. I do not exist for him, I am peripheral matter. I'm old. But he goes on, determined to learn what he can about Becker, and says, in a friendly voice, that's he's never seen Rick here before.

"I used to come a lot," Rick says, turning the pages of the magazine while the music plays on his tape deck, a hideous, discordant dirge—Claus Nomi making a camp mockery of that Dietrich classic "Falling in Love Again." The music Rick loves (Nomi, the Violent Femmes) is horrible, thinks Lark—it's not even music. It's music that makes fun of music, signifies the presence of a new generation, jaded, sarcastic, in love with Camp. That's all Rick has, he thinks: Camp. And a gorgeous butt. Thick legs, a wonderful body and—poignant in one who has not yet turned thirty-one—hair thinning already at the crown. Oh, well. We are all packages, and my package isn't what it used to be. "I used to come and photograph the graffiti," Rick says. "I was going to turn the photos into a line of postcards. But I haven't been back since then."

"Ah," says Lark, "I'm somewhat more addicted."

"You should be careful here," says Rick. "It's dangerous."

He's already been warned by people who come here that you can be assaulted, murdered, or arrested by plainclothes policemen; he's been told his license plate is on file in Tallahassee now; he's seen the face of a sweet, good-natured, gentle Episcopalian minister he became friends with two summers ago plastered on the TV screen last month during the eleven o'clock news, along with the story that the minister had solicited sex from an off-duty cop at another boat ramp, near Ocala—career ruined, family devastated. Lark's had an irate father, who said his son had been propositioned, threaten to put a bullet in his head and scream at him, "Why can't you people meet in each other's homes?" (Ah, thinks Lark, that *is* the question.) But these all mean nothing, compared to the consequences of what really happened: meeting Becker.

"Well, I'm . . . careful," says Lark, "to never . . . intrude upon anyone. And we keep each other posted, the people who come here."

"Do you know a guy named Ernie?" says Rick.

"Oh, yes," says Lark. "I think I know him."

He does not say, We're librarians, so to speak, catalogers of the place. We live here, like the owl.

"He's a nice guy," says Rick.

"Very nice," says Lark.

"But this place is kind of pointless," says Rick, as he leafs through the magazine while Lark peers down through the aperture in the roof, thinking, His fingers are thick, that's a good sign. And I love the tattoo. "I mean, nobody asks anyone back to his home, because that would destroy his closet. Nobody ever kisses, from what I've seen. It's like dogs sniffing each other under a bush. Then they go back to their house, or wife and kids. I guess what I am trying to say is—sucking a dong in a men's room with cigarette butts in the urinal and sometimes a turd is not my idea of love."

"Well, of *course* not," says Lark. "But what *is*?"

"I don't know," says Rick. "I was dating this twenty-one-year-old last month, but he was too nuts."

Lark's heart lurches between the pleasure of hearing a homosexual evaluate someone's character, rather than his penis, and the pain of learning that the artist was attracted to a human being who is twenty-one years old. Well, he thinks, that leaves me out. "I guess that's why I'm here now," says Rick. "Though I can't say this place looks promising." He glances up at Lark for the first time. "Do you think it's promising? Do you like it?"

"Like it?" says Lark. "I don't know. Sometimes I do. Sometimes I think it's a gift from God—an oasis in the desert, a sacred refuge, a place where one finds friendship and beauty. Other times I think it's a hideous little ant colony illustrating the most depressing principles of homosexual life, since it reduces everyone who drives in here to two things—a penis and a car. It makes sense mostly, I think, for people who can't hack it in Gainesville, much less in New York or Paris. But you," he says, leaning down to speak directly into the cab of the little truck, his cheek against the cold damp roof, "you *should* be in New York or Paris. You're still young. You're handsome, you're bright. Like the man I met here a year ago, whom I've only seen once—the night we met. Who's never been back, so far as I know. Though I still hope he'll be here, every time I come in."

"That's not good," says Rick. "You have to put yourself in

the arena again, find somebody else, forget him. The only way you get over someone is sleep with other people."

"I know," says Lark. "But that hasn't worked: Even though I have gone out and, as you say, slept with other people, it all means nothing. This place means nothing now."

"And you haven't seen him in how long?"

"A year, on April twenty-fourth," says Lark.

"God! Get over it!" says Rick. "It's obvious he doesn't share your interest. You're—how old?"

Lark takes a breath, presses his chin against the roof, and says, "How old would you like me to be?"

"How old would I *like* you to be?" says Rick, lifting his head from the magazine. "I don't know. How old are you?"

"Too old to be gay," says Lark. "Too old to still be out. Let's put it this way—I'm about to exit the demographic group advertisers and TV executives find most desirable. I'm the reason *Murder, She Wrote* is such a hit. I'm about to qualify for AARP. I'm old."

"You're an antique," says Rick, leafing through the magazine.

"Yes," says Lark. "But unlike the furniture in the back of the truck, my value has not gone up, it has gone down. There are advantages to being a chair."

"So how old's the guy you met here that one time?"

"Thirty-four," says Lark. "The perfect age! Still young, but no longer shallow. Old, without the drawbacks of age. In other words, he can still go to the bars."

"Who wants to go to the bars? I piss away my money in them. I hate the bars."

"I hate them too," says Lark. "A more incestuous, alcoholic bunch doesn't exist! But I want to be *able* to go to them."

"Why?"

"Because when you can't go to the bars in Gainesville, where do you go?"

"The boat ramp," says Rick.

"Exactly," says Lark. "At a certain point in life, there is *only* the boat ramp. At night. Thank *God* for the boat ramp at a certain point in life. My point. Whereas you still have options."

"Like what?"

"Like going to the bars in Gainesville or New York. Men must endure their going hence, even as their coming hither: Ripeness is all."

"What's that?" says Rick.

"The Shirelles," says Lark. "Could I get in the truck with you?" he says, his legs suddenly aching.

"*No!*" says Rick—and then, before Lark, startled by his vehemence, can segue into his questions about Becker, Rick turns the key in the ignition and says, "I gotta go, I'm meeting a friend at the bar!" Lark stands back from the truck; Rick puts it in gear and drives out of the parking lot, leaving him in a little cloud of exhaust. I bore Rick because I'm too old, he thinks, and what's worse, I talk about it, which is as bad as talking about your hemorrhoids or bunions. I used to listen to older men complain about their age, and think, I will never do that. I also said I would never turn thirty or have hair on my back. But I did and I do, he thinks as he walks back to his car and takes up a position leaning against the fender. The minute he does, the old sensations of fear, criminality, and danger come over him, mixed with the beauty of the night. Let's face it, he thinks, Rick is right. There is something criminal, dirty, closeted, and self-loathing about all of this. That's how we behave, anyway, the men who come here: depositing our semen and driving off afterward, as if it were toxic waste. The way students from the university come out here and dump pets when they're graduating. Dogs that get run off by people they approach—because, Ernie pointed out, it's people who feed them—till they're as scattered, confused, and beaten down as we are. At least Ernie takes the dogs home, or has taken four of them. People have to fend for themselves. And that's why it's so furtive, skittish, guilty, wary here—for gay men and dogs. The boat ramp is a sort of spiritual dump. But in this dump is Beauty, occasionally, not to mention an abandoned dog or a human embrace.

It wasn't just Becker's approximation of a sexual icon, he thinks as he stands there feeling the chill enter him, it wasn't just the black T-shirt, the bulging crotch, or even Becker's theory that Lark's compressor was switching on and off because it was searching for freon and there must be a leak in the line—though these words filled him with aching desire. It was the long conversation that night as the two of them stood there in the cold—the dissolving of two separate solitudes, the instant rapport of kindred spirits, the relief of so many years of loneliness.

"Are you cold?" Becker asked Lark when he noticed he was shaking.

No, thought Lark, I'm scared, because I want you so badly. Instead he said, "A little—once it gets in your bones, that's it."

And Becker offered him the sweatshirt in his car, which Lark declined, because he knew full well that what had got in his bones was not the damp chill of April night air but his desire for Becker, like some virus that the body begins to fight with an initial chill—the way Lark's first roommate said he knew he'd gotten HIV, the night he brought that skinhead home from the Pyramid Club, the one who was so violent, so angry, during sex. Somehow Lark's body knew he would be standing here, on another damp cold night, a year later, trembling for real, waiting in the cold darkness for Becker to drive in, because even that was preferable to sitting home, warm but alone in that empty house, beside a telephone Becker was not using to call him.

Becker doesn't have to call or come here, or sit home alone, he thinks; he has his daughter, her homework, her clothes to wash, her dinner to make, her stories of what happened at school that day, her hour of practicing the clarinet. Her menstrual problems, her reading assignments. Let's face it, he thinks, standing there shivering, I have no life. I can't pretend I do. I'm standing here doing penance, eating ground glass, wearing a hair shirt, for some reason I can't explain; a reason Becker knows nothing about. Which is why he picked me up, ate me, moved on. Stopped his car, he thinks as he unlocks his own, had me, and drove on—leaving me flattened on the road. I am road kill, Lark thinks as he drives out of the boat ramp, turns onto the highway and heads home. A dead armadillo.

Becker's House

~~~~~~

When Lark leaves the boat ramp and returns to the town in which Becker and he live, he can't go directly back to his empty house anymore. He makes a left instead at an old, abandoned fishing camp and drives down the only paved road in town, where, after passing the high school—a low, modern, nearly windowless building that looks like a factory that makes missile parts—and a small pecan grove, he begins slowing down to give himself the maximum opportunity to look at Becker's house. He started doing this five months ago, after looking up Becker's address again in the phone book—the only record of his existence—when it became clear that Becker had no interest in seeing him: a silence, an invisibility he cannot tolerate. It is always at night that he does this. Sometimes the lights of one of the baseball fields—there are nine—are on. Mostly he has little light with which to see. Cars are in their driveways, but he never sees Becker's. All he has to go by is the curve in the road before it goes down a hill, at the bottom of which he can see the house in between the trees.

He felt an enormous sense of relief the night he realized this was Becker's house—that it did exist, that it was a house, that Becker did live in it. A red-brick house, dark red, with the bricks protruding unevenly on purpose to give the walls texture; and a sloping backyard planted with date palms and crape myrtle, furnished with a birdbath, a miniature windmill, a silver ball on a pedestal, and a rock garden surrounding a pool, where

Becker, who was once a navy SEAL, gives diving lessons. Finding the house was like finding Becker again. Or like finding—in a fable—the entrance to hell. Here it was, the place at which he'd entered Becker's indifference: a house, a red-brick house. A dark-red-brick house, with date palms and a fence. Where Becker had gone after leaving him, late that Friday night. Where Becker held the telephone when he spoke to him. Where Becker fed his dogs, did the laundry, combed his moustache, slept every morning of the week till the last minute before driving to Palatka for work. Where Becker answered the telephone one afternoon, saying he'd taken so long to pick up because he and his lover had been out in the backyard.

Sutcliffe always liked to go home with lovers. ("All that love!" he explained.) Becker's significant other was a salesman for hair care products who traveled a great deal by plane around the Southeast to salons and malls. Before that, he had worked as a dancer at Disney World. They'd met on the Fourth of July during a shoot-out at Frontier World. Becker had given Lark all the details in the grave, quiet manner of someone who was both proud of his partner and bored with the relationship; at least that was what Lark picked up. Indeed, they had been at a point of crisis the night Becker came to the boat ramp—the boyfriend had called to say he'd decided to move to Atlanta, so he'd be closer to the airport where he had to spend so much time changing planes. Becker thought he was losing him. That may be the only reason Becker went to the boat ramp at all. He was looking for a new love. Alas, Lark had evidently not filled the bill.

"Love is an opportunity for personal growth," a friend told Lark when he heard his tale of woe. Oh, please, thinks Lark. It is, unrequited, a form of death. The refusal of the father. The meanness of man. The silence of God. Becker refused my offer of my old travel magazines, he refused my invitations to the beach, because he knows it's not just magazines, he thinks as he drives slowly toward Becker's house, or a trip to the sea I want to give him. It's my love. And this he doesn't want. He doesn't even want the salesman to move in with him. ("I told him I'm about through raising one," he said, "and I'm not gonna raise another." This implied the boyfriend was irresponsible, impulsive, adolescent. Surely I am none of those things, thinks Lark. No, not anymore.) Though if you love someone or something—a lot—as I do Becker, thinks Lark, that should give you rights. Because love, real love, isn't that common in this world. Desire, real desire. The sort that lifts you out of yourself, the kind that amounts to inspiration. That isn't so common.

Unless you're Becker, he thinks with a sudden feeling of dejection as he passes the last baseball field, and just about everybody you meet is so inspired. *Quel* burden: Beauty. A curse, said Juvenal. And not just Beauty—that aspect of a person has nothing to do with sexual gifts; I've been to bed with beauties, thinks Lark, and wondered, How do I bring this to an end? "Beauty," his friend the bartender said when Lark complained, "seldom comes without a price tag." You bet, he thinks. In this case, driving past the house of a man who could very happily spend the rest of his days on earth without ever once seeing me again or hearing my voice. A condition I cannot approve. Lark knew the day he realized this was Becker's house that he would keep driving past it every night. And now that is just what he does every night when he comes home, whether he has been to the boat ramp or not.

He tells himself it is a shorter route to the post office, where he goes before heading home each time he returns from the nursing home—as if mail could provide what an empty house could not: something waiting for him. He tells himself it is more direct to turn left at the fishing camp, drive past the high school, and rejoin the highway at the corner where the bank sits opposite the video rental store. But that, obviously, isn't the reason. He goes to see Becker's house. He has to see if the windows are lighted or dark, if he's gone to bed, if the car is in the drive;

he has to say good night to Becker. He has to drive past the house on his way home because at night he cannot be seen.

The chicken-wire fence that encloses the whole yard was put up because of the dogs, yet he sees it in a different light, as the external manifestation of Becker himself, and the problem Becker has with men who fall in love with him: a fence to keep admirers out of the house where he watches his parrots and toucan, keeps the dishes and clothes clean, and talks on the telephone to men he never invites over. Biding his time, in prison as it were, like Lark; both held here by duty, the claims of Family—he, Lark, attached to a dying woman; he, Becker, to a growing girl: the consequence of a single orgasm, the one ejaculation that had, unlike all of Lark's, consequences; consequences in time. ("How did it happen?" Lark finally asked in an awed voice. "A stiff dick has no conscience." Becker shrugged, expelling a stream of cigarette smoke.)

Becker planned, he said, to get work in the Virgin Islands as a dive instructor when his daughter graduated; he felt no obligation to put her through college. Lark can easily see Becker on a beach, in the shade of palm trees, patiently instructing secretaries and tired attorneys on vacation in some cerulean lagoon. He'd be a gorgeous captain taking them out to the reef for a long day's swim among the tropical fish. He'd be a knockout, exactly what the passengers of a cruise ship spending a day in port would like. That evening they'd sail away, masturbating in their cabins. There would be no need for a chicken-wire fence, only the fact that the ship was departing for Port Everglades. Convenient denouement. That way there would be no hard feelings, stalkings, or embarrassment. Just a *Love Boat* fantasy. It all makes sense in the Age of Oprah, thinks Lark. And we are living in the Age of Oprah.

Sometimes when Lark drives past, depending on the hour he returns to town, depending on whether he's stopped at the boat ramp to see if Becker is there, the house is dark, and sometimes the windows are lighted. Most often just one is: a small window near the center of the house, with a thin white curtain, and a pale-blue swatch of wall that could, Lark thinks, belong to either a bathroom or kitchen. He chooses the former, because when everyone goes to bed, that's the room where people sometimes leave a light on. Other times the two translucent, narrow panels of glass that flank the carved wooden door are glowing, with the light of some small lamp in the living room. He takes this to mean Becker is out—has left one lamp on for his return. That Becker is out bothers Lark. He assumes it means Becker is having sex with someone. Possibly that big, beefy man with silver-gray hair who always goes to the grocery store on Friday with an elderly woman. "We had our queer moment," Becker said of him—meaning their eyes had met; but Lark does not know if Becker's use of the word *queer* was contemptuous of the man, or hip and ironic, since Becker seems to him hard to place.

Becker works outdoors, after all; he operates construction equipment. He does not read books, so far as Lark knows, or even watch TV. He has, on the other hand, referred to a lyric in "The Boss," a song by Diana Ross; read copies of *Out* the boyfriend brought him; and, Lark has to conclude, is just as gay, or queer, as any other man his age in the bar on a Saturday night.

Is that where Becker is now? Lark wonders whenever he sees those two panels glowing with light. At a friend's? At the boyfriend's? With a trick? Does he sleep over when he tricks? Or does he insist on returning home each time? Lark realized how proprietary he had become regarding Becker only when he tried to telephone him one night—a week after they'd met—because a movie about John Wayne Gacy, the serial killer, was on TV. This, he felt, he should tell Becker to watch. When nobody answered the phone, Lark nearly fainted. He hung up, heart pounding, wondering like some anxious parent whose child has not come home on time, Where is Becker at nine o'clock on a Monday night? Why isn't he home? Watching this movie? And he realized, with a sinking feeling, that he had no control over the man.

Then, a few months later, after a string of phone calls Lark made—long conversations that Becker always ended with "Thanks for calling!"—Lark called him up on Homecoming Weekend, to invite him to a party in Gainesville a friend gave every year, famous for its collection of handsome men. The phone rang. Nobody answered. He could hear the drums of the high-school band coming from the football field uptown, where the local athletes were playing; the floodlights blazed bright silver over the tops of the trees; he supposed Becker was in the stands, with his daughter, a father among many, watching the local team play. And he thought, Becker has a life of his own— football games to attend, parties to go to, bleachers to sit in on Friday night. I'm the one who has no life. And he never called Becker again.

Which means there is much about Becker's life he does not know—this life Becker is living without him, this life with a teen-age daughter he has to explain menstruation to, parents he has already informed of his homosexuality and politely listened to when they quoted the Bible to him in reply, in a town that he has known since he moved here in the third grade and that watches him now, he said, like a hawk. This life to which Lark is irrelevant. Why, he does not know, but the force of it leaves him breathless. We never know why we are rejected. Few people have the nerve to ask, he thinks. Fewer the courage, or indifference, to tell. ("You've got to follow them!" said Sutcliffe. "Follow them until you see the one they *do* go home with. Then you understand everything. Follow them home, if you have to; stand across the street until you see the trick leave. That's the only way you learn *why* you were rejected! Then you can go home and relax, and say to yourself, Okay, so I'm not a five-foot-four construction worker from New Jersey with bad skin. I'm me!")

The first time Lark realized he was not to see Becker again was the night he summoned up the courage to ask him over and Becker declined. "I'm tired," he said with a yawn. "I think I'll have a glass of water and go to bed."

"I'm being rejected," said Lark, "for a glass of water."

Becker laughed and said, "You tickle me!"

Lark was not tickled. He was bereft. He did not know if Becker was refusing him because he wished to remain faithful to his boyfriend, or because Lark did not appeal to him. So he told Becker it was possible to have just a sexual relationship, with no strings attached, no claims made.

"I know," Becker replied.

"Well then, why can't we do that?" said Lark.

There was the briefest second of silence. Then Becker said, "You're putting me on the spot." Meaning: You are forcing me to tell you why I don't want to see you again.

"I'm being ruthless, I know," said Lark.

To which Becker replied, "No, you're not," which was quite true; he was simply asking the archangel why the gates of Paradise had just been shut in his face. Lark still does not know. But, like everyone rejected by a lover, he is faced with two alternatives: Blame Becker or himself. *Blame* is the word people tell you not to use in the Age of Oprah. "It has nothing to do with you, personally," someone said. "You're just not his type." It is, in reality, the most personal thing in the world. Nothing, in fact, is more personal than the selection or refusal of a lover. That is why men go to mobile homes, shoot their ex-wives and then themselves. On the other hand, his friend was right—it is entirely impersonal too: One is either blond and blue-eyed or black-haired and bearded, young or old, educated or uneducated; the list of attributes is endless, the approximation of the other person's fantasy entirely out of your control. You either look the part or don't. Which leaves the question: Is Becker someone who would sleep with everyone—once? Or: Why *did* Becker sleep with him?

Simple: "He was between affairs," Ernie said. "You got him between people." Or: "He just wanted to see what was in your pants."

It's extraordinary, he thinks as he approaches the house, slowing down but not so much that someone looking out a window might wonder what he is doing, what people will do to save their egos. "If he's not interested in you, he's not worth bothering about," one friend said. (So simple, efficient, sensible.) And: "You can't know what's in his head. All you can do is move on." And: "If you don't fill the 'bill, just accept it." And: "The nicest thing you can do is leave him alone."

The gift Becker wants! Instead Lark has become a successor to the poor alcoholic professor from Gainesville who crashed into a tree opposite this house, which has become a sort of temple for them both, apparently—set in the pine barrens in its little patch of ranch houses with tricycles abandoned on the sidewalks, the translucent glass panels on either side of the door glowing chastely in the night with a soft pearl-colored radiance, like that of the votive candles left in a shrine—while the god is out, bringing ecstasy to mortals. Lark needs Becker more than he needs anything else, it seems, unless it is God. That's what Becker has become, he thinks, what takes the place of God in the late twentieth century. Though he's more like the gods of Greece than the God of Christianity: willful, stubborn, capricious; subject to moods, fatigue, thirst, boredom, hernias; descending to earth to have sex with mortals, then retreating to Olympus. That somehow describes what has happened better than any other myth. The times are pagan, it's time to bring back the gods, he thinks as he drives past, noticing each time something new: a rusted swing, two turquoise seahorses attached to the bricks, three strands of barbed wire that top the chicken-wire fence like something in a military compound, festooned with the hearts and genitals of Becker's admirers. Still, when Lark sees the lighted panels on either side of the door, or the central window with the swatch of blue wall and the thin white curtain blowing in the breeze, when he drives past at night, something floods his heart and he says out loud in wonder, amazement, gratitude, and despair, "I love him! I love him!"— amazed more than anything by the durability, the persistence, of the emotion.

Sleeping Alone

~~~~~~

They're words, at least, he never expected to hear himself say again; not here, at any rate, not after leaving New York. Every time he leaves his mother in the nursing home, she says to him, "I love you a lot," and he says to her, "I love you a lot," but the words are—even if he means them—bound up with a love that does not count. Of course he loves her, and she loves him. To love another man is the problem. He went to New York in 1970 to find someone he could say those words to, and he did, three times, though they were always more understood than uttered; speaking them seemed to him to invite the malice of the gods, who were only too willing to provide a future moment when, looking back, you would remember saying them to someone you no longer even spoke to. Speaking them seemed to him dangerous—or at least entailed in his mind a strong promise, the deepest of all loyalties; something that should not be taken lightly. Eventually he realized you had to take them lightly or not at all; because by then he had refused more than once to move to the county to live with someone in a house with a stack of firewood by the door. By then he had ended up living with Joshua and a cat. And habits that once constituted the pursuit of love were now just a set of habits. Or so it seemed one Saturday night as they all sat around the table in the kitchen of his apartment, talking about Love. "Don't even use the word," Sutcliffe told Joshua. "What most gay people need is not a lover but a dependable, regular sex partner. That's all. Love has nothing to do with it."

"I *beg* to differ, darling!" said Joshua, home early from the baths down the block, already washing dishes in his underwear and sling-back pumps and bath towel wrapped around his head as a turban—a domestic parody of some Jayne Mansfield movie Lark always enjoyed. "That's *all* I'm looking for. A Hot Daddy whose mind and character I will cherish as much as the balls he insists on stuffing in my mouth. I know what I'm holding out for. Real love from a peer whose mutually supportive esteem for *my* best qualities entails a certain commitment, a belonging *to*, and an ability to listen. I'm holding out for the Big L, dear— *that's* why I go to the gym for three hours a day, that's why I read François Villon in the original French, that's why I'm learning how to make squab *à l'arlésienne,* and plan to do three hundred and forty-five push-ups at the gym tomorrow, instead of a mere, paltry three hundred."

"But you were just at the baths!" said Sutcliffe.

"Mais oui," said Joshua.

"And now you're home by yourself!"

"Because my entire gym was there," said Joshua. "And I can listen to Jack Heifetz do Carol Channing imitations tomorrow, when we're working out. What's a gorgeous guy like you doing alone on a Saturday night?"

"Going over to a colleague's to write a grant proposal that's due Monday," said Sutcliffe, standing up and going to the door. "Otherwise I'd be at the baths, with the rest of your gym."

"You should be married," said Joshua. "You're such a catch!"

"You sound like my mother." Sutcliffe smiled, and he was out the door, in his black chesterfield.

"Well, he should be," said Joshua after the door closed. "He's so smart and so nice," he said, resuming his post at the kitchen sink. "Why isn't he married?"

"Good question," said Lark. "Maybe because Irish-American Catholics of his background aren't supposed to marry other men. Maybe because he has too much fun going out. Did you have sex at the baths?"

"Not exactly," said Joshua as he began rinsing a plate.

"What do you mean?"

"Well, I wouldn't say we had sex. I'd say we . . . came in the same room."

"But you came?" said Lark.

"I was the rain arriving in Jaipur," said Joshua, looking over his shoulder, pressing one hand to his nipple. "I brought life to the delta."

"No!" said Lark.

"You're right," said Joshua, turning the faucet off and putting the plate into the drying rack. "I didn't come. That would require a connection between the mind and body I haven't had since third grade. Don't be ridiculous," he said, as he pushed his mattress out into the middle of the floor of the front room. "Me? Have an orgasm? I'm sorry, Red," he said, using a nickname he had taken from some old Katharine Hepburn movie, "I guess my problem is, I have standards. Nobody else at my gym does, God knows. They've *all* slept with Mark Glass. Maybe I just have to wait. Maybe it will all make sense to me when I'm old," he said, pausing to put a Valium on his tongue and washing it down with a sip of water. "I can't wait to be old! I'm going to be such a wonderful old man. I'll teach French to young people in some little town in Vermont, and cook elaborate, complicated meals all day long."

"I didn't know you were fluent in French," said Lark.

"My French is sensational," said Joshua, lying down on the mattress. "I can talk dirty in French. On both a dark and light level," he said, sighing, and pulling the cat to his chest. "It's so odd. I love my job, I love my friends, I love New York; it's just that, gee, I'm going to bed with my cat, because I have no personal life. Good night, Red," he said. "I've taken my Valium and I'm going under."

And that was their discussion of Love. Twelve years and many deaths later, he watches at the nursing home the young woman with useless feet and hennaed hair going around the hallways after everyone else has gone to bed, filling her cup at the water fountain, pushing open the door to the lounge in which the vending machines sit, getting a late-night snack, and he thinks, *She lives without Love. She lives for those peanut butter crackers in the vending machine. We can all scale down. You have to. I can't feel sorry for her. She has accommodated.*

Later that evening he sees another patient, a handsome old man who always sits on the patio with his tray of food before him, staring down at his plate with an ironic, meditative expression as he smokes a cigarette—a silence, a stoicism, a reserve Lark finds touching. That night the man is sitting alone in near darkness in a corner of the enclosed patio that leads to the garden. He looks so forlorn in the gloom, with no one around, the summer wind fluttering the napkin on the tray of food no aide had yet removed. Lark calls out, "Isn't it too hot out there for you?"

The man looks up and says, "No!" in a sharp voice. In other words: *Leave me alone.*

It's the same with Becker, Lark thinks, walking back to his mother's room with a copy of *People* magazine that promises the inside story of Charles and Diana's marriage. If I call him because I feel sorry for him, because I assume he is as lonely and sex-starved as I am, I might be completely wrong. He is probably neither. I am projecting. You have to be careful whom you extend pity to—they may not want it; they may look up and say, "No!"

Becker said nevertheless when they finished having sex, "I hope you enjoyed that as much as I did." Then he sprang up out of bed and went to the bathroom while Lark lay there trying to decipher these words. Were they polite? Sincere? He knew something was wrong when, after he asked Becker if he wished to take a shower, Becker went into the bathroom and closed the opaque glass door behind him and turned the water on. A moment passed while Lark listened to the sounds; then he got up and found himself tapping on the glass door so that Becker would let him in. I shouldn't be tapping on the glass door, he thought. I should be in there with him without having to ask— if he enjoyed it as much as I did, that is. In fact, Lark hadn't enjoyed it much at all; he had been too perplexed and awestruck, asking himself, Why is this god having sex with me? So Becker's remark was doubly enigmatic. Lark stood in the tiled shower behind Becker and watched him soap himself, then took the bar of soap and began spreading suds across Becker's freckled back. And when he did not turn around, did not embrace him, did not return the favor by soaping his stomach and back, Lark had the distinct feeling that—though the opaque glass door had been opened, and he was now next to Becker in the shower—he was still outside the door. Then when Becker dressed afterward, as quickly as a fireman going to a fire, and went back to the bedroom to find his lighter, Lark had another intimation that Becker was putting this episode quickly behind him—and moving on. "Call me anytime," Lark said fervently as he embraced Becker at the door. "I don't feel I can call you, with your daughter at home."

"You can call," said Becker, raising his eyebrows, as if to say, She doesn't run my life; it's my house and my telephone.

And so begins the summer, and so ends the cool, wet spring. Each morning he awakes and wonders, if it is raining and chill, What is Becker wearing to work, and does he have hot coffee in a thermos? Or, if it is 95 degrees, How will he protect himself from the sun out there? Becker's silence becomes synonymous, somehow, with the frustration of caring for his mother. Lark goes around the house saying, "I won't let her kill me, and I won't let him either!" He makes lists of things, including ones headed "What I Like About His Body" and "Is He Happy or Unhappy?" The first one reads: "(1) His hands. His enormous, beautiful hands. (2) His long, lean arms. (3) The musculature of his back, the muscle so close to the surface of the skin, the leanness. (4) His slightly narrow chest, completely unspoiled by a gym. The nipples. (5) The iliac crest—the Greek Muscle, where the torso joins the pelvis. (6) The enormous balls, flowing down the inside of his thighs like a waterfall. (7) The penis, big, long, bent. (8) The whole incredible package: the long, lean body, the enormous hands, the narrow flat chest with its light sprinkling of hair, the iliac crest, the huge soft gonads." But mostly he thinks of the still, melancholy, quiet watchfulness on Becker's face as he had sex, that serious, sad, profoundly attentive expression on his beautiful, sad face, as if this was what he lived for, this was what was most important, most wondrous to him, this was the stillness beneath all things.

On balance, it looks as if Becker probably is happy; yet what attracts Lark to him was the opposite—his melancholy face that night as he watched Lark adore him, the fact that every now and then he has to call in sick to work because he is too depressed to go in. Becker! Depressed! That gorgeous man! With all the perquisites of Beauty! Depressed! Why not? thinks Lark; this town, Florida itself, is a machine for manufacturing depression. He's seen it drag so many people down, including his own father. (Or was that old age? "Old age is hell," his father used to say—often.) Whatever the cause, Becker gets the blues, frequently, and this only makes Lark want to call him up and say, You're depressed, I'm depressed, let's be depressed together! Instead he looks out the window at the little bit of sky, the air above the houses that lies between his and Becker's, which seems to him as solid as lead, as impermeable as a glacier, a mass of rules, regulations, courtesies, taboos, and one

single overwhelming fact—that Becker does not desire him—
and then turns off the light.

That summer it begins to rain again, the way it did when his
parents first moved here; the daily thunderstorm that arrived like
clockwork every day at three is gone forever, Lark thinks, but at
least it has been raining. The gray margin of the lakeshore that the
drought exposed between the weeds and water has now disappeared, and the rainfrogs rasp in the flower beds at night. (Only
when it's wet are they able to search for a partner. Our wetness is
Youth, thinks Lark, and I'm running out of that.) One night he is
walking past Becker's house and is surprised to look up and see
Becker himself sitting shirtless and shoeless on a small bench
next to the front door. His body is a dark reddish brown. (The last
time Lark saw it, in April, it was white.) Becker sits there staring
silently ahead, with slumped shoulders, exuding an air of weari-
ness and solitude. Lark is so shocked by this apparition, and the
tenderness he feels at the sight of him, he does not know what to
do. He keeps walking into the light cast by the front door. Becker
looks away; Lark keeps going. He rushes back to his house, sits
down, and writes a letter asking Becker why he looked away the
moment Lark came into view. Then he puts it on the dining room
table and wonders if it would be a mistake to send it. He had no
right to intrude on Becker's solitude—even if Lark still thinks of
him when he wakes in the middle of the night, and in the morning
when he rises.

The next morning he awakes before dawn, gets into his car,
and drives out on the highway, thinking he might see Becker's
car on his way to work. When he gets to the nursing home that
afternoon, he is not very alert. "Are you mental?" his mother
asks him as he stands in the middle of the room with her tooth-
brush in his hand, unable to remember what he is supposed to
do next. Yes, he wants to reply, Becker won't speak to me. Their
sex lasted no more than half an hour; Becker's refusal to repeat

it goes on and on—through the long, breezy May afternoons, the twilights, and the nights. The phone does not ring. Becker does not ask, What are you doing? My mother, thinks Lark as he pushes her around the hall after supper, envies people in wheelchairs because they can use their arms—sits in her blue Geri-chair in the hallway all day when I'm not here, completely paralyzed, while madwomen and madmen go past her, their bony white hands moving the wheels of their wheelchairs—and she thinks, If only I could do that. If only I could use my hands to move a wheelchair and feed myself.

And he walks behind her thinking, as he rounds the corner by the nurses' desk, If only Becker would love me. If only our sex had been better. If only I had a gigantic, irresistible cock. If only I were Al Parker, the porn star, who's dead.

Rejection, thinks Lark, as he pushes his mother around and around the corridor ("You're fast!" the aides laugh when they reappear again), is so much more castrating when you are older. It seems then like a consignment to Hades. The underworld itself. Whereas all I, and everyone else in this atheistic age, want is to remain among the living. Where there's so much to envy. Like Becker, his youth, his penis, and his hair, he thinks as he sits beside his mother's bed after their ride, wiping the drool from the side of her mouth that follows a coughing spell, thinking of precum emerging from Becker's penis.

Seven years I waited to meet him, Lark thinks as he drives across town afterward, seven years since someone first pointed him out to me in the Melody Club. Seven years. The same period of time Jacob worked for Rachel's father before he could marry her. Forty-seven years, more precisely, of my life, education, and experience, consumed in twenty minutes, like the fossil fuel that lay for aeons as decomposing carboniferous swamps, deep in the earth, burning up in a millisecond as I drive this car. What locusts we are, consuming millions of years of Time in a drive to the grocery store; eating one another in bed in seconds.

And then moving on. Human potato chips. He reduced me to a trick, he thinks, as he pulls off Sixth Street into the strip mall where the two gay bars are located, past a drag queen using the pay phone in the parking lot. She actually looks good, he thinks. She's wearing a dress that reminds Lark of a Charles James creation, the sort Suzy Parker (born in Palatka) used to wear. I should stop and tell her that she really looks elegant, he thinks, no kidding. She would probably appreciate that enormously; it would make her day. But he's so leery of drag queens at the Melody Club—the egos are so out of control—that he parks the car and walks into the Ambush without performing that particular random act of kindness.

He orders a club soda and stands in a corner of the bar Becker goes to every Saturday night (Becker told him) and tries to understand the milieu in which Becker takes his pleasure, as if that will help him understand Becker. He stands there watching men play pool, looks around at the other patrons, and wonders, Would Becker find that one attractive?

"I'm a very sexual person," Becker told Lark. You bet, he thinks, standing in the Ambush, trying to see the people there with Becker's eyes. That's what Lark has to figure out. Does the crowd bore him sexually? Has he already slept with everyone he wanted to—just once—except the boyfriend, who is often away on a trip to Tampa, Charleston, Atlanta? Or does he see someone new every time he comes, someone he wants and almost always gets? Lark can't imagine Becker being rejected; just as he can't imagine Becker sitting home depressed, alone, and bored—though he knows in fact Becker calls in sick a lot, not because he is physically ill, but because he is depressed. The week before they met, in fact, Becker had called in sick; then called the boyfriend, who told him he was flying out that afternoon. Thirty minutes later, the boyfriend called Becker back to tell him he had changed his flight, to come on over. "And I did," said Becker that evening, as he sat across from

Lark in the lamplight, nervously smoking cigarettes with those huge, graceful hands. "And he was waiting for me. In bed."

"Do you have good sex still?" said Lark.

"Fan*tas*tic!" said Becker. "The sex is fantastic!"

Crueler words were never spoken, thinks Lark as he watches the men in the bar around him: the little pods of alcoholics who all seem to know each other and actually like sitting in this place for hours, looking up each time the door opens to see who is coming in. I feel like a penguin on an ice floe, he thinks. I feel like a yokel who just walked into a used-car showroom— they know everything; I know zilch. Southern men. Strange species. It's like that bumper sticker, he thinks, that lies beneath everyone and everything down here: WE DON'T CARE HOW YOU DO IT UP NORTH. Exactly. A culture unto itself. He thinks of what Ernie has told him about the men he's had affairs with over the years down here: the married electrician from Ocala; the bag boy from Lake City; the construction worker who, after leaving Ernie to return to his wife, lost both of his legs in a car crash and wrote a postcard to Ernie saying, "Those were the happiest months of my life."

"What do you expect?" Ernie said. "He was Church of the Nazarene—where they tell you your sins are back home, rotting in the closet, while you run around all day in godless pursuits." The rules governing relationships with these men, Ernie said, are: Don't ever ask for their number; don't think you can call them; don't wait for the phone to ring. Simple. Just hope that every three or four months they may call and come over. Just hope that somehow, through the deadening haze of boredom, ritual, tradition, shame, discipline, religion, family pressure, and small-town surveillance, they will dial your number.

Lark knows exactly what Ernie was referring to—only Becker does not fit exactly into that category; he is a mixture of things Lark cannot quite figure out. He doesn't have the opportunity to; Becker makes himself invisible. He's like that village in

Brigadoon, thinks Lark as he leaves the bar, the one that appears for only one day every hundred years—I walked into it, and now it's gone.

Or perhaps it's not Brigadoon but Chernobyl, he thinks as he drives across the hot, windy, dark countryside toward home—as the town he lives in glows above the line of trees on the horizon. And still when he's home, he gets out of the car and stands motionless in the driveway, listening for the telephone; every time he comes back to the house and unlocks the door, he listens for that sound, hoping it might be Becker.

In fact, Becker called only once after their tryst—when he telephoned late Sunday night, while Lark lay reading in bed, as his mother slept in the bed beside his. They spoke for a long time, until his mother awoke, asked, "Who's that?," and Becker, hearing her voice in the background, said, "Is that yours?" and Lark said, "Yes." That's mine, he thought, Becker understands.

Becker never called again. Like the old man on the patio who was not too hot, Becker didn't need Lark; and, not needing him, he could not be approached. Lark started calling him once every two weeks, or driving past his house around eleven o'clock at night, wondering why the window was lighted and what was going on inside. Eventually Becker ruined the town for him. Like Americans who were taught that segregation laws were keeping blacks and whites apart, only to discover, once these were gone, that there was a psychological antipathy much harder to overcome, Lark had always assumed his loneliness was geographical; now that Becker was living five blocks away, it was worse.

In the middle of July, a woman who substituted for teachers at the grade school in town drives to her boyfriend's house on Lake Pearl and fires five shots at him with a gun. The news makes the front page of the local weekly; Lark reads it and thinks, He was dumping her. So she went there with a gun. Lark does not go to Becker's with a gun; he drives by around eleven and sees the translucent panels on either side of Becker's front door, and wonders where he is—having sex with someone, or simply shaving so he doesn't have to in the morning, or putting dishes away. ("I keep a very clean house," Becker said. A bad sign, thought Lark when he heard it, though it meant that Becker himself was very clean—that lean immaculate body, already naked when Lark entered the bedroom and caught Becker looking at himself in the mirror, the mirror Lark has since removed since he can no longer stand to look at himself.)

Lark takes his walk every night that July, setting off a series of barking dogs as he goes, like a string of firecrackers, but he never sees Becker sitting tired and solitary in the driveway outside his house again. One night he comes upon Becker's daughter's name etched into the cement of sidewalk block near city hall, and thinks, So she is a normal girl like any other. Then he walks home through the suffocating air, the reek of fertilizer, the rank odor of gardens, wondering why he can't walk to Becker's. But he cannot. The line between what is called appropriate and inappropriate behavior is thin but definite, he thinks; the schoolteacher should not have taken five shots at her boyfriend, and I must not be found crouching in a hedge under Becker's window. Though what is demented is that people accept so little ecstasy in their lives. Including Becker—his youth and beauty rotting in this little town—unless (this is his real worry) Becker has managed, as Lark has not, to find erotic life here, in all this peace and quiet. He probably has, Lark thinks—and the thought is painful.

In fact, maybe I don't want Becker, he thinks; maybe I just want his allure. That quality of self-possession, insularity, confidence, masculinity. He remembers what Becker said about disciplining his daughter: "I can be quite cold and callous." Oh, let us be cold and callous together, he thinks—instead, the weeks since they last spoke lengthen, and the incredible, never suspected comes true: He realizes he is never going to sleep with Becker again. He's been dropped. And he thinks, The ability to withhold love from another is the most astonishing ability of all. Which makes the fact that Becker gave himself to me freely, intentionally, unashamedly now seem the cruelest fact of all; because he then took himself back.

By the end of July, Lark thinks he actually hates Becker—his youth, daughter, huge dick, sensitive nipples, iliac crest, dark hair, enormous hands, high buttocks, and ability to get along completely without Lark—because he is losing sleep over Becker, and still thinking each time the phone rings it might be Becker. But it isn't.

At night he lies in bed listening to a jet pass overhead, slowing down for the descent into Gainesville—that high, faraway, hoarse sound that seems so far above the daily grind of life on earth—and he imagines the people inside the plane fastening their seat belts, preparing for landing, and thinks, That is the salesman's flight, that is the plane carrying the penis Becker *does* love ("I'm not a size queen," Becker said that evening, "but I went into the john and saw this guy standing there and it was huge"), the person who can bring pleasure to Becker ("We have fantastic sex! The only problem is when we're done, I want to start over again, and he never lets me"). Some problem, thinks Lark. Eos, he thinks, goddess of dawn, had Polycrates stung to death with scorpions for refusing her. But I lie in bed in an empty house, listening to Becker's lover's plane descending from the sky, fold my hands upon my chest, and wait for sleep.

A week later he is driving home from Gainesville and the boat ramp at such a late hour that he does not think driving by the house can hurt—it will simply be dark, and Becker will be sleeping. So after picking up the mail he drives past Becker's. The carport is empty. The windows are dark. It is 11:38 P.M. Becker is sleeping elsewhere. With whom? Maybe someone he met on his computer. As if gay life were not fractured enough into ages and types, rural and urban, men with/without HIV or

AIDS, the pierced and the nonpierced, the pissfreaks and religious, he thinks, I now have to deal with computer chat lines. Let's face it, thinks Lark as he drives home, I was depressed before I met Becker, I was alienated from homosexuality before AIDS, I can no longer try to figure it out.

So it has all ended here, he thinks as he lies in bed, the long journey, the attempt to be happy, to have a life. And it has failed. Joshua committed suicide in New York because he got to the Loneliness before you did, the loneliness you are now finally tasting—the one that cannot be ignored, the fact that it is unavoidable, especially in this town where Becker lives like the only other gay man at the Arctic Circle, and still will not see you, does not want to be with or know you at all. The final failure to "take." The final failure to adhere, to connect, to form a union, that stands for all your failures to do so, in all the years you spent looking in New York. Becker gave you one last taste of Hope, of Happiness—one last illusion that you could have what you dreamed of—and then the door closed, he disappeared, and now you have to conclude you were used, as *you* have used people, for temporary relief, quick fixes, release of lust and loneliness, and nothing more. The end result of the life you have led is this, he thinks: lying here in this house, in this town, thinking of Becker. God help us get to the grave with neat clothes and a cheerful face.

Then it starts to rain again, and he thinks that even in the midst of sorrow, justified or not justified, self-indulgent or unsought, there is the sound of rain on the roof—the beauty and wonder of life.

The Letter Song

~~~~~~

By August he's so anxious that he starts visiting Ernie at night—
after driving home from Gainesville with a sense of urgency, as
if, once home, in the same town as Becker, he at least has a
chance of solving his problem. Ernie will explain it all.

The weather itself adds to his depression. Late at night the
wind rushing through the car still feels hot. Heat lightning
flashes over the treetops east of Highway 301, and along the
highway the wind forms small spirals that scatter dead leaves
across the asphalt and blow them into the car, as if a tornado
is coming. Five miles farther it's utterly still, and the convenience stores at 301 sit in pools of light the color of lemonade;
he stops to buy a bottle of cold water and linger in the air
conditioning before going on. Everyone in the store is barefoot,
in Levi's cutoffs and faded tank tops. The dogs lying on the
cement walk outside do not even lift their heads to see who's
walking past them.

Beyond the pecan farm east of 301 the sky seems to open
up, get bigger, but the boat ramp entrance is hardly visible—
only because he knows where to look does he see the dark road
disappearing into the furry trees, like the entrance to an under-
water cave—and then he drives right by. When he gets home
he unlocks the door quickly, as if the phone were ringing, but
it's not, and he opens the door on which no one has left a note
either and goes inside, wondering, Why don't I hear the phone?
(When the phone did ring during the day, he picked it up think-

ing it could be Becker; instead a woman on the other end of the line asked him if he was pleased with, or had any questions about, his AT&T service. He went through the polite dialogue thinking, Yes, there is something wrong with it. Becker doesn't call.) And then he leaves the house and walks up the road to Ernie's.

Ernie's two-story house looks dark when you pass it on the sidewalk; like a New England spinster saving heat in winter, he has the light on in only one room downstairs, which you see only when you're past the last holly tree planted in a row along the highway—which means Ernie is still up, watching television. He walks down past the greenhouse in which Ernie raises hydroponic tomatoes, his satellite dish, the cage in which he keeps rabbits, and a potting shed, then rings the doorbell. Ernie sleeps intermittently, having to get up and pee during the night, turning on the TV once he's up to see if some old movie is playing. The minute Lark presses the doorbell, the dogs jump up, run into the hall, and hurl themselves against the wall. The cats remain hidden. Then Ernie, a moment later, shuffles to the switch and turns on the light.

"Hi," says Lark, thinking, I'm trying not to walk past Becker's house, and since I can't talk to him, since he won't see me, may I come in and talk to you instead?

"Hello," says Ernie in a low, grave voice, and lets him in. The dogs sniff Lark's legs, desperate for data from the world outside, finding odors on his ankles and socks that constitute advertisements from other dogs. Then, having sniffed him up and down with surgical delicacy, they follow Ernie and Lark into the dark living room and, after Ernie turns on the lamp, lie down and put dolorous faces on their paws—as if holding him responsible for their boredom, as if they find the town dull too.

He thinks of his mother as he leans forward in his chair to speak to Ernie. He thinks, I must get her out of here somehow.

But how? She's sleeping at the nursing home; he's at Ernie's, talking about the boat ramp. Some life for both of them.

Ernie and Lark sit now in a puddle of light, surrounded by the dim shapes of antiques and books Ernie has stored here. The house is filled with furniture he has purchased over the years, the detritus of other people's lives, which ended up scattered among the pawnshops, estate sales, and flea markets of the state, like the books that sit in boxes on the porch, books he bought thinking he would read them when he retired, and his collection of carnival masks from Brazil. The last time Lark was here, he asked Ernie to shave his back. It's impossible to live completely independently, Lark thinks.

Ernie offers Lark a drink; Lark watches him go to get it and wonders, How do you sit home at night alone? On paper, Ernie is the nightmare of homosexuals—living by himself in a small town with his cats and dogs—but in fact he seems content. Good-humored. Realistic. Healthy. Only the odor of dog pee on the rugs and the white powder Ernie has sprinkled over the spots make an unsavory impression. And all the unread books. Becker never reads. (If he did read, Lark would want to know what; that would tell him everything. If only we were friends, he thinks, or had continued having sex, then I would see exactly why he isn't what I think. But no, he cut me off before that could happen, and so I'm investing this uneducated, rigid, small-town bore with all sorts of sterling qualities. Because he's now the only real repository of romantic reverie: The Man Who Got Away.)

When Ernie returns with his glass of iced tea, Lark asks him how the foot he cut wading in the lake feels. "I should have gone to a doctor when it happened," Ernie says as he sits down, "but now it's on the mend, though not entirely closed. I hope it will be better by the beginning of next week. That's five more days." Who's counting? thinks Lark. Time rots when you live in Florida. He can feel the lake down the slope of grass—can feel the whole town, its darkness, its silence, its torpor, its placidity, all around them in their pool of lamplight. He can feel it most in the fact that he sits here, talking to Ernie, instead of Becker. He imagines the rest of his life in the two dogs sleeping on the carpet covered with dog hair, and the light in the library full of opera records. Ernie has accepted all this. Lives alone, with his dogs and cracked recordings of Kathleen Ferrier and Geraldine Farrar, while the dogs pee on the rugs and the town slumbers around him.

Lark leans forward. "You know, I've had an experience with a man in this town," he says. "A man I met who I thought would then be a friend. But in fact the opposite happened. He didn't want to have anything to do with me. Do you think that's because this is a small town?"

"Of course," says Ernie. "People in small towns have got to watch what they do, and whose car is in their driveway. Everyone *knows* you in a small town. It's wonderful if you have children—because your children will never get lost or hurt. Someone in town will call you up if they are," he says. "When I grew up, I knew everyone, and everyone knew me."

"Do you consider this a small town?" says Lark.

"I do and I don't," says Ernie. "Let me put it this way. If you grew up here, and if even one of your parents still lives here, then it is."

"Ah!" says Lark, thinking, Becker meets both requirements. Perhaps he's being a model homosexual, which does not include giving Them something to talk about. Perhaps, perhaps, perhaps. All I can do is speculate and obsess. It's like Madame Bovary, he thinks: her night at the château. Becker was my night at the château; the windows were broken to cool the dancers; I can't forget, even though I'm back to reality, and Becker is invisible, as unrepeatable as that one magic night. He is never at the grocery where I once saw him—standing in Produce, his huge hand gripping an entire head of cabbage, glancing up at me, when I came around the corner, with that perpetual alertness of the homosexual and the sexual sixth sense that some people in life like Becker have—or at the boat ramp, where we finally spoke. He is never anywhere. He's a noctural hunter that reveals itself only when it wants.

So now I sit here, thinks Lark, on this hot, dull, sultry night, with Ernie, not Becker (why do we always love the young?), imagining the phone ringing back at the house, hearing Becker's voice on the other end, saying, "What are you doing?" Those signal words that hold an entire universe of sexual pleasure in them. *What are you doing?* Those four words that summon up the bottomless ennui, the isolation of that town, where people settled because they thought it was a good place to raise children, who were in fact bored to death by the town and left it after graduation never to return, unless, like Becker, they had children themselves they wished to raise, repeating the cycle again. *What are you doing now? Nothing,* thinks Lark as he watches Ernie scratch one of the hounds behind her ears. *And you? Nothing,* Becker said that night at the boat ramp. *Then let's go.* That was the sequence, the open sesame to Becker's body, Becker's embrace.

Becker is saying those words to someone else now, thinks Lark as he stares at the dog. Even as we sit here. The fact that I've lived in New York means nothing to him: The years at Flamingo, Fire Island, the Everard earn me no credit in his eyes. It's like a currency that's no good once you cross the border. I'm in another country now. My life up there doesn't translate into the local language. The people here wouldn't even get the references. My mother has no idea what I've done with my life. She at least wonders; Becker doesn't. He couldn't care less. He's not interested. He never was—he never wanted to live in New York. And what did I accomplish with all those years in the city? Why should Becker care that I was at the first White Party, or the Fellini Ball in the Rainbow Room? Those were my fantasies, not his. He stayed home, content with the flowers out back, his daughter, his boyfriend, his trips to the bar. The fact that we both live in the same town now means nothing. Or rather, the opposite of what I thought it should mean. I thought it should mean we had something in common. Becker thought it meant we must leave one another alone.

Truly sociable people move to the city, thinks Lark. It's the stubborn, self-reliant types who prefer small towns. The real American is a loner—like Becker. Who just happens to drive me crazy. If I were truly to express how I feel about him, thinks Lark, there would be nothing left on the bed when we got through but a little pile of bones, like the relics of a saint. That's all. Gone. Devoured. Consumed utterly: his hair, his lean muscles, his huge, soft balls. I'd be sitting there belching quietly and picking pubic hair out of my teeth, he thinks, like a fat man after eating six dozen oysters. Perhaps that's why he stays away—he knows this is what awaits him: extinction, he thinks as he picks up his glass of iced tea.

"Did you go to the boat ramp today?" says Ernie.

"No," says Lark. "Did you?"

"I was there for about an hour," says Ernie.

"And?" says Lark, thinking, We're like my neighbor Helen and her friend Penelope, talking about someone's hip replacement. Or granddaughter's wedding. Or hysterectomy. We're like two old men talking about the Lions Club.

"The man who drives the cement truck was there," says Ernie. "The one who masturbates while he reads porn magazines on the dashboard, sometimes with the door open, sometimes with the door closed."

"Oh?" says Lark.

"I'll never get with him again. It's really not worth the trouble. The only exciting part is getting him to let you in the truck. But once you're inside, it's rather a disappointment. I'd give him at most a C-plus."

"You mean the penis?" says Lark.

"No," says Ernie, "size doesn't really matter to me. He has a nice, average cock. There's just something about him. As the woman in the joke said, 'He just don't 'peal to me.' " And he laughs and scratches the hound's ears. "Has it been too warm for you to bother going?"

"No," says Lark. "I'm in love."

"In love!" says Ernie. "Goodness!"

"With someone I met there," says Lark. "The man who lives in town, the one I was just telling you about. For a while I went, hoping I'd run into him again, and now I'm *afraid* I will—so I just stopped going. You know, it could be so nice. In a movie, I'd return from all those years in the big city—which were, I see now, a kind of war—I'd come back to this little town . . ." he says.

"Like Barbara Stanwyck," Ernie says.

". . . after all that effort, and find True Love here in a small house on the edge of town, far away from the plague, settle down and help Becker to raise his daughter. That's what would happen in a movie."

"But this isn't a movie," says Ernie. "*These* are movies," he says, holding a hand out toward the floor-to-ceiling shelves of video cassettes. "By the way, when do you want to see *Pride and Prejudice*?"

"Not now," says Lark. "Why *can't* life be like a movie just once?"

"Because I told you," says Ernie, "you can fall in love in your twenties, and perhaps your thirties, but very rarely, if at all, in your forties and fifties; and if it does happen then, well, there are complicating factors."

"Such as?" says Lark.

"Oh, you're older, stuck in your ways, not as attractive as you used to be, and therefore at a disadvantage. Your life is mostly behind you, while the other person's is not. That's why we become invisible to certain people. That's why you probably, on some level, resent the young. That's why it upsets you when someone you want at the boat ramp drives off after seeing you get out of your car."

"But why doesn't that upset you?" asks Lark.

"Because I'm not competing," says Ernie.

"But you can't stop competing! When you stop competing, what is there?" says Lark.

"This," he says, reaching down to scratch the dachshund behind her ears. "Isn't she a pretty thing? And so overweight, like me."

Lark chooses to ignore this demonstration of affection. "Up north, people may seem rude, but they're honest," he says to Ernie. "Down south, people are polite, but you *never* know what they are thinking. They don't let you know."

"He evidently let you know," says Ernie. "That he didn't want to get with you again."

"But it's my *destiny* to end up here with him. My life has led to this," says Lark. "This is why I survived."

"Maybe it's not a movie you're thinking of," says Ernie. "Maybe it's an opera. *La Forza del Destino.* Would you like to hear my favorite aria from Act One?"

"No," says Lark. "Thank you. I wouldn't mind hearing 'The Letter Song' from *La Périchole,* though."

"Oh?" says Ernie.

"Because I'm thinking of sending him a letter."

"Don't. A letter would be one more embarrassment. Nothing's more annoying than someone who won't accept no. If the man who drives the gray Cadillac comes up to my car one more time, I'm going to be rude. And I don't like being rude! As I am sure yours doesn't either. The best thing you could do now is leave the man alone! And leave the letter writing to La Périchole," says Ernie. "Would you like to hear it in English or French?"

"Neither," says Lark. "I'm too depressed."

"Over that man in town? Don't be absurd. If someone doesn't want you, move on. It's nothing personal."

"It's the most personal thing in the world. Didn't you ever love someone?"

"Oh, my, yes."

"And who was he?"

"A bank teller I met in Portugal, when I was stationed there. I was happier with him than I've ever been with anyone else."

"Then what happened?"

"I was transferred, to Saudi Arabia."

"But can't you get in touch with him now?"

"I have no idea where he is, or whether he is still alive."

"But that's so sad!"

"Life is sad," Ernie says. "Because you never know what you've got until you lose it. You know the saying, Life is lived forward, but understood backward."

"But the point is to understand it now, so we make no mistakes!"

"Good luck!" laughs Ernie, as he rubs his dog's belly. Lark says nothing as he stares at the carpet. Then Ernie says in a polite voice, "Would you like me to shave your back?"

"No," says Lark. "You know, Turgenev wrote a story called 'First Love,' in which some men sit around recalling the first woman they fell in love with. He should have written one called 'Last Love.' Because it's much more painful. We fall in love less, but when we do, it's much deeper." They fall silent, and the dog in Ernie's arms looks dolorously at Lark. "Who was *your* last love?"

"Oh," says Ernie, as he scratches the hound's belly, "some nelly little queen in Fort Lauderdale. But he was blond and had the most beautiful teeth you've ever seen and a little terrier who ended up behaving much better than his master! He looked a little like that boy Henry was obsessed with," he says, as Lark rises with a sigh. "Whatever happened to that boy Henry was obsessed with at the boat ramp last spring?"

"Sandy?" says Lark as he walks to the door. "His father sent him back to Iowa."

"Why?" says Ernie.

"Because he was getting into trouble, running around with Henry, stealing and taking drugs, and of course having sex with Henry and his lover."

"Well, good," says Ernie as he walks Lark to the door. "If I remember correctly, Henry said Sandy was bisexual, and if he goes back to Iowa, maybe he'll go back to women, and that's to his advantage."

"What does Iowa have to do with women?" says Lark.

"I've always thought that Florida drew a trashy element," says Ernie in a delicate voice as they pause at the door. "Too many drifters, too many people escaping something, too many people on the lam. There's just something trashy about the atmosphere down here, or there has been recently at least, with all this growth. Back in Iowa, Sandy may return to his relatives, his roots, and women, and as I say, that would only be to his advantage."

"You mean—" says Lark.

"I mean this isn't a life I'd wish on anyone," Ernie says.

"Why not?" says Lark.

Ernie laughs. "You go to the boat ramp and you ask that?"

"I love the boat ramp!" says Lark. "It's the only place you can get out of your car, in this insane culture based on driving and watching television, and actually meet people! It's where I've met all my friends down here, it's where I met you!"

"Well, yes," says Ernie, "and I'm glad you did, but you must admit it can be rather stressful sitting there at times. And gay people are not always very nice to each other. And straight people wish we would lock ourselves in insane asylums. Don't you agree?"

"I suppose," says Lark. "But that's why I love Becker. He doesn't go to the boat ramp! He went that one night just to see what it was like. And he's never been back since. He said he liked to talk to people first. He's the exception to the boat ramp. An escape from the boat ramp."

"There is no escape from the boat ramp," laughs Ernie. "Not at our age."

Our age, thinks Lark. That elastic phrase: so comforting when the person using it is younger than yourself, so cold and cruel when older. Like *sir* in the wrong hands, he thinks. I knew I was old when people in stores started calling me sir.

"And of course I'm grateful for it," says Ernie as he turns on the outdoor light for Lark. "Like you, I've met all my friends there. But still," he says, "it isn't a life I'd wish on anyone."

"Well, that's encouraging," says Lark.

"Oh, I don't mean to discourage you," says Ernie. "I don't mean that at all. It's just that sooner or later, you'll stop falling in love, and when you do, there's always a dog at the pound who'd love to have you."

"Well, thank you for having me," says Lark, and he walks up the sodden slope, onto the dark sidewalk, happy that it is too late to even think of going to Becker's now. He has accomplished something: He has made it through another evening.

Confused and Alert

~~~~~~

By three o'clock the next afternoon, Lark is back at the boat ramp, killing time before going to the nursing home. If Becker doesn't want to see me, he thinks, my mother does. He pictures his mother in the hallway just outside her room, where the aide has left her in a blue Geri-chair, watching people go by. He's always pleased when he rounds the corner and sees her gradually focus on the figure walking toward her. Her son. He loves bending down to give her two kisses and hearing her start to murmur, like a person coming out of a coma, those words that make his heart swell: "I'm so happy you're here, thank God you've come! I have so much to tell you."

In truth she does. If he has nothing to tell her ("I went to the post office today and Becker wasn't there!"), she has lots to tell him. The cook's boyfriend broke into the kitchen and went after her with a knife. Billy, the other quadriplegic, who moved in with Nancy, a nurse who used to work here, had to dial 911 with his nose after Nancy began starving him to death. Joyce, a very bright nurse who for some reason cannot look directly at his mother, yet talks to him all the time, has been dating Neil, a male nurse on the night shift; after sending him a New Guinea impatiens in a hanging pot, she opened the door of her house that morning and found the impatiens upended on her steps, stripped of its blooms, reeking of cat piss, a twisted mass of dirt and broken twigs, with a note attached: HANDS OFF, BITCH. "It's his ex-wife," Joyce explains calmly. "She's a Filipino. They take these things more seriously than we do."

All the nurses bring their lives into the nursing home. Half of them are divorced. Two have been married to the same man; they talk about his chronic constipation in the hallway. Betty, who promised Lark she would take the medicine cart she pushes around the halls twice each shift and wheel it down the hill into the duck pond the day she won the lottery, wins the lottery and does just that. A thousand dollars' worth of narcotics goes to the bottom. (She thinks everyone is overmedicated.) Then she drives off to California in her red Mazda sports car. There is always something going on in the nursing home, unlike his life.

That day he arrives on a very hot afternoon and finds the place locked tight; he bangs on the door, rings the emergency bell, and finally someone opens the door a crack and tells him that two students have been discovered dead with their throats slashed, so the staff locked the doors. Everyone is exchanging theories about the killer; one of the dead is the granddaughter of a woman on Hallway One. ("The killer is after young women," he tells Joyce, "not *old* ones!") Even that is part of the indignity of old age, he thinks. Nobody wants to murder you. But all that week the patients at the nursing home suddenly seem more valuable; they are spoken to with unusual warmth. The next night he rushes back to the nursing home to be where the action is, to share the latest news, and has to ring the emergency bell to get in, and bang on the door like a peasant trying to find shelter in a castle.

"I've so much to tell you," his mother says to him when he bends down to kiss her on arriving. "Hurry, get me up!" Her day depends mostly on what the nurses and aides have done or not done—all of it discussable. ("He treats me like a human being," she said one day of a favorite neighbor who had just left after a visit; it was that simple.) His mother has her paranoid fantasies—she imagines one nurse dislikes her—though most often she is right. And in general she is far more realistic than he is. One day he dressed her, then removed her blouse and put on another. "Why did you do that?" she said.

"Because it makes you look like a little old lady," he said.

And then, a moment later, out in the hallway, she replied, "But that's what I am!" Indeed. Not in his eyes: She's still thirty-five, perfumed, beautiful. He's the one who can't surrender her to the depredations of physical decline; he's the one who dresses her like a doll and presents her to the world; he's the one who panics when she's not eating well, or says the light hurts her eye (cataracts), or seems lethargic or sad. He's the one who storms down to the desk whenever he finds her too relaxed and demands to know if the nurse has given her a tranquilizer. (It would be easier to give them all tranquilizers, stash them in one big room, and close the door.) He's the one whose heart accelerates when the phone rings at home, and it's a nurse—obliged by law to inform the family—telling him that his mother has a skin tear (the skin on her arm looks like the outermost layers of a very old onion) or a bedsore (Lark and his mother's bête noire) or (he will never get over this) a broken arm that no one noticed until they moved her one night for supper. He is the one who wants her to live forever.

She merely wants to go home—or, failing that, some company. When a class of students has been at the nursing home— mostly young people taking a course given by the local junior college with a week of on-the-job training—she is radiant; the young bring an energy, an affection, an optimism and degree of attention the people who do this five days a week can seldom muster. (He wants a law passed requiring high-school seniors to work part-time in a nursing home; it would help both the patients and the students.) His mother's happiness seems to depend largely on who her aide is. When she likes her aide, she's happy. When she does not, she isn't. Whichever mood he finds her in, no matter what his own, he feels relieved, restored, the moment he rounds the corner and sees her there. Once she was confused and said to him when he bent down to kiss her, "Would you please go to the nurses' desk and have them call my son?"

"I am your son," he said.

"Oh," she laughed. And they were off.

His greatest joy is simply moving her from her bed or Geri-chair into the wheelchair, which is much easier to push around the hall, and taking her for a "spin," her paralysis momentarily obliterated, her stillness exchanged for motion, her mobility now superior to that of the other patients moving in their own wheel-chairs, with much effort, around the corridor. That moment is incomparable: He feels like Jesus, raising Lazarus from the dead. It is worth everything else. Even if, in an hour or two, they are bickering, negotiating her constant demands—to wipe her nose, to take her home permanently, to make sure the nurse knows she wants a Restoril and two Tylenols at bedtime—that single, brief moment when he first swims into her vision and she awakens like a flower in some speeded-up film, blossoming before his very eyes, is sweet. And so, he began to realize his twelfth year visiting the place, is all that goes before and after it—the jokes with the aides as he walks down the hall to her room ("She's waiting for you!"); their favorite nurse ("She told me to call your house if you weren't here by five-thirty!"); the handsome aide who works in the Dementia Unit and who can be seen cheerfully shepherding his charges down the hall back through the double doors meant to keep them in; the madwoman who always holds out her hand to him and squeezes it shut in a kind of wave; and finally, around the corridor, his mother, the princess he has come to waken from a long, dull sleep.

Only Roy, the bearded fifty-five-year-old queen from Archer, with a knowing smile on his face as he watches Lark proceed down the hall, sees right through him. "She's all excited, she's waiting for you," he will say in a flat, sardonic voice as he lifts the top of the yellow plastic laundry bin and drops a load of dirty diapers in, as if to say, I know you have no one else in your life.

His mother says, as he bends down to give her two air-kisses, "Get me up quick. I've been lying here since one o'clock. Not one person has come in to move me." And sure enough, the pad beneath her is soaked with a dark aureole of urine. Full of disgust and righteousness, he rolls her to one side and bunches the diaper up; then rolls her on the other side and removes the wet pad, like a waiter in a restaurant taking off the tablecloth, proud of his skills; he can change a patient with the best of them. In five minutes he has her dressed and in her wheelchair, her hair combed, ready to set out on a tour of the nursing home.

The others, the ones who can move their own wheelchairs, are always, when Lark and his mother turn the corner into the Medicare hall, exactly where the aides left them. Where the aides leave them baffles him sometimes—especially when the aides are busy or distracted; he saw one wheel his mother's roommate, Charlotte, into their room after dinner and leave her in the corner facing the closet door. Not because she was being punished, but because the aide had forgotten to turn her around toward her television set, and then turn the set on. It's like musical chairs: Wherever the aides leave them is where they stay—sometimes for hours, until another aide on a new shift comes to retrieve them. This evening the patients are all in their usual places near Station One: The same cluster of women in wheelchairs turns toward him with hopeful faces when he enters.

Lark supposes no one will ever come to visit him if he ends up in a nursing home—I have no son to do for me what I'm doing for my mother, he thinks as he wheels her past the young lady at the telephone. This is the fact that explains the expression on Roy's face when he saw Lark coming down the hall at five-fifteen. Roy knows. He sees, thinks Lark as he smiles at Roy, that I have nothing else in my life. Not at this age. Queens can tell. When she goes, I'll have to hit the road. Mexico City for Christmas, Quito for July Fourth—that endless string of holidays to be celebrated without a family. That's all American life is: holidays. For which you need Family. I'll leave the country for Christmas, he thinks, register in a hotel in Oaxaca—and wait incognito for Christmas Day to pass. Till then, I'm Lochinvar, coming to rescue a damsel in distress.

Wheeling his mother around, he sees the red-haired woman who cannot use her feet back in her room now, slowly typing on a small portable typewriter on the chest of drawers. "She's writing a novel," says an aide who notices Lark looking into the room. About what? he wonders. The present or the past?

For a while Lark read books aloud to his mother—the last one they never finished, a paperback biography of Katharine Hepburn—and then they became news junkies because that was easier, and because they had so little news of their own. She was paralyzed; he couldn't tell her about the boat ramp. So they watched CBS. By the end of the twelve years they had become so familiar with its conventions, etiquette, and formula, the compulsion to watch national news was gone, unless there was an investigation going on: the Iran-Contra, Robert Bork, Clarence Thomas hearings have spoiled them. They're used to scandals, to inquisitions.

He brings magazines or *The New York Times* with him to read during some of the television they watch—even though it is rude to read during *Murder, She Wrote*. That is something they do together. Sometimes he reads her an article from *Time* or *The New Yorker*. (When they ask me what I did the past twelve years, he thinks, I'll say, I read magazines.) "Do you miss New York?" she sometimes asks when he arrives with a fresh copy of *The New York Times*. The question always makes him pause. He can't tell anymore. He has been gone for so long. It's like the Stockholm syndrome: After a long enough confinement, you grow attached to your kidnapper. Besides, New York is a place he cannot miss, in a sense; his city is dead. The local news seems comforting in comparison—shots of crime scenes, fires, a few investigative pieces (city councillor runs up huge bills on his car phone), and finally the obligatory closing clip about the birth of an antelope at the zoo or a rescued whale, dolphin, or bald eagle—as if, no matter how many murders, stabbings, robberies, instances of revenge taken on former wives, battered children, it is reassuring to know we still care about our wet and furry friends. Then the national news with Dan Rather. News that in retrospect merely serves to mark a decade doing, really, nothing.

In fact, by the end of the twelve years Lark is no longer a news junkie; the news seems repetitive, depressing, and ultimately hopeless—like everything else, the older he gets and the more time he spends with the decrepit and the dying.

Occasionally, when he enters the nursing home, he sees on the wall a hand-lettered sign announcing a memorial service for a resident he and his mother came to befriend, a death that has upset even the nurses, whose demeanor is always a giveaway after someone they have come to like has died. Ruth, the lovely, soft-spoken women from Omaha, who chain-smoked, dead; Rita, the one they watched *Wheel of Fortune* and *Jeopardy!* with, dead; Aurelio, the Cuban man followed everywhere by his Cuban wife—the dapper fellow who had bruises on his face where she had struck him because she was convinced he was flirting with another woman—dead; and three of his mother's old roommates—a very old woman who lay in bed all day calling "Pain pill! Pain pill!" as brittle as a crab; a demented ex-schoolteacher who threatened to hit his mother one afternoon and was quickly moved; and Cora, who called his mother "my baby" and stuck up for her, and then went mad, threw trays of food at the nurses, and died in another wing—all gone. Very few patients leave the nursing home alive—unless they are there merely to recuperate from an operation or undergo physical therapy. Mostly they leave on a stretcher, wheeled down the hall by the paramedics.

Lark and his mother have spent twelve Christmases here, however, serenaded by choirs from the Boy Scouts and nearby churches; when flocks of people of all ages assembled in the foyer and then set out, as nervous as a platoon of soldiers on reconnaissance, down the hall, singing carols against the roar of TV sets, stealing glances into the rooms they were passing— glances that revealed, of course, worse than the Ghost of Christmas Past, everyone's nightmare: being old and crippled in a nursing home. Once Santa Claus came in and sprinkled candy into the room as he walked by, like a priest flinging holy water in a procession, and Lark found his mother, when he arrived for dinner that evening, covered with candy canes and gum drops, like a German Christmas cake studded with candied fruit. Another time he found her choking on the communion wafer a real priest had just given her before moving on to the communicant in the next room. For two or three years a mysterious couple from the local Catholic church came in every Wednesday to talk to his mother. An elderly man who played the piano in the dining room at dinnertime came in every afternoon at three to have tea and cookies with his mother's roommate. ("He completely ignores me," his mother said. "I might as well not be there.") Lark is delighted when he learns someone else has come in to visit—an apprentice nurse's aide or a nurse who used to work here—because he knows how it relieves the long, dull day.

The truth is he often has to make himself get out of the car and walk inside—screwing himself up for the scene that awaits—as if descending into a tomb. The first month here, a nurse told him paralyzed people appreciate breaks in their routine; but he soon learned his mother counted on his usual schedule. Accidents, you might say, are a disruption in the order of things; and since her accident, the one that left her paralyzed, order has been very important. (On the other hand, whenever she slips through his arms onto the floor, or he takes a fall, she bursts out laughing. *Real* disruptions in the order of things thrill her, and he wonders if he should start leaving banana peels around.)

Otherwise, he and Angela Lansbury are the two points on which her universe rests, two permanent points of stability—even if, he notices, Angela has aged far less than he since he started coming to the nursing home. His mother asked one night why he didn't let his hair grow long. ("Because I'm losing it.") She even said, another evening, "You've gone gray," in a wistful tone that made him think his aging was as much a blow to her as it was to him. Then it dawned on him, She has more hair than I do now. Time has not stopped. He is losing his looks in the nursing home, at the boat ramp, on the highway between the two. What difference does it make? he wonders. I'd have to lose them somewhere—here or in the bars. And the bars are no longer home. The nursing home is.

The nursing home now constitutes a group of people with whom he can talk after a day spent alone in his house; he has become dependent on the place, and the scenes that terrify Christmas carolers and drop the jaws of children whose parents brought them here to see Grandma are as familiar to him as a pack of playing cards—images that have eventually become amusing, even hilarious, so dramatically do they depict, as in some tableau, Dejection, Fatigue, Distress, or Shock. As he wheels his mother around the halls, they pass patients lying in their blue Geri-chairs with mouths open in a silent scream, a perpetual expression of outrage, as if they have been irradiated, frozen, by some rude nurse's aide, or simply Life itself. Or both, since Life, at this point, *is* a rude nurse's aide. (Rarely are any of them fired, so understaffed is the place. Americans don't want to pick fruit or vegetables, dispose of garbage, or take care of old people in nursing homes. Such snobs, he thinks, for a democratic country!)

If you navigate the halls regularly you learn, like a pilot on the Mississippi, to spot shoals and eddies, fallen trees and momentary traffic jams, before you even come close—though sometimes he has to slow to a crawl behind two madwomen taking their own sweet time to move down the hall side by side. It would be rude to shout at them, even though his mother urges him to; there is quite enough shouting in the nursing home already. "I don't *want* a man to undress me!" another woman is yelling to an aide who stands there with a nightgown in hand, as Lark, completely blocked, comes to a stop outside her doorway.

"Don't worry," snaps the aide as he bends down to remove the sock from her right foot. "You ain't got nothin' *I* want, lady!"

Ah, thinks Lark. That's why I hate the bars now. The tragedy of all of us when we lose our looks. The only thing anyone could want from most people in this place is money. The money their family, or the federal government, is paying for the bed they occupy. Too true, too cruel, the lessons of the nursing home, he thinks, as the women blocking him finally separate, and he carefully pushes his mother's wheelchair through the intervening space. The great, the primal fear of human beings: Nobody's going to love you when you're old and gray, he thinks as he pushes his mother into the hall on which the mad patients live—the ones who aren't in the Dementia Unit. The Dementia Unit is for Alzheimer's; the rest are just gaga. (His mother has become fond of both groups of residents. She likes to stop and talk to each one, those who are gentle and kind, at least; for people, when mad, do not lose their personality, their character—and in the ruins of some faces, kind or beautiful originals could still be seen.) His mother's attitude toward dementia is ambivalent; she used to say quite often, as he wheeled her around the hall, "They're better off not knowing where they are." But she nearly leaped out of her chair the evening he wheeled her by mistake toward the Blue Dining Room—where the gaga are fed.

The word the staff use is not *gaga;* the two categories are *confused* and *alert.* Outside the nursing home, at the boat ramp, for instance, the categories are different: young or old, handsome or ugly, well hung or small. Here it's much simpler. When his mother first arrived here, it was very important to have a roommate who was alert; as the years went by, he's come to realize alert patients have preferences, opinions about things the confused are quite indifferent to, like which television program they want to watch. His mother's current roommate is a perfect example of the fact that the mad can be charming, civilized, easier to live with. She even seems to have a prescience that ordinary folk lack. Once, when Lark was very tired, discouraged, and angry with his mother, and he had just learned that morning that another friend had died—when he was standing in the middle of the room between the two beds wondering how he could go on—he looked up and saw Charlotte staring at him. "Don't worry," she said. *"God is watching."* He never forgot the remark.

He reminds himself that it is very easy to find someone else's mother's madness charming. The few times when he suspected his own mother was becoming "confused" terrified him; if she lost her mind, he thought, he would lose her utterly. He admires Charlotte's daughter—the professor who comes in to converse as best she can with a mother who is mentally a shadow of her former self—and the cheerful determination with which the daughter conducts visits that Charlotte only dimly perceives, on some diluted level.

He is grateful Charlotte is so easy to get on with—that she asks no questions, does not find his own devotion odd. (He assumes the rest of the nursing home does; he is used by now to answering the question aides ask him, "Are you an only child?" As if that could be the only explanation for the frequent visits.) At three o'clock every day an old man—who lives in the same apartment complex Charlotte once lived in—eats Danish butter cookies with her from a tin, until it too is added to the stack of empty tins on the table beside her bed, and drinks coffee, all the while ignoring Lark's mother's requests for help; then, after the old man goes down to the dining room to play the piano for the residents eating there, Charlotte throws up, just in time for dinner. During dinner, they all watch the news on Channel 4. "The country's in trouble," Charlotte said one evening not long ago, midway through the broadcast, her fine, patrician features wrinkling with concern, her right hand held up in the air, like a piece of Roman sculpture, for emphasis.

"I agree," Lark said. "Something very terrible is happening in the United States. Nobody seems happy anymore, and I don't know quite why that is. Is it the media that gives that impression, because television likes conflict, or is it reality? Whichever, the result is the same. An impression of unease, unhappiness. It's just extraordinary," he said, turning to her, glad there was someone he could vent these thoughts to. "We won the war, we settled the problem of the Bomb, we beat the Russians, we've expanded liberty to groups never before even acknowledged in our own country, and still people are bitching. The culture seems sleazy; everything is tacky; people hate it and don't know how to change the situation. There is this terrible sense of godlessness—this feeling we're all alone, we're all we've got. I think Nietzsche was right. The death of God, he said, would not be felt for two centuries. Sometimes I think we're beginning to feel it now. Now that this country is so rich and overdeveloped, we have nothing to do but face the emptiness of life. Our problem is that we have no problems. Nobody really cares about the inner cities, or even saving the rain forest. We just drive cars and watch TV. And TV has destroyed everything! Theater, social life, a sense of security. Everybody's moving into gated communities and working on their abs. It's very narcissistic. Plus we have no sense of adventure anymore, of the future. There are no worlds to be discovered, and since most of us are not going to outer space, we stay home and eat fat-free fudge. Integration seems to be the main project the media has for the rest of us. But integrating blacks into American life is just not an exciting project for the race that wiped out the Indians and settled the West. It's like making them eat spinach. I don't know what the future of this country holds—I suspect white Americans are basically bored to death. And not at all happy with the way things are going."

"And the country is in real danger," Charlotte said, gently stabbing the air with her forefinger.

"Yes, I agree," Lark said, thinking she was more lucid than they believed.

"Because the crows are not being fed," she said.

"That too," he said, looking out of the window at the birds crisscrossing the lawn, thinking, What do I know anymore? She could be right—*these* crows, on *this* lawn, outside our window. Perhaps Charlotte is one of the Four Horsemen of the Apocalypse. Perhaps we're in a novel by Stephen King.

When the news is over at seven, the aide comes in to undress Charlotte and put her to bed, at which point Charlotte always undergoes a severe shift in personality. The minute the aide touches her, she lets out a scream so bloodcurdling, a cry so riveting, that aides who are doing this for the first time drop her arm, step back, and sometimes burst into tears; at which point obscenities begin pouring from Charlotte's mouth. (When his own mother cursed him with "Goddamn you!" he called her on it, and she said, "It's my roommate. That's how she talks all the time.") "What are you goddamned people doing to me, for God's sake!" Charlotte says that evening.

"Nothing," the aide replies in a tiny voice.

"Yes, you are!" Charlotte cries. "You're tearing my arm off!"

The aide goes ahead, gets Charlotte's nightgown on, draws

the curtain between the beds, and begins to clean her bottom. "There's a place in hell for the likes of you!" Charlotte yells. Silence. And then, in a perfectly calm and quite sarcastic voice, "Could you tell me please if this is leading to anything?"

Yes, Lark wants to say, yes, it is: On a practical level, to your eventual falling asleep tonight. On a more cosmic plane, to Extinction, Obliteration, and Death.

That is the end product of the place—and one of the reasons he refuses to let his own mother remain here weekends. He is afraid that she will die if he simply leaves her here. God knows what would have happened, he thinks, if she was on Medicaid. Poor Billy, who was, could not leave the nursing home more than one night a month when he lived here; those are the rules—if he'd gone home any more than that, he would have been disqualified for assistance. Only private-pay patients are allowed to come and go as they wish. Coming and going—even if it feels on many Sunday nights as if he has just rolled Sisyphus' stone up the hill only to have it roll back down again, even if he feels each time he has to return her to the nursing home as if he is shoving her into an oven—is crucial to his peace of mind. To leave her here seems too much like abandoning her to Death. The real nightmare is that she should die here alone.

How decent and humane it looks in the daily obituaries, he thinks, when at the end of someone's little paragraph—the nine lines of type most lives are reduced to—the words *died at home* appear. Everyone wants to die at home—even men in prison— on the front porch, whether they have one or not, in a rocking chair, ditto, falling asleep while the grandchildren play in the yard and the smell of a fresh-baked apple pie set on the windowsill wafts from the kitchen, surrounded by family and friends. What family? What friends? Most of us die in hospitals—connected to tubes, at three in the morning, without a nurse or a relative in sight.

"I get a chill every time I see one of those," his mother said one evening when they passed a stretcher the paramedics had parked in an alcove. "That was the door they took Mrs. Rollins through," she said as they went around the corner. And then: "I'm going to be cremated, you know." And then: "But make sure I'm dead, before you do. I might just be in a coma."

People vanish overnight. They go out on the stretcher and are never seen again. In a few days, other patients are in their rooms, and their little collections of plants, books, family photographs (when young) are taken down from their Hall of Memory. Or one day a thought occurs to you—you haven't seen Mrs. Rollins in quite a while—and you have to conclude, She must be dead.

The daughter of his mother's roommate Cora appeared in their room not long after Cora died, and began taking down the samplers, collages, framed photographs, and potted snake's-tongues that made up her mother's side of the long chest of drawers that ran along one side of the room. That night Lark was feeding his mother dinner. They were sad that Cora had died; they had gone down to the Dementia Unit the last month of her life, after she'd been moved to a room there—he'd wheeled his mother to the bedside and she'd said, "Cora, Cora," but got no response from the woman lying there, digging deeper and deeper into madness. It's like a prison, he thought—the inmates become friends with one another. A week later she died, and two days after that, her daughter—a thin, pretty, morose woman, who, with large glasses and a soft voice, looked like Joyce Carol Oates—came into the room to get Cora's things.

Lark told the daughter how loyal she had been and how much they would miss her mother—and then the daughter, standing between the beds with her mother's teddy bear in her arms, said, "Thank you. That's more than my brother can say. Now I'm paying for the funeral he won't even come to. I tell you," she went on in her clear, thin voice, "I realized when I was married, taking care of other people doesn't mean they will take care of you. When I was sick with peritonitis in the hospital for six months, my husband used to scream at me for leaving him alone with the kids. They were all furious with me. That's when I said, I'm getting out of this. That's when I decided to go to college, learn computers, and get divorced. I've raised my sons to be different, I hope—to take care of others. I did my best with Mom, but it wasn't enough. She died because I left her alone this summer for two weeks. I explained to her I had to move because the carpet in my apartment was mildewed, and I hurt my back moving furniture, and I had a rush deadline at work. But when I stayed away those two weeks—she took it personally. She started to deteriorate then."

Still clutching the teddy bear, she looked at Lark. "I let up just once in five years," she said in a toneless voice. "Of course Donald, the administrator, told me families hang on sometimes, and that only makes it harder for the patient." Lark frowned at her over the bowl of pureed pears he held in his right hand, his left gripping the spoon poised at his mother's lips. "But you can't help but hold on," she said, "because you love them."

His mother shook her head, miming an expression of impatience, her lips pursed, as the woman continued to stand there with the teddy bear in her hands; Lark had never heard the daughter talk like this. That's because it's all over, he thought, all the things that were kept down can now come out. He was glad his mother had probably not heard most of what she'd said (her hearing was going)—it was a nasty comment on their own relationship, after all. They were both hanging on to each other, for reasons he didn't even want to examine.

"Well," said the daughter, coming to life again, "I've left a few nightgowns in the closet; if you want them, they're yours. Good-bye and good luck," she said, and turned and left with the teddy bear.

"I thought she'd *never* shut up," his mother said, the moment she was out of the room. He was glad his mother was still alive, but the idea that he was sustaining his mother, jailing her, keeping her behind on earth, in this lamentable condition, because *he* couldn't let go made him again wonder, Who is imprisoning whom? ("But what about your own life?" Sutcliffe had asked him one evening at the Wordsworth. "What life?" said Lark. "I don't have one." And neither do you, he thought at the time, looking across the table at his friend.)

When his mother said once in a calm, dispassionate voice, like that of a scientist observing the behavior of a hamster, "You'll never leave me; your conscience won't let you," she was right. The evening he came out of the snow and into the rehabilitation center two weeks after her accident, and then walked down the long corridor lined with young men in wheelchairs who'd dived into shallow swimming pools, or been shot in hunting accidents, or smashed up in auto accidents, all paralyzed, all watching him walk by; and he saw, at the corridor's very end, his mother, in her wheelchair, like a little bird, her arms raised as three aides attempted to put a sweater on her; and she caught sight of him and began to cry his name over and over again as he came closer—that evening, at that moment, while the snow fell outside past the enormous window, and the paralyzed men watched him walk by, and the aides started to laugh at his mother's repetition of his name, over and over—he knew: We are linked together now, in some way, that only death will end. And so it was. "I'm holding you back, aren't I?" she said, years later, out of the blue, when the excitement, the newness, of the rehabilitation center had been replaced by the dull ordinary routine of real life—when the rehabilitation center had become a nursing home, and their being together claustrophobic at times.

But he liked it too; that was the odd part—shopping for diapers with the young mothers at Pic 'N Save, getting eye drops and Kleenex and Q-Tips and bandages; planning menus for the weekend (which loin of pork is leaner?), washing her clothes and hanging them on the line. He was, at last, what he'd always wanted to be: a parent. Life grants us what we desire in ways we never imagined. "Is she your wife?" the woman clutching a plastic baby would say as he went by the cluster of harpies by the nurses' desk, pushing his mother in the wheelchair with her name, written in Magic Marker on a piece of adhesive tape, stuck on the back. Yes, he wanted to say, as he and the nurses laughed. He could see the headline in the *National Enquirer* now: WHEELCHAIR CEREMONY—I MARRIED MOM!

It was Roy who burst that little fantasy balloon, who reminded him where all this was heading. "Sit down and watch," he said to Lark one sultry summer afternoon as Lark walked through the Garden Room on his way to his mother, and found Roy in one of the wrought-iron chairs, smoking a cigarette on his break as he watched a family barbecue on the grassy central courtyard outside the screen door. "They're both from my hometown. Cousins. One loonier than the other. The old lady in the wheelchair is the tall one's mother. She's ninety-three years old, and tired of the whole business. But they want to do a barbecue. With the mullet and grits they used to eat when she cooked for them God knows when in Crystal River. They're so desperate," he said in a low, calm voice as he sat there watching them through the screen, "to keep her alive, and she just wants to go. Look! She's crying," he said, as he raised the cigarette to his mouth. "She's just *exhausted,* the poor thing, because they want to re-create some picnic in the past when they were eleven, and you could still swim in the river, and there weren't no condos on the riverbank, and it was Old Timey Florida. So they are cooking the mullet and serving the grits and she's too tired to even eat," he said, as the other residents began lining up at the screen, watching the family barbecue in the courtyard, like ghosts at the banquet whom no one has invited.

"The *scandal,*" said Roy, as the tall one, the son, served his mother's plate, wiped her eyes with a napkin, and said something to his cousin. "It's not the age and decrepitude of the mother, which are considerable, but the depth of *their* loneliness and fear of abandonment, *their* desire to cling to the Past. You'll see," Roy said, stubbing his cigarette out in the ashtray and standing up, "what it's like when yours is gone. You'll go back to that house, and it won't mean a thing. All that furniture, her clothes, all those rooms. There'll be a sense of freedom, and then—Loneliness! Big time. That town won't know what to do with you—the only reason you visit people is because of her. They're *her* friends, not yours, and she got her status from your father. You'll be a social zero when she dies. None of it will have any meaning. No one will even *ask* you for Thanksgiving, unless as Christian charity. Children will *avoid* your house on Halloween, or you'll draw the drapes and hide in the closet till they're gone. We're *monsters* as far as they are concerned. And, when it comes time for *you* to be admitted to a place like this, you'll be what they call a Problem Placement," he laughed. "Try dealing with that," he said, taking his timecard out of his pocket and punching it. "I haven't got a living relative. I've got nobody to take care of me when I get old, and my family once owned the entire *town* of Apalachicola."

And he swept out of the Activities Lounge, leaving Lark with a message so stark he declined to follow Roy down the hall and went instead onto the patio, where, politely ignoring the cousins gathering up the remnants of their barbecue as a nurse's aide wheeled the mother back inside, he crossed the lawn and came to a stop beside the window of his mother's room. There she lay, turned toward the hallway, half watching *Wheel of Fortune*, half watching the doorway for his return. As he put his face close to the glass and looked in at her, he felt such a wave of love and tenderness all he could think was, You may be paralyzed from the neck down, you may have itchy skin and only one good eye, you may wake up every day still paralyzed, still in this nursing home, you may not be able to feed, bathe, or dress yourself, or brush your teeth or wipe your butt or walk or dance or drive a car or take a shower or do one thing you may want to do, including scratching your nose, but you can't die, because everyone else has and you're all I've got.

"Your Gums Are *Always* Bleeding"

〜〜〜〜〜〜〜〜〜〜〜〜〜〜〜〜〜〜〜〜〜〜〜〜〜〜〜〜〜〜〜〜

In the bar are the usual suspects: one of them a Cuban drug pusher on the far side of the bar and, in the back room, two men playing pool. They are drunk. One of them is so drunk that each time he completes his shot, he stands up and starts to sway; then his knees buckle and his partner comes over and straightens him up with what looks like the Heimlich maneuver. The next minute the man manages to sink the eight ball in the designated pocket. Lark finds a perch on the banquette just inside the pool room—from this vantage point he can look at the men playing pool and, through the doorway, the men at the bar—and nurses his club soda. He doesn't drink alcohol here because he knows he has to drive; he doesn't understand how any of these men drink as much as they do, sink a pool ball with unerring accuracy, and then drive home. He doesn't smoke, he doesn't go out in the sun anymore, he avoids fats and red meat, he exercises at the gym three times a week and goes to bed every night by midnight, and he still looks like Andy Warhol. It's the old joke: The people at Mother Earth (the health food store in town) all look ill.

The room begins to fill up. The Muscle Pod comes in—a trio of men in white T-shirts, with big biceps, chests, and buzz cuts who talk only to each other. One of the T-shirts says, NO PECS, NO SEX! That's about it. Rick, the sculptor from Waldo, comes in next, with a trio of young blond students in baggy shorts and T-shirts; at thirty, a confirmed chicken queen. Then an old man with white hair and glasses with thick black rims sits down next to Lark, introduces himself, and tells Lark that he is eighty years old and his daughter has dropped him off here while she goes shopping. Never bitch about your age, a man told Lark years ago; there is always someone who would be glad to exchange his for yours.

Rick sits on a stool surrounded by the young blonds with haircuts made popular by the film *Another Country*—the English Schoolboy look. That rarest of expressions on his face is firmly in place: a smile. He's generally so unhappy Lark has stopped calling him. Even after their interview at the boat ramp, Lark tried to be Rick's friend—drove him to the beach one day last month, went swimming with him, talked. All Lark remembers of their outing is the young knockout who passed them as they strolled the surf, and looked not at him, but at Rick. When, on the way home afterward, Rick blurted out, "My life is a mess!" Lark put his head back and laughed. He sees now this was cruel. At the time he couldn't react any other way—the idea that life could be, at the age of thirty, a mess seemed risible. How could anyone be miserable at thirty, when being thirty is the deepest source of joy there is—it got you cruised on the beach? Now he reflects, At age thirty my own life seemed a mess too: stagnant, slimy, stalled. Over and done. Going nowhere fast. Rick, with debt on his credit card, his art piling up in a trailer in Waldo, driving thirty miles round trip to the bar every night, getting drunk so he can talk to nineteen-year-olds: Perhaps his life is a mess. But he looks happy now. Chicken queen that he is, in the very henhouse, surrounded by *jeunesse dorée*.

The *jeunesse dorée* isn't really, not down here. Gainesville isn't Princeton, but it is a large, rich state university that can no longer accept everyone who applies; the students are not stupid. And they are, for the most part, children of affluent families. He's watched them for twelve years now, in various bars—the Loading Zone, before the owner's cocaine habit pissed that place down the toilet; the University Club, its pale successor; the Melody Club, the grandam of them all. Talking to one another with a certain intensity, their glasses of booze and cigarettes cocked at a sprightly angle, they all look as if they were wearing T-shirts that say, AWAY FROM HOME FOR THE FIRST TIME. On our own. In Nightclub Heaven. At last, adults, in a gay bar. There is in Gainesville, Rick said bitterly one evening, an unspoken assumption: "I'm important here for four years." It lends the students who go to these bars a certain sense of superiority: the tourist in St. Thomas, while the cruise ship, floodlighted, nine stories high, waits in the harbor.

Of course it takes a certain guts, Lark supposes, to leave the dormitory, the fraternity house, the student ghetto, and go to a gay bar. It can't, he thinks, be easy. Not really. One is still going deeply against the social grain, disqualifying oneself from membership in the tribe, pursuing a part of oneself that doesn't fit with the rest. Not all the gay rights marches, novels, support groups, and enlightened university policies can change the significance of what one is doing when one walks into the University Club. And to come to the Ambush is really slumming. Far from the harbor where the cruise ship sits, all floodlighted and air-conditioned and clean. To come here, thinks Lark, means you are leaving the safe perimeters of a bar near campus where everyone is twenty-one, to go to a bar where ages are mixed; where you might find a thirty-year-old sculptor, or a corroded thing like me, he thinks, or the eighty-year-old grandfather on my right. You might find Life. With all its unpromising messages and mixed forecasts of what lies beyond the Great Divide of Graduation. You might find: Old Gay Men. Eeeek! The thought that this is what lies at the end of the road. He avoided older men himself when he was their age. Averted his eyes.

Now, still sophomores, they keep their distance in that and other ways. They belong to their own discussion group at the university. They go almost exclusively to the University Club. Or, if they come up here at all, go into the Melody Club first—where students had to come before there were any bars downtown, where drag shows (so reassuring to the young) are held once a month, and women mix with men, and R.B., the owner, sits nursing a cigarette, a heart condition, obesity, diabetes, and the question, Should he close the bar now and retire and pay some attention to his health, or have cardiac arrest on a barstool with the Miss Florida pageant onstage?

The Melody Club is separated from the Ambush by a small garden-courtyard and a covered walkway. The *jeunesse dorée* usually enter the latter, smaller, western bar via the garden route—enter and sweep through the front room in a pack that does not stop until it reaches the safety of the video games in the pool room; or they stop right inside the door and conspicuously speak to one another under a pencil spotlight. It is a pose he struck himself years ago. It is based on an underlying assumption: You are Young, and therefore people are watching you. It is Your Turn now. The others in the wings, on the dim bleachers, would have you if they could. But you won't let them. You won't even look—except at one another. Part insecurity, part conceit—part fear and part vanity; embedded in a deep soil of self-consciousness. Their beauty is astonishing, but the rest is of no interest. His Tadzio is older. Men in their thirties floor Lark. He can dismiss the college crowd; they won't come into their own for another fifteen years. Men in their thirties have discarded the silliness of youth but still retain its privileges. Men in their thirties are It. But now even men in their thirties are, alas, receding from him with each passing year, like islands in the wake of a passenger ship at which he can no longer disembark. He notices the eighty-year-old gentleman has started talking to the man on his right; Lark slips off his perch and purchases another club soda, with lime.

When he retrieves his perch on the little bleachers in the

corner, he pretends to watch the pool players and tries to imagine Becker standing over there, in that corner, smoking a cigarette. (Becker's only breach of discipline. His daughter wants him to quit; he went to a psychologist in Gainesville about it, and she told him he referred to himself in the third person—a piece of information Becker found worth passing on to Lark the night they had that long, sweet precoital conversation while the still spring night dampened the leaves on the driveway outside. But Lark didn't know what to make of it.) He tries to picture Becker over by the jukebox, tall, skinny, handsome, serious, watching the pool game while someone speaks to him. He is surely well known in the bar; he's been coming here for years. (Indeed, Becker told Lark he was thinking of going to the bars in Jacksonville instead—like a salesman who has already used up a particular territory, thought Lark at the time.)

There was another problem he had with the Ambush, Becker told him. "Sometimes people don't understand our conversation is just social," he said. Ah, thought Lark, you mean the idiots who actually believe one's friendliness, not realizing it is mere good manners, an attempt to demonstrate that not all handsome men are stuck-up queens with Attitude. It must be a problem being Becker, he thought. Having to extract yourself from the muck, to pick off the leeches, so you can go after the person you really want. Of course what had impressed Lark about Becker was his straightforwardness, the night they met; he'd pulled up beside Lark at the boat ramp, got out of his car, leaned against the fender, and actually waved when he saw Lark glance at him in the rearview mirror. He'd lighted a cigarette and waited patiently while Lark, frightened, listened to the final movement of Beethoven's Seventh Symphony. And then, legs shaking, stomach lurching, Lark got out of his car, walked up to Becker, and lied when Becker asked him if he was cold. Yes, he said—though the real reason for his trembling was merely the horrible apprehension that he wanted Becker so badly he was shaking like his roommate's cat when it crouched on the fire escape in New York, looking at the fat pigeons it could not reach on the windowsill of the building behind them: shaking with desire.

Ah well, all ancient history now, thinks Lark as he sucks an ice cube. Being exactly what everyone wants is a problem. Though now the problem is different: There's a virus. Becker must be petrified of getting AIDS. He has a daughter he's responsible for, he thinks as two young men come into the pool room, and as they walk past Lark, the tall, dark Mediterranean stud turns to his younger blond companion and says in a deep voice, "Your gums are *always* bleeding." Then they take a seat on the bleachers opposite. Is that it? Gainesville is probably as infected now, in the core gay community, as New York—these people have buried lots of friends. Is that why Rick is sitting there, enthralled by the trio of nineteen-year-olds? Bodily fluids that have not yet been tainted? Of all the conversations people are able to have, the AIDS conversation is not one of them. "Don't ask, don't tell" applies far more to tricking than to the military. It's the motto for sex in the nineties. People are embarrassed, or afraid, or just don't want to know; the etiquette of extracting this vital information has never been developed, much less evolved. As with the rest of life, the most important things are left unsaid. Becker told him the night they met that he'd been tested, and, when asked if he'd been nervous at the time, shrugged and said, "No. Why should I be?" Silly boy, thought Lark. Then Becker glanced at the TV table covered with jars of Vaseline, eye drops, and gauze bandages that Lark used for care for his mother, just before they were about to retire to the bedroom, and asked if he should bring the bottle of petroleum jelly. "No," said Lark, thinking, Does he not know that condoms are incompatible with oil-based lubricants? He wasn't sure how savvy Becker was about the virus, but he wonders now if that's not the reason Becker dallied with him once and no more—because your gums are *always* bleeding.

On the other hand: Becker comes here every Friday night—Becker told him that. It's the only reason Lark can be here this evening: the knowledge that Becker is back home. He wants to see Becker again, but not in this environment, among the cruelest in the world—though Rick looks happy at this moment. That's because Rick gets bombed. After five or six beers, he once told Lark, you can say those stupid opening lines in the bar that seem so ludicrous when you're sober. After five or six beers, he can talk to the person sitting next to him.

"But what do you do about driving home?" Lark asked him.

"I drive home with some guys and sleep at their place," he said. "No sex. I'm too smashed. I just sleep." This seems as poignant to Lark as Rick's having to get drunk in the first place: He's not even having sex.

"But how do you get them to ask you home?" said Lark.

"Once I get my hands on them, they are usually mine."

"What do you mean?" said Lark. He sees the answer now: Rick is massaging the upper back of the blond next to him with his strong, thick hands. "And what happens when people do insist on sex?" Lark asked.

Rick said, "They're usually jerks. This guy told me last night he picked me up because I had a big chest, but boy, when you show the slightest bit of sensitivity, when you are yourself, they don't like it."

Ah, thought Lark, nothing changes; it's the same old story—everybody's looking for a Man. The old-fashioned, politically incorrect kind. The one who chops down trees, kills Indians, clears the forest, and runs the mutual fund. Poor Rick, he thinks. He looks, with his broad chest, big legs and butt, his handsome swarthy face, like an Italian quarry worker, a German peasant. Inside, he's a boy who was scrawny all through high school, and played alone in a trailer as a kid while his mother stuffed envelopes for extra money after work; he read comic books, unable to play outdoors because she was terrified of snakes and lightning. Now he's a bodybuilder, eats health foods, lives alone, uses a blowtorch, loves Eydie Gorme, wants a lover, and goes home with nineteen-year-olds who like his big chest and want to rake their fingernails across his back. Ah, Gainesville, he thinks. Ah, humanity!

Ah, Michael Jackson! He turns now to look at the television above the bar in the main room, as the eighty-year-old man gets up and leaves with a man who looks about forty. He wants to stand up and scream, Doesn't anyone *know*? Can't they *tell*? *This man is a drag queen!* Instead he puts down his empty glass, leaves the banquette, and walks silently to the other room. Just before he reaches the door, Rick swings around on this barstool and says, "That guy you're interested in, he was here Friday night."

"I know," says Lark, glad for a moment, as he bends his head, to be part of the general roar, the bar tableau, the cluster of convivial customers. "He only comes on Fridays."

"I don't know about that," says Rick. "A friend of mine saw him at the baths in Jacksonville too, last Sunday."

"Aha," says Lark, as someone shoves against his back. The pressure of people leaving is too great; he says, "See you later," and lets himself be borne along the current out of the door, thrilled and dejected at this dreadful news.

At the Fontainebleau

~~~~~~

It's funny, Lark thinks as he drives home, how I used to worry about Sutcliffe's opinion of things: He was my Voice of Reason, if not the Voice of the Upper East Side. Surely he would find Becker handsome. Surely he would love his thick, rich, melancholy voice, his manners, his hands, even the way he smokes. Sutcliffe might have fallen in love with Becker. Or he might have dismissed him curtly, as a small-town queen who did not read books, much less exemplify the sterling qualities I have attributed to Becker. Who knows? It's too late to find out now. Sutcliffe is dead, and I am stranded here.

One New Year's Eve, Sutcliffe told everyone sitting in his front room before the fire that a friend of a friend from San Francisco was on his way over to explain to them how to unite Love and Sex. In those days they actually believed someone from San Francisco might be able to—San Franciscans were better at sex, gave more time to it, were advanced homosexuals, offered a course in how to get in touch with your anus.

He never came. "Maybe he got lost," Sutcliffe said finally.

"Or maybe he met someone on the IRT and went home with him," said another guest.

"Or maybe he went to the Mineshaft," said another.

I'm still wondering, thinks Lark. Those first two years in New York, he would linger whenever he could at Sutcliffe's after the other guests had gone; the two of them would sit before the fire and, as the winter evening deepened, Sutcliffe would hear his

Confession. These moments were the kernel of their friendship—the still center on which everything else rested: those firelit requests for advice.

About his own problems Sutcliffe was not forthcoming. Why does anyone drink? Lark wondered. Because they're unhappy, said a friend of his who'd drunk for years. If Sutcliffe was unhappy, Lark thought, why was he unhappy? Whatever the reasons, by the early eighties Sutcliffe was no more able to go out without a bottle of white wine than Eddie was without portable oxygen. After Lark left the city, he heard from a friend that Sutcliffe was still going to Tea Dance every day in summer, by himself, but now he was drunk when he got there, and began crying when friends came up to greet him; crying because yet someone else had died. Lark was glad he was not there to see it. It was painful even to hear about. "He looked like an old drunk," said the friend, who'd had his own trouble drying out, "tears streaming down his cheeks, those cracked lips. He looked *awful*. And I always thought him the most elegant, the most impeccable man I knew." By that time Lark was going to New York twice a year, in the spring and late fall. In March the city was grubby and everyone was tired of winter; in November it was exhilarating. Both visits Lark was so glad to be back that when the plane landed at Newark, he wanted to get out, kneel, and kiss the runway, like the pope. He could hardly bear the thirty-minute journey between the terminal and midtown. Once back home, however, merely walking the streets, he began to realize the city had turned into a vast cemetery.

There was no place to go anymore. Joshua, his roommate, was celibate and going to macrobiotic cooking school; the St. Marks Baths on his block were closed by order of the city—two slender black doors plastered with advertisements for punk rock bands, like the doors of an embassy in a country with which diplomatic relations had been broken. Lark rushed instead to a pornographic theater on Third Avenue five blocks north of his apartment, and plunged into the darkness like an amphibious creature returning to the sea. When he brought a Pakistani tennis pro he met there back to the apartment one afternoon, when he thought his roommate was at work, Joshua opened the door, and Lark felt a withering blast of disapproval.

Joshua disapproved of everything then, it seemed; each time Lark returned, Joshua had less of a sense of humor. The man who had liked to walk around the apartment in sling-back pumps, Jockey shorts, and a towel turban wrapped around his head, imitating Bette Davis, Katharine Hepburn, Julie Andrews, and the entire cast of certain films by Satyajit Ray and Ingmar Bergman, was now to be found sitting in a Brooks Brothers ensemble of cords, vest, and striped shirt after work, eating, when Lark arrived, his macrobiotic dinner—a strand of seaweed suspended before his lips between two chopsticks. He did no imitations. He made no jokes. He spoke in a low monotone, communicating only what was practical and necessary; even the cat was addressed in a clipped, cold way; and when Lark took down a pot to steam vegetables, Joshua asked him not to use that one, because he used it for his own meals. It was like a divorce. Lark suspected the reason: He had chosen Florida over Joshua. "How's your mother?" Joshua would always ask immediately after his return, with strict politeness; and Lark, at a loss, would say, "Fine," since her condition wasn't one that— absent Jesus performing miracles as He walked about—was likely to improve; thinking, at the same time, In some ways, better than you. One day Lark took down one of the older pots, an ancient, begrimed, encrusted one that had been hanging from a nail in the brick wall since he moved in; and when the nail fell out and a cascade of brick dust fell into the air, he was somehow not upset: It symbolized the general disintegration that was going on.

It wasn't a happy time. He could feel the gloom in the apartment as he steamed his vegetables in the old pot, and Joshua worked overtime copy-editing a manuscript at the kitchen table; and when Lark turned and expressed his joy and excitement at being back, Joshua looked at him and asked, "Are you on a drug?"

"No," said Lark, "I'm just excited to be back. You remember excitement—or at least the concept! I couldn't wait to be here."

"Why?" said Joshua with a cold, deadly expression on his face.

"Oh, I don't know, Joshua," Lark said impatiently. "I guess because I've been away. Do I have to explain it?"

"No," said Joshua. "I just hope you don't plan on having fun here. That would not be too wise."

Not even Sutcliffe disagreed with that; since taking home a drunk Polish sailor he encountered on First Avenue on Labor Day, Sutcliffe had been chaste too. Sutcliffe and Joshua were scared, and regarded New York City as a sort of radioactive pile. That was why Sutcliffe was home when Lark dropped by, sitting with a glass of white wine and a cigarette at his desk. "My sex life is in the closet," he told Lark. "Literally." And he opened the door and showed Lark a black plastic garbage bag filled with magazines. "Dutton is supposed to come over if anything happens to me and get it out of here," he said, naming his oldest friend, an attorney with Shearman & Sterling. "I've agreed to do the same for him. We've made arrangements for everything. That's all we do now, Dutton and I—we go out to restaurants and talk about perpetual trusts and life insurance. Have you made a will? You've got to take care of all that stuff. Medical insurance, will, who evacuates the porn if anything should happen to you. All this dreary, grown-up insurance stuff. I hate it. These are my boyfriends," he said, plucking a magazine from the garbage bag and leafing through the pages for Lark, who stared at the big black bag and thought, That's what being gay means now to both of us.

Lark had his in his closet too, in brown paper grocery bags. They were always there, docile, waiting for him, whenever he wished to take one out. He had so little sex with other men because there were so few where he lived. Sutcliffe had stopped having sex in Manhattan because it was dangerous—the deadly isle—and confined himself to that garbage bag. Then he went away, as soon as he could, each winter, for a month in some sunny place untouched by the plague.

The geographical cure assumed the disease was located in New York and one could fly to places where it had not yet arrived: Rio de Janeiro, Honolulu, Miami Beach. Sutcliffe stopped going to Rio when the disease started appearing there, and he did things at the baths he later regretted; he stopped going to Honolulu when the long trip west became too exhausting. The winter Lark told him he couldn't come to north Florida, he ended up in Miami Beach, where one evening he phoned Lark, home watching a documentary on gazelles on the Golan Heights. "And what are *you* doing?" said Lark.

"Nothing," said Sutcliffe. "We can't go out. They rioted again last night downtown. They've put up the bridges from the mainland to Miami Beach. We're trapped. I'm sitting here with a book by Danielle Steel. I read it all day today by the pool at the Fontainebleau."

"But the sun is bad for your skin," said Lark. "You can get skin cancer."

"I know," said Sutcliffe. "Everything's forbidden—sex, the sun. I'm calling my memoirs *Sunlight and Sperm.*"

"Is there anyone down there you know?"

"No. Just Sterzin."

"And what will you do this evening?"

"Go down to the Eden Roc and sit in the lobby with my Danielle Steel. Did I tell you that you can buy reading glasses in the drugstore now? There's a nice guy from Charleston who works at the Eden Roc who tells me what's going on. I asked him what was left of the Angelo Donghia renovation, and he showed me. And Jim Bailey is in the nightclub, doing Judy Garland."

"What's that like?"

"Just what you picture it to be. The alternative is an AA meeting. They've got it as organized down here as a kibbutz. But they talk about AIDS, which I don't like. In New York, they keep the two issues separate. Booze and death. You go to one or the other."

"But are you enjoying yourself?" said Lark. "Are you happy there? Do you wish you were in Hawaii?"

"No, no," he said, his voice rising, almost in panic. "I'm glad I came. They have concession stands on every block here. In Rio and Waikiki you have to walk for blocks. I love the concession stands, and I love the Cubans at the desk, and I have a terrace with a view of the ocean and the river for sixty-five a night. And I've got my Danielle Steel and my glasses from the drugstore."

Lark excused himself.

"Where were you?" said Sutcliffe when Lark returned to the phone.

"I went to the bathroom," he said.

"I started to panic," said Sutcliffe.

"While I was in the bathroom?"

"Yes. I'm not so good at being alone, at the moment."

"You're not alone," said Lark.

"I am alone," said Sutcliffe.

"How could you, of all people, be alone?"

"Everybody's dead," said Sutcliffe. "I got up yesterday in New York and I got the *Times* and there was a headline on the front page: 'Everybody's Dead.' Actually it said 'Everybody I Know Is Dead.' By Henry T. Sutcliffe. Though actually it should have read 'Everybody I Know Is Dead, or Might as Well Be.'"

"What do you mean?" said Lark.

"I mean nobody goes out!" said Sutcliffe, his voice rising. "We live in the most wonderful city in the world, and nobody goes out! If you're not going to go out, believe me, there are a lot more pleasant places in this world than Manhattan to sit home in a room by yourself. The point of New York is to go out of the room. To mix, to mingle, to create something nice for other people. Nobody's doing that anymore. They stay home; they say they have to get up early in the morning when you ask them to go out."

"Why?" said Lark.

"Because they're depressed!" said Sutcliffe. "Let me put it this way: The ones who are dying are going out. To doctors, to support groups, to restaurants, to parties. The ones who have escaped stay home."

"What about Dutton?"

"We don't speak."

"Why not?"

"We had an argument. About a can of caviar. Several cans of caviar. He stayed in my apartment over Labor Day and when I got back all the caviar was gone. When I mentioned it to him, he hit the roof. He told me I was cheap. He told me I had the values of an Irish maid. He said I had no concept of what friendship means. I said, 'Yes, I do. It means leaving some caviar behind.' He was livid. Twenty-five years of friendship down the toilet over four tins of caviar. As if there weren't more important things going on right now."

"It's because there are that the caviar was a big deal," said Lark. "Nobody's saying what they're really thinking these days."

"You mean AIDS?" said Sutcliffe. "Don't blame the caviar on AIDS. Dutton did things like that long before the plague. AIDS doesn't change people, it just highlights certain aspects. Dutton thinks he owns the Book of Right and he always has. I haven't got time now for bad manners. Maybe that's why I'm all alone. Maybe that's why I'm here in a hotel room reading Danielle Steel."

"But I can't believe this!" said Lark. "You, of all people, shouldn't be alone! How did this happen? You have more friends than anyone!"

"Had," said Sutcliffe. "Had more friends than anyone."

"Well, can't you go out?"

"I went out," said Sutcliffe. "I went Rollerblading in South Beach with Sterzin. Sterzin is coming over in a few minutes to take me to the Cardozo to interview models."

"See!" said Lark, seizing on some shred of evidence that his friend was still living. "You're going somewhere! You are having fun!"

"Nobody is having fun," said Sutcliffe. "Not really. Everybody's dead, or might as well be. It's easier for me, in a way. I'm dying," he said. "But what are *you* going to do?" Lark said nothing. There was a knock on the door. "There's Sterzin!" said Sutcliffe. "Gotta run!" And there was a click. That was the next-to-last conversation Lark had with Sutcliffe.

How could this be? he wondered as he took his walk later that night around the sodden, sleeping neighborhood. How could Sutcliffe be in Miami Beach all by himself in a hotel room? Because he wanted more, thinks Lark, taking the same nocturnal walk years later. Because he didn't want to stop. Like Eddie, the day they went to nine restaurants in one afternoon—walking in, demanding a table, telling the staff the air conditioning was set too low, ordering a meal he ended up stubbing cigarettes out in, not eating a thing, then asking for the check, having Lark hail a cab, and going to the next one, where once again he demanded a particular table, demanded the air conditioning be adjusted—and all of it was granted, all of it, because he looked like Death in that Ingmar Bergman movie *The Seventh Seal,* because he was that sacred object, a Person with AIDS. Eddie, who was the nicest, the gentlest of men, was impossible to please the day they started out at Food and went to the Union Square Cafe, and then for old times' sake the Lion's Head, and then Spaghetteria, and then 103 Second, and then Meriken, and then the House of Szechuan, till finally he lost all hope as Eddie stubbed yet another cigarette out in yet another uneaten soufflé, and said in a voice that carried through the restaurant, "Let's go! I want to see the Beauty Boys! Let's go somewhere where we can look at the Beauty Boys!"

And they got into another cab, whose driver Eddie ordered about in the same peremptory diva's voice he was using on the waiters and the maître d's—because he was a diva, he was dying—in a madman's tour of the city they loved, until finally, on their way to the Four Seasons, a friend they hailed on the sidewalk at a stoplight took one look at Eddie and said, "This man needs to be in a hospital," and they took him to Payne Whitney; where, sitting in the lobby downstairs, and then later, in the cool clean hallways covered in linoleum upstairs, Lark surprisingly felt the same peace he does when he goes into the men's room at the boat ramp on a spring day and listens to the faucet dripping and the wind shifting in the trees, clean and quiet and removed from life. That was why Sutcliffe kept traveling. For the same reason Eddie went to all those restaurants the day they put him in Payne Whitney for observation: because they wanted more.

That's all people can want, he thinks as he walks around the suffocating park. Because we don't believe in the afterlife anymore. Oh, sure, people talk about the dead looking down on us, or rejoining their friends at some great disco in the sky, but it's all a sentimental affectation, a nice thought that is all we have these days to mitigate the horror of human extinction. But nobody believes there's anything more after this—this rich cornucopia of consumer products, this spectacle called Life. Sutcliffe kept traveling and Eddie kept taking another taxi because they didn't want to stop. They didn't want to surrender.

And that's why Ernie still goes to the boat ramp, and my mother won't die, and I'm in love with Becker. We all want more. As Susan Hayward put it, I want to live.

Then he stops in the middle of the road and looks around the little park at the houses fronting it, and their lighted windows, and lists: one breast cancer, one hysterectomy following an ovarian tumor, neither child married, no grandchildren, extreme obesity, prostate cancer, macular degeneration of both eyes, dizziness and fatigue, two divorces, widow, widow, widow, divorce.

He cannot bear to think of the places certain lives are leading. He cannot bear the idea that there will be no happy ending.

So he heads up onto the highway, turns on Lemon Street, and continues past the mostly dark houses, the municipal swimming pool, the yards of people he does not know, and finally stops behind a clump of azalea bushes across the street from Becker's house—walks into the middle of them, gets down on his haunches, stares at the two translucent panels glowing in the night, and thinks of the folded laundry, the washed dishes, behind them. "I keep a clean house," Becker said, and while Lark worried at the time this meant he was anal-compulsive, the thought of it now soothes him as he crouches there staring at the house of a man and his daughter, so far as he knows, not yet disfigured by Life.

Picking a Roommate

~~~~~~

The next day his mother's roommate has a small stroke; nobody notices till Lark points it out: Charlotte is not quite herself. The daughter comes in the following week to see her. This time she brings a friend—a woman her age—and tells Lark that they live together in Montana, not Gainesville; she pretends she's just driven over from the house in Gainesville she actually sold a few years ago, after putting her mother into this nursing home. (There are advantages to Alzheimer's.) On the last day of the daughter's visit, Lark suddenly realizes that she may never see her mother again, if she is returning to Billings; and he gets up, turns off *Murder, She Wrote,* and takes his mother out for a spin around the hall so they may be alone.

And still it's a shock when he comes in the next Saturday and finds Charlotte's bed empty. His mother doesn't even know that Charlotte died during the night. His mother has always said she cannot sleep at the nursing home—he's afraid even to think about this: lying in bed awake all night, paralyzed, till dawn— so he can't understand how she failed to notice her roommate's death; although, with the mere drawing of the curtain between the two beds, many things can be done quietly, including expiration. Thank God, after she learns the news, he can whisk her away for the weekend. Thank God it's Saturday. As if to prove her statement, his mother falls into a deep sleep within thirty minutes of their return home—a sleep that continues intermittently till he awakens her for the arrival of the priest who comes to give her communion at six o'clock. It is a time of profound peace; he lies on the floor next to the sofa she is sleeping on and stares out at the lake, the butterflies darting over the plumbagos, and thinks, We're safe here, for the moment.

Then the telephone rings and he jumps up and runs to get it before she awakens; it's Frank, calling from San Francisco, his breathless, hoarse, rapid speech telling Lark he's been up all night at an orgy on crystal meth, and can't get two of the people to leave his room at the National Hotel, what should he do? "Tell me how it happened," Lark says, like a shrink. He tells Lark how it began at a sex club the night before, and how he's in love with a Russian speed freak who's so emaciated he looks as if he has AIDS; that he's attracted only to people who look like that. Lark listens until his mother wakes up and begins calling his name, at which point he tells Frank he has to go. "Wait!" says Frank. "I want you to hear something!" Lark listens. "That's Yuri's penis being slapped against the phone. Bye," Frank says, and then hangs up. When Lark returns to the porch his mother is asleep again, her mouth open, and he resumes his place on the floor beside her. Then the telephone rings again. People call because they know he's home, a fixed point in their lives. They call because they're lonely, bored, depressed, and they know he'll pick up.

"Who's on the phone?" his mother asks when he returns this time.

"A friend from New York," he says. She closes her eyes a moment. And then, "Why are your callers always men?" she asks.

Sleep pulls her under again, not even bothering to close her eyes entirely; her lips part and she begins to doze, as he writes a letter to Charlotte's daughter saying how much they both admired and liked her mother. He reads it to his mother after she has taken communion and is wide awake.

The next day he goes out onto the porch and writes more letters. They're bored with *This Week with David Brinkley*—besides, she has a cataract in her one "good" eye, and the glare off the screen hurts her; so he takes her onto the porch, tips her wheelchair back against the armrest of a chair, and goes to the table and types. Then she closes her eyes, as he looks over at her and thinks, I am boring her to death. She can't possibly be sleeping; after a while, one can only sleep so much.

When she used to fall asleep, he would say to her after she awoke, "You were sleeping," and she would vehemently reply, "I wasn't asleep, I was just resting my eyes!"—as if to have been caught napping was wrong. Now, she really is just resting her eyes, because they hurt. The doctor he asked to look at her said that her neck is fused at an angle that makes it impossible for him to perform a cataract operation, so, he presumes, she is going blind. Lark can't imagine how she feels about it; as sad as the fact of her cataract, perhaps, is the way he spoke to the doctor as she lay in bed, as if she were not there, or were a child too young to make a decision. He has now come to the point of doing something he saw others do early on, and that he silently vowed never to do: talk as if his parent were not there. She is there, alas, quietly contemplating the facts herself, since she is an intelligent woman; she knows the cataract cannot be removed, she knows what that means, and so, when she closes her eyes now to rest them, he feels an infinite pity, a deep sense of helplessness. What can she do but close her eyes? It is the last activity left her on earth: resting. What else is there for her to do?

He sits there typing letters to friends scattered now all over the country—Leigh in Chicago, on lithium; Eugene in San Diego, trying to find a lover on the computer when he's not counseling drug addicts and alcoholics for an HMO; Lewis, in San

Antonio, running sex ads in *Daddy* magazine, and getting so many responses he keeps going out to the mailbox where the children yell *"Puta! Puta!"* at him while he takes out his mail; George, in New York, three hundred pounds, no longer going out except to eat because clients have stopped spending money on pre-Columbian textiles; Hal, living on Fire Island through the winter with someone he hates because he has no other place to go. All nice people, good men—it's just that they're lonely. ("Are you there?" his mother said once while a friend from Los Angeles was on the phone, heartbroken after a man twelve years younger had said he just wanted to be friends. "Yes, I'm here," he said to her, at which point his friend sighed into the phone, *"I* want to say those words to someone.")

"Keep typing," she says, when he stops.

"Why?" he says.

"Because then I know you're there."

That's all she wants: someone in the room with her. (That's all his friends want, for that matter.) Which is why they have to find her a new roommate, fast. He knows the front office is trying to find someone suitable, but she can't wait. She makes him call the social worker to hurry it up. She doesn't want to spend one more night in an empty room. ("Your mother is afraid to die," his cousin's husband said. Who isn't? thinks Lark.) He loves going in, the week after Charlotte dies, and having the room all to himself and his mother—even if both of them feel sad. The social director, the nurses, tell them which women are available as roommates—and they go up and down the halls after dinner, stopping before the women's doorways and looking in. The inspection makes them feel forlorn. The first candidate lies on a bed tilted up; all that is visible in the gloom is her open mouth, breathing; she is so old, so pale, covered in a clean white sheet, she seems to be wrapped in a spider web. (She dies a week later.) Another lady they've passed for years in the hallway, an "alert" person whose current roommate screams; the third is someone they have seen pushing her wheelchair around the halls for years—it's odd to connect names to the faces they have seen for so long a time. None of them rings a bell.

His mother has only one desire: a body in the bed next to hers. Her horror is being alone. (Mine too, thinks Lark, though as a middle-aged queen, I'd better get used to it.) The next requirement is someone in the bed who can ring the bell for the nurse. The staff knows the effect losing a roommate has on the patients: The nurses watch Lark and his mother with sympathetic smiles as they go up and down the halls looking for the rooms with possible roommates in them. It's horrible, he thinks, as he stops before yet another open door and he and his mother look in at the woman lying sound asleep on a hospital bed. I'm taking her to select a roommate, the way you'd go to the pound to find a pet. This shouldn't be happening to her; she shouldn't have to do this.

They both feel depressed as they traverse the hall. How has she lived here all these years, he wonders, in these surroundings? They miss Charlotte more and more. She looked so lovely. Her hair done every week, a smile always on her face, a measured air of dignity and poise; she had that even when the aide had left her sitting in the hallway after dinner. Now she's gone. And they are still looking at Mrs. Berkowitz, who seems to be covered in a silver spider web, barely able to breathe through its silk cocoon: all that is visible is her open mouth, on that pyramid of whiteness.

He has never been so dejected as he is on this tour of the decrepit and the dying. His mother, on the other hand, has lived here for more than a decade and is inured to it, or realistic about it, in a way he isn't. "I don't care who it is," she says. And so they agree to leave the pleasant room she shared with Charlotte and move two doors down to Mrs. Klein, who is here only to recover from a fall, who goes to therapy every day—a program his mother surrendered a decade ago when it was decided she could make no more progress—and even swims in the pool. Mrs. Klein is totally alert: an intelligent retired nurse from Kansas who likes to watch *The Waltons* from seven to eight, a period during which Lark now takes his mother out of the room because he can't bear the sentimentality of the show, and reads magazines to her down in the reception room, killing time till *Murder, She Wrote*, which, thank God, the new roommate also likes.

The week they change rooms, he reads her the cover story in *Time* magazine devoted to the murders of Nicole Brown Simpson and Ron Goldman. As she grows more indifferent to life, the goings-on of those still on the planet have to be ever more extreme to catch her interest. Just like my father, he thinks, who gave up the *CBS Evening News* and started watching cartoons at six-thirty instead. That brilliant man. Odd; when it comes time to die, you relax all the little things, he thinks—the habits of dress and diet—that seem so important to us when we're in our prime: like exchanging your robe and pajamas for daytime clothes, watching the news, eating a balanced diet. His father gave them all up toward the end. He ended up watching westerns at four in the morning, eating big bowls of vanilla ice cream slathered with slabs of peanut butter.

When you are about to die, Lark thinks, you might as well eat peanut butter and ice cream—like John, cashing in his insurance and going to Bermuda, where he went to a local soccer field every day and just sat there, with five T cells and a Visa card, admiring the calves and thick wind-blown hair of the players running after the ball, a living example of the philosophy of the advertising campaign Just Do It. (Some people can't till they are dying.)

Now his mother is loosening her grip. "My body is tired of being my body," she said to him one afternoon as she lay on the sofa at home. Lark said nothing. There was nothing he could say. He knew what she meant, or thought he did. This body that she had not made use of for over a decade now, that had hung suspended from her neck all these years ("The Talking Head," one of his friends called her), limp and shriveled, was a burden. And she was tired of it. Tired of her body, the body that is our soul's representation, our agent, in Life; the body he takes to the baths to show to other bodies in the hope a spark will pass between them. The body that seems to have no other purpose except to produce another body, something she did—and made, he fears, the real achievement of her life; something he has not done, thereby reducing her achievement. She's tired of her body. She's tired of it all.

So thank God for O.J., he thinks, as he reads the horrifying details to her in the blue reception room—he's hit pay dirt with the murders. She's actually interested. She cares. And he goes on reading till it is time to wheel her down to the room for *Murder, She Wrote.*

The Dejected Pugilist

~~~~~~

After *Murder, She Wrote,* he gets his mother ready for bed while they watch Larry King interview two defense attorneys, and by the time he's brushed her teeth, watched the nurse give her the nine o'clock medicines, adjusted her arms and legs, kissed her good night again, and walked out of the room—even though she's still asking him to do something else—he feels likes a diver whose lungs almost burst rising to the surface; so he's furious when, after exploding out the side entrance into the warm air, he walks to his car and finds the front left tire flat. Leaving his mother behind—especially as she's saying, "One more kiss, one more kiss!"—is so stressful he likes to drive away immediately on leaving the place she is trapped in; and when as now his flight is detained, he panics. Car trouble, he feels, is all that stands between him and insanity; or rather the absence of car trouble. He's been reduced to this one machine: It's all that remains of his self-esteem. His car.

He sits there on the curb for fifteen minutes, in despond, gazing at the hills covered with the roofs and parking lots of Burger King and Service Merchandise and Red Lobster and Shell, which glow like pieces of charcoal on a grill, like armies bivouacked in the hot night, beneath a gigantic spotlighted American flag, undulating slowly high above the Shell station. Then he takes the tools out of the trunk and tries to change the tire. He can't; somebody has warped the plastic antitheft nuts on the tire, and the little wrench won't budge them. So he goes back inside and calls AAA, and waits for the mechanic, hoping it will be a handsome young man, which turns out to be the case; he's towed to a nearby gas station on University Avenue, and then, an hour later, arrives home so angry he gets out the typewriter and writes a letter to Buick describing exactly what happened. Then he writes a letter to Senator Graham suggesting the farm subsidy program be abolished and in its place a new one, which pays people not to have children, be established. More corn, okay. More people, no. Then he writes three letters to friends whose long caretaking of other friends with AIDS has just come to an end. He says the same thing in each one, because he can't, at this point, think of anything original to say. There has never been anything to say, he thinks. AIDS, despite its sadistic cruelties, is, on some level, as meaningless as influenza. Then he decides to go to the baths but, because he wants to be well rested the next day, makes himself go to bed instead and sleep.

He can't sleep. It's the summer, he thinks. The summer is always the worst. Nobody visits. Nobody calls. If I can just get through the summer, if I can just get her to fall, we'll make it, he thinks; because right now both of us are depressed.

When he wakes up the next morning, he lies there looking out the window at the still, sodden garden, and thinks, I might as well be living in an igloo at the Arctic Circle—that's how it feels in Florida in the summer. Up north in winter people stay inside to keep warm. Down south in summer they stay inside to keep cool. There should be a day in May, he thinks as he listens to the cool air issuing from the vents along the floorboards, when the priest blesses all the air-conditioners in town, like the shrimp fleet at Tarpon Springs. If there are any shrimp left.

He gets up and wonders whether to write another letter to the newspaper about overfishing and overpopulation and over-development, even though he knows these sentiments have a snowball's chance in hell of saving what is left of Florida. It would be like pointing out the editors' misuse of the adverb *like*. The distinction between *as* and *like*, he assumes, is going the way of the shrimp, black bear, and panther. The whole world is collapsing; it's just as well his father got out as quickly as he did, leaving him and his mother alone. ("I miss your father," his mother says from time to time, when they pass the chair he always sat in, or he asks her what is wrong when he sees her lying there with a strange expression on her face.)

In summer they always feel alone. In summer they feel like one of the small, green tree frogs he finds clinging to the interior of the mailbox he opens every day on the road outside; hiding, like him, from the world. His mother wants him to write a letter to CNN saying Michael Kinsley on *Crossfire* is smug and conceited, but he tells her this will make no difference; it will just prove that someone is watching the show. His mother still gets angry watching television. He doesn't. "I'm a very patriotic person!" she says when emotion gets the best of her. He isn't. Or rather, he is, in a cynical and subdued way. I'm the anal-compulsive, jaded offspring of a heroic generation, he thinks, and a better, more credulous time. He'd rather watch the Weather Channel than CNN. He sits watching the weather and thinks, What if Princess Diana was driving to Disney World with her two sons, and the car broke down, and it was late and stormy, and they needed shelter and knocked on my door? And I had to put them up for the night, and cook them breakfast in the morning? What would I cook? Or: What if Donna Karan was driving through town and had a blowout, and needed a place to sleep? Or Emanuel Ungaro or Carolina Herrera? And he would imagine playing host. This never happened, however; he simply went to bed in an empty house, and woke up to another session of depression.

I could get into the car and drive to the bar in Reddick, he thinks, and lip-sync "Vision of Love" in a red dress. But he doesn't. He imagines instead his mother lying in the nursing home, waiting for his next appearance in her doorway, and thinks, If only she knew I am lying here too, waiting for my next appearance there. He used to count the hours in the nursing home till he could leave and drive to the bar; now he has stopped going to the bar, and can't wait to get to the nursing home. He realizes she is suffering, like Jesus on the Cross; she thinks she is suffering for her sins. He can't imagine what they are. Jesus suffered for mankind; his mother is suffering for him. He doesn't know what in either case could justify their pain. So he goes to the boat ramp and continues to think about her— lying in bed, or on her blue Geri-chair in the hallway, entertained he hopes by student aides talking a class that afternoon, most probably ignored by everyone except a stray fly or two. He thinks of her long, patient, uncomplaining acceptance of this awful situation—God is punishing her!—as he sits in his car in the still soft afternoon, watching the young man who takes his small preliterate son into the rest room with a mop and pail and scrubs clean the messages on the walls. He thinks of her thirty miles to the west, the two of them in separate places, both atoning for their sins.

"Are you a homosexual?" she asked him years ago. "Of course not," he said and left the room. "Are you what they call a homosexual?" she amended it to last week—trying to find the right combination of words that would allow him to be honest. He said nothing. But I am, he thinks, I am. It has been, in fact, the biggest fact of my life, the one thing I've been unable to assimilate or integrate with my upbringing. It has actually become my whole existence. I am sitting here thirty miles from her too embarrassed to admit the truth, the prey of passing police, the patient spider waiting for a fly, as she waits for my next entrance. God, life turns out badly in some cases—so very unlike what one hoped it would be! We should go on *Oprah*. Devoted son comes out to paralyzed mom on national TV, he thinks. There wouldn't be a dry eye in the house! Plus she'd get a trip back home to Chicago, and she could see snow once more before she dies.

He goes home instead two hours later and finishes the day watching Oprah reunite a mother with a daughter estranged from her family by a problem with crack cocaine. He sits there wondering how his country went from "Some Enchanted Evening" to "Me So Horny" in less than fifty years.

It's part of the decline and fall of practically everything, he thinks. AIDS is just one more piece of pollution on a planet swarming with too many people. Even the Windsors, he thinks, watching a documentary on the royal family that evening: nothing but trapped animals—pet hamsters—entertainment for people in nursing homes and houses like his. He wants Diana to find happiness, if she can.

A woman telephones asking for his mother, who's being tracked by a breast cancer survey out of Washington; he says, "She's not here now." Another woman calls an hour later to ask if he is interested in visiting a brand-new resort in Apalachicola. A thunderstorm begins to rumble in the distance. The boy who lives down the street goes past on his bicycle, wearing a helmet that resembles a small flying saucer. Lark gets up and walks in circles around the living room, wondering how he can make his mother happy. Then he lies down on the floor and closes his eyes and savors the peculiar construction of her new approach to the question: "Are you *what they call* a homosexual?" It sounds to him like the inquiry of an anthropologist or a lost tourist deep in the Amazon: Are you what they call a cannibal? A vampire bat? An herbivorous ungulate? He can't imagine answering "Yes." That brief declaration is beyond his powers; though he can imagine what worlds, what galaxies, its enunciation would open up. The freedom, the relief, the conversation that would follow—the confession of his life, how friends have died, and he like Ishmael alone survived to tell her.

He cannot say it. And being unable to say it, he surrenders

to her some peculiar power; he remains her hostage, because he cannot predict how they would regard each other in this altered state—of Truth. So there the matter rests; half answered, half admitted, the subject lies between them like a dead fish, a stinking carcass, a whale rotting on the beach; and they have to work around it, pretend there is no dead whale in the living room. The resulting stench is that of boredom. I am boring my mother to death, he thinks again. And so we go on in this twilight of understanding, this implicit knowledge of each other, everyone hiding—until the telephone rings, and the truth intrudes on our hermetic little world.

And then the phone does ring, while he lies there by himself contemplating the wreckage of his life, and he picks it up and hears a thick, rich voice that is not Becker's but is like Becker's in some ways—depressed, and sexual. It belongs to another single dad, only this man, the same age as Becker but rather pear-shaped and afflicted with eczema, is divorced and lives with a woman he says is his aunt in a small house near Lake Sampson. Lark met him at the boat ramp one afternoon and gave him his number after their encounter. A week later the man called, and thus began a relationship that has been going on for almost a year now, and helps remove some of the sting of Becker's ongoing ostracism of him. In other words: I have always depended on the kindness of strangers, thinks Lark after he hangs up and runs into the bedroom to dress for their date. In other words: Sometimes there's God so quickly! In other words: Life is what happens to you while you are planning to do something else. Bob is what happens to me, thinks Lark, while I'm pining for Becker. Bob wants to see me, Bob will sleep with me again, Bob may be a part of the great sea of clinical depression, which covers the pine barrens of north central Florida, but boy I'm glad he calls when he does, every three or four weeks, even if I have to drive right past the road on which

Becker lives with his daughter and their two dogs to get there. Because Bob lets me come to his little cottage, and we've become friends in a way, even if he always has to get bombed before he calls.

The first six months, Bob always met him at another boat ramp on Lake Sampson, a quieter, sunnier, open parking lot without a public rest room, but with a small gazebo down by the beach. They would meet in the parking lot and then drive to the forest down a rutted dirt road Bob knew of that led to a canal; and there, on the bank of the canal, littered with beer cans, cigarette packs, cans of soda, and used condoms—the litter of the rural picnic— they would spread a blanket beneath a cloud of yellow flies and mosquitoes. Bob liked to have sex outdoors. Sometimes they had sex at the boat ramp itself, in a grove of pine trees along the channel; the lake was so deserted on a weekday afternoon that even though Lark felt naked at first, he was eventually able to perform with nothing between him and a cluster of retirees' ranch houses overlooking the boat ramp but the fenders of Bob's old white Camaro. Lark never had an orgasm. Bob was utterly passive. He always asked Lark to drive to a convenience store first to get beer and cigarettes. Lark did not have Bob's phone number—only Bob could call and suggest they meet; but this took all the responsibility out of his hands, let Bob make the decisions, and if two or three weeks passed between encounters, that seemed perfectly right to Lark.

Bob said his aunt made him sleep on the sofa in the trailer and refused him the use of the television and the ceiling fan; he made a living doing odd jobs for the elderly people in the nearby trailers. He came from upstate Michigan, had moved to Tampa and then to the woods to get away from cities. He is blond, with a big beard and beautiful eyes, well built despite the pear shape, and a drunk; one afternoon while sitting in the car putting away beers, talking about his daughter in Detroit,

Bob began to cry—and Lark, deep into middle age, thought, This is rarer than semen. Now I love him.

The day he cried was also the day when Bob came to the parking lot on a bicycle and told Lark he'd had his license taken away, after a policeman stopped him while driving drunk to the lake one afternoon—so for the first time Bob put his bicycle into the trunk of Lark's car and let Lark drive him home, down a rutted dirt road into the woods where a small blue house stood in a clearing beside a blueberry patch, a vegetable garden, two decomposing cars, and a van. The house was filled with tools and the detritus of renovation; the only finished room was the bedroom. A chair blocked the doorway to keep the dogs out— inside, a big double bed with pale lavender sheets floated in the radiance of the sunlight pouring in from the yard outside, as clean as the altar in a church. As they lay down, Bob told Lark his real name was not Bob but Henry, and he lived here not with an aunt but a girlfriend; a fact Lark regarded skeptically till ten minutes later a blond woman walked through the door after returning from work in Gainesville. She and Lark were polite to each other. Lark didn't know how much she knew. They both knew, however, that Bob/Henry was drunk, and Lark did not hear from him for months after that.

He has been telling himself this was fine too, but in fact he has missed his friend, and when Bob (he reverted to that name) calls again—drunk—Lark is thrilled to drive over immediately and take him out for more beer and cigarettes. He is glad Bob called, sad Bob had to get drunk to do so. "I'm a facilitator," Lark tells him.

"No," says Bob, searching for the right word as he opens a can of beer, "an enabler!"

"That's right, that's right!" they say together as they drive off from the convenience store in Starke.

The sex back at his little house in the woods saddens Lark— it has saddened him since the day Bob told him, "You're my only friend." He stares out the window over Bob's head at the weed-choked vegetable garden behind the house drying up in the sun while they make love, as far away from Bob and the little bedroom as it is possible to be. Then he drives Bob afterward to the cemetery in Hampton to meet two men he beat in a fistfight the previous week, who told him they were bringing another man to whip him. I'm in a co-dependent relationship with my mother, thinks Lark as he drives off, looking in the rearview mirror at Bob seated on the stone wall waiting for his fellow pugilists, and with a drunken bisexual who has to get bombed before he can call me up, and has to have a fistfight after we have sex. But hey, beggars can't be choosers. Better than being alone. As Forster said, Only connect! And Lark drives home past the houses in the countryside he always imagines hold happy couples, and decides to look for Becker tomorrow at Biven's Arm.

Biven's Arm

~~~~~~

He drives to Biven's Arm down Main Street, where he stops at a Pic 'N Save that is so different from the one on the west side. The one on the west side is huge, new, full of lawn furniture, potted plants, clothes, groceries. The one on Main Street, the first in town, like everything else on Main Street, is Gothic in comparison—small, shabby, stocked with far less merchandise on the much smaller shelves, and with far stranger customers. Even the women at the checkout counters are odd. Diane Arbus would have a field day in here, he thinks when he enters. The sad air of the ghetto hangs over the place; even the security guards seem melancholy.

The first thing he looks for is his mouthwash; for some reason they have stopped carrying Viadent. Some mouthwashes, he read somewhere, are so strong they shock the cells and can cause cancer of the mouth. But then, what can't? His dentist told him to put just enough mouthwash into a glass to color the water in it, and use that. So that's what he does when he is out of Viadent. Teeth, hearing, cataracts, lower back; all these things, in his late forties, have begun to be concerns.

He buys Listerine and then, as always, pauses in front of the hair dyes. To dye or not to dye, that is the question, he thinks. Dutton did it once, in the toilet of a Sabena 747 on its way to Brussels—he could not bear the thought of traveling through Europe as an old geezer. He used Lady Clairol, and he left it on too long; when he got off the plane he looked like Dracula.

There is something deeply depressing about dyeing, or painting, your hair, he thinks. He doesn't know how women put on makeup without feeling cheap. On the other hand, there's Lewis in San Antonio, running ads in *Daddy* magazine, buying the rubber gloves and chemicals, mixing them, and painting his own hair once a month. ("Do it for yourself!" he says. "Because it makes *you* feel better!") He can't. I've got to stop internalizing the oppressive values of a youth-oriented homo- and heterosexual consumer culture, I've got to stop internalizing my own oppression, and I've got to get Q-Tips, he thinks. The trouble is, you are what you look like—you do get the face you deserve— and mine is basically that of a queen whose last nerve is being worked. As Dutton once signed a postcard, "The Wreck of the Hesperus."

A black couple down the aisle is examining trusses; Lark is still in front of the hair dyes. He always does this: stares at the Grecian Formula, the Just for Men, the Lady Clairol, and then leaves. Lewis says men always make the same mistake: They dye their hair too dark, while women know to go *lighter*. Lark agrees. He prides himself on being able to spot men with dyed hair. It's all right to dye your hair, he thinks, if and only if nobody else, not one single person in the whole wide world, can tell. Because if one single person anywhere knows, then you're a fraud: a vain man terrified of losing his looks, his youth, his virility. Pathetic. Patrick, the first time Lark dropped by his apartment in New York and found him, like some mad scientist or brain surgeon, with his rubber gloves on, and the dye cooking under a rubber shower cap on his hair, told him it was the only way to go; made him look years younger, people couldn't figure out why; then, ten minutes later, after rinsing it out in the bathtub, Patrick came into the room with his new color and Lark had to suppress a gasp. My God, he wanted to say, you look like Mary Pickford! But he did not. And three or four years later, on one visit to New York, he had to admit while walking down the street with him: Patrick finally got the color right. It takes time, he tells himself, mistakes, errors, practice. Just Do It.

But he doesn't. He walks away and pays for his mouthwash, marveling at the young mother pushing her deformed child up and down the aisles in a stroller. He knows what it's like to take someone in a wheelchair, someone physically grotesque, out into public places. He's used to watching the faces of people coming toward him when he wheels his mother down the corridors of the Oaks Mall, though it takes a certain preparation, a certain willed equanimity, each time he takes her there to buy a hot dog and to look at people. She likes people. He doesn't—in crowds, at least. And that's the only way America offers them anymore: as crowds.

He watches the security guard collecting shopping carts people have left out in the parking lot, as he unlocks his car, wondering again if the heat isn't warping all his music tapes. Then he drives out onto Main Street, and, because he's in town an hour early finally to get the results of the blood test he took—results he realizes now he still prefers not to get—he keeps driving right past University Avenue, thinking, I will not let that cool, calm lesbian in a relationship of eleven years tell me I've got HIV, and as for learning I don't have it, I don't think I can stand the emotional upheaval—the guilt, gratitude, obligation to rededicate my life to something meaningful—of that either. In other words, leave me alone, he thinks as he drives past the square, which used to have a nineteenth-century courthouse but now, like so many towns and cities that entrusted themselves to urban renewal in the sixties, has two cereal boxes facing a plaza broken up into different levels, like Copley Square in Boston; so that what was a majestic open space now looks like a bunch of children's building blocks stacked on a playroom floor, building blocks nobody sits on but the homeless or the few stray, sullen people waiting for that most ignominious of things in a car culture like America: the bus. There is a bus that runs the length of Gainesville, but the people waiting for it all look as if they have just had barium enemas at the hospital. It's the shame, the humiliation, of waiting for a bus.

Nobody comes downtown anymore, except the students, after dark, going to the clubs and dance bars. The town has moved entirely to the west; at least all that is new, state of the art, expensive, up to date—like the Pic 'N Save across from the Oaks Mall. So goes Pic 'N Save, so goes Gainesville—ever expanding, ever renewing, ever abandoning its past. Quaint survivors like the pool hall on Main Street he drives past now, or the bookstore around the corner, or the old post office now a theater, do not make up for the fact that, as you drive south, there is something vaguely seedy, down-market, and abandoned about this part of town. A quality he likes. Here there is still a forlorn, quiet, sleepy quality—that aspect of Gainesville one encounters every now and then, in between semesters, when most of the students are away. *Then* the town returns to its bucolic southern self. Otherwise it's Booming Plastic Florida, a mere addendum to I-75, he thinks, as he passes a store where his cousin bought the mattress on which he sleeps now, after declaring his old one pathetic.

Lark loves the old, hates the new, which must be an aspect of necrophilia, which must be connected to the sterility of homosexual desire, he thinks, as the buildings thin out and he begins to hear the hum of his tires on the pavement and he finds himself driving past—curious anomaly over here—expensive houses set on several acres behind walls of woods. Gainesville is all trees. You can't even see the city when your plane lands—you look out the window and see a forest canopy broken only by the Seagle Building (the single skyscraper, downtown), the football stadium, the radio tower. Otherwise, you might be landing at a river camp in Ecuador. He has to give the locals credit for that: They respect, they cherish, their trees. The road is flanked on both sides by forest all the way to the small nature preserve he stops at, called Biven's Arm.

Biven's Arm: a patch of forest surrounding a stagnant pond, with an observation deck, a boardwalk, and dirt paths through the trees. He parks his car in the small parking lot, gets out, and walks toward the entrance.

These places are either the most humiliating or the most thrilling ones on earth, he thinks, as he steps out onto the deck. Or both. A young woman who was murdered in June was found not far from here, buried in the woods; the police had searched the park for days in vain. Since then the publicity has died down, but still the place has a reputation, among the men who cruise here, of danger—a reputation that is part of the lore surrounding all the parks and boat ramps Lark goes to down here. The reputation for danger does not bother him; he suspects there have been undercover cops here in the past, but he also suspects that era is somehow over, at least for the moment.

What he does fear is not the reputation the place has for policemen, but something much more frightening: chicken. Biven's Arm, he has been told, is for the young. In each other's arms. For good reason: The park closes at sundown. The young can stand daylight. The old cannot. That is why, he thinks as he crosses the deck of the reception area, the Boy Bar opened in New York in the early eighties with brightly lighted rooms. The point was obvious. And that other bar on Second Avenue that looked like an art gallery—a bare room, blazing with light, behind a big plate-glass window, Both bars pushed back to the dim margins, like a vampire reeling from a crucifix, anyone who could not stand the glare. It was a form of discrimination, he thinks now as he waves away a cloud of mosquitoes, discrimination by Light—though he doubted, whenever he passed the bar on Second Avenue, he could bring a lawsuit based on wattage.

Though of course it wasn't just the wattage that made him feel unwanted—New York was dying, even before AIDS, under his feet. It was the whole point of the Boy Bar: a certain contemptuous edge. If the sixties were about peace, love, and flower children, and the seventies about track lighting and a vase of gladiolas, then the tiny moment between the seventies' end and the onslaught of AIDS was about Sid Vicious and the Boy Bar—which then became gyms, Calvin Klein, and Hitler Youth. What an amalgam! What a continuum! No wonder I spend most of my time alone in this car, going to places like this, he thinks—New York's a tough town, especially when you're too old to even walk down a street in Manhattan without silently apologizing for your appearance.

He does not look at his reflection on the glass when he stops before the illustrated panels describing the ecology and vegetation of the marsh. He concentrates on the words and pictures beneath the glass. His reflection has frightened him for some time now. He has not looked in a mirror in years, except to shave, and even then he positions himself so that he sees only his jaw. Like Senator Dole, who told Steve Kroft on *60 Minutes* that, one day after being hospitalized for wounds he had received in World War II—a hospitalization that lasted three years—he caught a glimpse of himself in the mirror and was so horrified he has not looked in a mirror since.

You also have to avoid unsuspected surfaces, lying in wait, assassin-like: toasters, plate-glass windows, the fenders and bumpers of cars. People's faces reflect too; when you grow old, as his mother pointed out years ago after a visit to the mall, you become invisible. Being invisible is not like being attacked or beaten or jeered or insulted—it's just like being dead. That's all. He walks around the panel now to read the opposite side and sees two men, one bald, one silver-haired, seated on a bench, watching him.

People ask, What is the soul? What is the irreducible quality of the human being? *Your hair,* he thinks. *You are your hair.* Which is why youth makes so much of its. He stands there reading about the scuppernong, the bloodwort, the hydrilla, the herons and egrets—the long list of plants, reptiles, birds, mammals that leaves out, he thinks, the species truly native to the park (homosexuals)—while sizing up the men on the wooden platform. There are five of them altogether. Three sit on the long wooden benches of the pavilion, two reading, one staring into space.

He is used, by now, to no longer inspiring immediate interest, much less a sensation. He receives instead the bare minimum accorded every homosexual whenever he enters a bar, a room, a park in which other gay men have gathered: an inquiring glance. The appraisal that all human beings, God bless them, receive simply because each one is—for a mere nanosecond—a New Face. Attention must be paid, and is. In bars, at night, Lark can still create a certain undercurrent. Here, on this deck, he gets a cursory glance. Which may be due to the more constrained atmosphere of the place, of course; though there are five other homosexuals on the observation deck, they look to him like people waiting to see a dentist—a scene he has viewed often in Gainesville, where doctors' practices flourish like the hydrilla in this marsh. The men have wiped all emotion from their faces; the same air of constipated, genteel quiet, of people leafing through back issues of *Metropolitan Home, Architectural Digest,* prevails. Only they are waiting in fact for someone they want to have sex with to arrive, to get up and follow them into the woods. It's like a bar with a back room, he thinks, or a brothel where the prostitutes sit in a lounge waiting for a customer to choose one of them. Only in this case, the customer does not select the prostitute; the prostitute selects the customer!

At any rate, cruising in the middle of the afternoon is somehow depressing, he thinks: like going to a movie in broad daylight. He steps off the observation platform onto the board-walk. The boardwalk becomes a path, and the path is lined with quotations from writers—Eudora Welty, Annie Dillard, Oliver Wendell Holmes—printed on laminated plastic rectangles screwed to small wooden posts. He stops to read them all; he still feels he might find on one of them the secret of a happy life. Most of the quotations deal with solitude, nature, or the oak tree. They always overdo these plaques, he thinks; the ped-agogic vice, the proselytizing instinct. The desire to pass on one's favorite *aperçu*—till the poor forest is burdened, is weighed down with print, turned into another lousy book, he thinks, as he straightens up and continues his walk.

I have read quite enough, he thinks; I need to live. It is quiet in the forest; the woods resemble those that border the southern edge of Payne's Prairie, a gigantic plain a few miles from Biven's Arm; a mix of palm and oak, pine and palmetto, grapevine and coreopsis—lush, delicate, beautiful, the broad green fans of the palmettos shining silver in the filtered sunlight, the purple beauty-berries on bended branches near the ground. He imag-ines himself from a distance: a figure on a leaf-strewn path, in the pale, silvery, filtered light, the suffocating, soaked air, some-where between quotations from Oliver Wendell Holmes and Saint Bernard. When did I age? he wonders. Why, in the last three months. In the last three months, for some reason, I changed categories. Because my hair has now turned silver and begun to thin like leaves falling from trees: Nature's notice that you've had enough time to attract someone and reproduce. Na-ture cries with one voice, "Do it now." Ignore this at your peril. The greatest sin: to live life as if it will never end.

Does he really think his mother can lie there forever, waiting for him to do something with his life? Does he really think he will always have the chance of falling in love, meeting the right man? Life offers you these invitations only once—the option is limited, like those discount coupons at Miller's. I'm Old, he thinks. And being Old means you've had your chance. Being Old means not being considered for purposes of reproduction anymore. Being Old means not liking to show yourself off, in a *paseo* that is based on looks. I should get a wig, he thinks. Like Warhol. Carry a wig in the glove compartment for places like this. Do Biven's Arm in a wig—that's the solution.

Suspended, like a golden leaf in a shaft of sunlight, he comes around a curve, looks up, sees the boardwalk and, on the boardwalk, coming toward him in another shaft of sunlight, a young Filipino with black, black hair and black, black eyes, who glares at him with an intensity he has not seen on a face in years. The young man grunts, "Hello," and Lark, astonished, can barely manage a "Hello" after he has passed. That glare, that intensity, he thinks, can mean only one thing: Food. The youth has spotted Food. Him. In the great food chain of Life, the Filipino wishes to devour Lark's protein product, like a dragonfly eating a water bug on the surface of the pond.

He pauses to read the quotation from T. S. Eliot before he realizes he has no interest in sex with this person at all. He is too depressed. He misses his mother. Passion has dried up, like the water that covered Payne's Prairie in a shining sheet in the eighteenth century—a vast blue lake crowded with water lilies and giant alligators. He has been left dry and sunbaked like the lake bed itself, the levees the gators lie on in the winter, basking in the heat. Which allows him to walk to his car, leaving both the Filipino and the wisdom of Western man behind, without much pain, regret, or wounded vanity. It does not matter, he thinks; I did not survive for this. As Sutcliffe said, "After twenty years, meaningless sex becomes, well . . . meaningless."

I'm too old, he thinks as he starts the car and exits the parking lot, noticing a big white police car at the curb spring to life and fall in place behind him. (Ernie says they keep a list of license plates in Tallahassee; Roy says thinking you're on a list in Tallahassee is something people do to make their lives more dramatic. Lark doesn't know whom to believe.) I'm too nervous, and too old, for this, he thinks as he slowly drives north in front of the cop. This is something Sutcliffe never had to face! He stayed in New York and kept his thick black hair right to the end—until he started to vomit his own blood.

The Thing No One Mentioned

~~~~~~

And Sutcliffe's memorial service! he thinks as he drives slowly
north on Main Street, keeping the police car in his rearview
mirror, the police car trailing Lark with the tenacity of a great
white shark. (Funny, he thinks, I'm so happy to see cops in New
York City, they're so reassuring, so hip; but down here they just
mean Trouble.) His memorial service! By the time Sutcliffe died,
Lark had been to so many. He sat there with the same feeling
he'd felt at the very first one: *This isn't really happening.*

At the very first one—Eddie's—at the funeral home on Second Avenue, he'd felt disoriented by the mere fact of the gathering. It was the first one of them any of them had ever gone
to—Eddie died in 1983—and when Lark got to the funeral
home, he was startled to see the men he'd been watching for
years as they got on and off the boats to Fire Island, now in
suits and ties. Looking very handsome, indeed. He kept thinking, as the rabbi spoke above the casket at the head of the aisle,
that Eddie would sit up at any moment and say to the man in
the front row, "I *love* your unconstructed jacket!" Eddie did not,
and instead the rabbi, a man Lark had known formerly as a
whirling dervish on the dance floor of the Sandpiper, gave a
eulogy that seemed as odd—the fact of it—as the suits and ties
on the men around him. Clovis sat in the front pew, crying, and
Clovis came from a world so artificial, controlled, and concerned
with appearance—Seventh Avenue—that Lark could not decide
if the tears were real. They seemed to be. So did the funeral

parlor and the other faces, even if Lark refused to believe that this was happening.

Sutcliffe sat beside him, further proof that it was, though all Lark could think when he glanced over at him was that Sutcliffe looked distinguished. But then Sutcliffe always looked distinguished. Sutcliffe was the one man he had seen in a suit and tie all these years—coming home from work in the afternoon, so handsome in his blazer on Madison Avenue, with the irises he always put on his mantel upstairs.

How vain we all were, thinks Lark, taking pleasure in each other's looks. Physical vanity, he realizes now that it is all over, was the foundation of our lives in those years, as it is of youth, period. They liked to walk down the street to buy flowers, to enter rooms, to catch the boat to the Pines. They had, without ever acknowledging it, that bank account everyone possesses once that makes real money for the moment secondary: Youth. New York was a city for the young—something they didn't think about when it belonged to them—rushing across the park, or uptown on the subway, to have cocktails at Sutcliffe's, where the room was always immaculate and the irises on the mantelpiece, and someone always knew where they were going next—usually downtown.

That was why it seemed doubly odd when they left the memorial for Eddie on Second Avenue and did not know where to go next. They didn't want to go back to the apartment on Fifth Avenue where Eddie had died, listening to Mozart during a snowstorm. They didn't know which of the cafés where the younger generation sat writing poetry in notebooks—shades of the sixties!—was the one to go to. But the sight of them in their berets and turtlenecks at the small round tables behind the windows on St. Marks Place looked to Lark like a cartoon by Jules Feiffer. So they wandered north, up Second Avenue, not knowing where they should go, feeling like displaced persons, and found themselves on Fourteenth Street in front of the Metropolitan Theater—a moviehouse that still showed pornographic films to a largely homosexual clientele—went in and stood in the lobby, looking out across the street.

"I knew someone in that building," said Sutcliffe, nodding at the tenement across Fourteenth Street.

"Who?" said Lark.

"A carpenter from Ohio," said Sutcliffe. "I don't remember his name. We met in that park in Fifteenth Street and went back to his place. He took off all his clothes and then his glasses and I fainted. A week later I ran into him outside the St. Marks Baths, where he was working on the renovation. He was sitting on a fire hydrant eating his lunch, and his face was covered with bright red sores."

"Chicken pox?" said Lark.

"Herpes," said Sutcliffe. "He said it probably had been triggered by his trick the night before, when he ate the man's ass." He turned to Lark. "Now here's how times have changed. Did I wonder if I'd been exposed to herpes? No. Did I wonder why he hadn't told me he was a carrier? No." Sutcliffe pushed the glass door open and they went out onto the sidewalk. "All I could think was, Why didn't he eat *my* ass? Wasn't I a turn-on? I went straight home and did butt exercises for an hour. All the cow really wanted—forget the Ph.D., forget the promising career," he said to Lark, "—all I *really* wanted to be was . . ."

"What?" said Lark.

"A Hot Man," said Sutcliffe.

Didn't we all, thinks Lark.

By the time Sutcliffe died years later, they had been to so many wakes, so many memorials, they were connoisseurs: numbly comparing the space, the music chosen, the eulogies, the food. He went to six in the Ethical Culture Society auditorium on Central Park West, four in the chapel at Citicorp Center. He heard string quartets by Mozart he'd never heard before, and rushed out to music stores afterward to buy.

Clovis's memorial resembled a graduation day in June: taxis across a sunny park to a flower-filled apartment on Fifth Avenue crowded with family and friends, a dappled terrace, women in hats. Everyone behaved well—even those about to graduate themselves.

Sutcliffe's was held in a lecture hall at the university; at five o'clock, like someone taking an adult extension course, Lark found himself pushing through throngs of students going home after class—these creatures Sutcliffe had instructed all these years, whose corporeal existence Lark had never before witnessed. (Or even thought about till Dutton came up to him and said, "AIDS didn't kill Sutcliffe. What killed Sutcliffe was open admissions at Hunter.") Then he took his seat in the lecture hall for yet another version of *This isn't really happening*, and sat there while colleagues and former disciples recalled the special efforts Sutcliffe had made to shepherd and mentor graduate students, his devotion to the school, his remarkable ability to obtain grants, his original work in setting up tours of the South Bronx for visitors, the exhibit of architectural details from destroyed buildings on the Grand Concourse.

The one person who might have spoken about Sutcliffe's private life—an erstwhile lover, a man still in his twenties who had come to New York to paint—could not; a few sentences into his remembrance, he choked up, excused himself, and sat down. Effective, thought Lark, with the detachment of the theater critic. Then, as speaker followed speaker in tribute to Sutcliffe's university career, each one acknowledging first his mother and sister in the front row, Lark began to wonder, Is no one going to say he was gay? And the overwhelming immateriality of this aspect of their lives struck him. This central aspect of their years left no concrete effects—children, family—behind; was not even something there was a customary language for, terms you could use in its description. All smoke, all invisibility, all silence and evaporation—the deep desires, the happiness of those years.

That was the strange thing about this life, he thought. When you admit you are homosexual, when you come out, you feel you are striking a blow for Life (your own)—for truth, authenticity, honesty, candor, freedom, reality, happiness—and you are. But further down the road, much further, if you survive the warts, herpes, syphilis, gonorrhea, mononucleosis, Epstein-Barr, hepatitis, HIV, and habitual uprooting of every object you fasten your heart to, you have to face the fact that you are left basically with nothing. Nothing, that is, but that decision to come out. The rest—the late nights, laughter, moments of intense pleasure, dressing up and undressing, faces on the subway, lips beneath your own—leaves no impression whatsoever. No trace of its existence. Except what friends remember. Friends who may not be able to recall these memories in public when you die, because they are based on something considered unfortunate, if not shameful. Something best left unreferred to. And so you all sit there, scattered among the audience, like the mistress of a man whose wife does not want to be confronted with your existence at the funeral. All extramarital sex is illicit—and always will be.

When a well-known activist suddenly rose from his seat, Lark leaned forward, alarmed that he would say something; but the man left the hall. "I had to keep myself from screaming," he told Lark at the reception moments later. Speaking to Sutcliffe's mother—the past to which his present could not be reconciled—Lark could not imagine anyone's referring to this fact. ("I married her at age six," Sutcliffe had said of this tall, elegant woman of eighty who stood in the mezzanine afterward, receiving expressions of sympathy. "That was my lover," he would say, after hanging up one of the daily phone calls during which he and she discussed everything but That.) Lark could think of nothing to say to her now, no condolence, no sentiment that could put in a better light this irretrievable loss, or even indicate his own relationship with her son—that frail word *friend* felt so weak at moments like this. He used the usual words, then stepped back and dumbly watched men he would probably never see again, now that the friend they had in common was gone, come up to her one by one, and then he left the building that gray winter afternoon and decided to walk home.

As he did, the city again turned into an open-air cemetery; corners, canopies, apartment buildings made gravestones superfluous. We are all dead, he thought, even the ones walking away from Sutcliffe's service. Down Madison Avenue on the corner where Sutcliffe had been kicked by the young man in the front of Givenchy, he glanced over at Sutcliffe's old apartment building—the dim doorway, now framed with graffiti, through which Lark had passed, like Alice, into Wonderland, in 1971. Then he walked to Fifth Avenue and turned south along the park—that stretch of expensive apartment buildings whose dignity and doormen always calmed him down—and looked south, where the city, lights blinking behind a scrim of naked trees shifting in the winter wind, began to seem glamorous again; an impression that disintegrated after he crossed Grand Army Plaza and, starting at Fifty-seventh Street, entered a crowd of pedestrians in which he could no longer expect to meet that welcoming, that interested pair of eyes in the face of a perfect stranger that had always made him feel he belonged to these people. Now he was simply a nondescript man in a dark suit and tie, overcoat, and scarf, avoiding his reflection in plate-glass windows, preparing an expression on his face that would allow him to run the gauntlet of all these uninterested people with a minimum of self-consciousness. Not till he got to Madison Square, and he glanced over at the windows of Metro's loft, where a pair of rings on which his friend had practiced handstands used to be visible, did he relax, in the deepening darkness, the thinning crowds, the return to what was, despite Metro's death, a familiar sight.

In the old days he would have stopped at the park—sat down for ten minutes at least, or taken a walk around the path—just to see who might turn up; the last time he had sex here, with a strange-looking man in a black raincoat, the man, instead of walking away afterward, stood there in front of Lark and said, "Well? Are you going to swallow it or spit it out?" How dare you force the issue, Lark thought at the time; then he leaned over, opened his mouth, and let the sour semen fall into a rhododendron bush. Satisfied, the man in the black raincoat walked away, while Lark remained on the park bench, thinking, I am spiraling downward. Why?

He had no answer then or now; so this evening he kept going, and felt himself vanish once again in the dozens of pairs of eyes that did not bother to seek his. I do not register, I'm not on the radar, he thought. I am a ghost, I am invisible. In winter with his cap on, and his collar pulled up around his ears, he imagined his age to be hidden—his face reduced to merely a pair of inquiring eyes. I can cruise New York after dark, he thought, in winter, during blizzards and extremely cold weather. But this evening it didn't seem to work—people were too bundled up themselves, too intent upon reaching their destination and getting out of the cold, to return his looks. Then he caught sight of the canopy of Eddie's building at Fifteenth Street, and then the crosstown bus that Rhodes used to take before he went back to his mother's in Philadelphia and died of diarrhea.

"Think of the wonderful men we know," Sutcliffe had said when talking about the future one afternoon, "who we'll visit, who are just getting better and better as they age." Not now. The ones whose doorways still might be used to reach them, as Lark walked south, were all shell-shocked, he thought, in one form or another: determinedly obese ("That way they won't even look at me") or reclusive ("I don't go out till after dark") or dyeing their hair ("Someone came up to me at a party and said, 'You must be a vampire; everyone is dying and you just keep looking younger and younger!'"). They had all reached the point now where there was no reason to go out.

At St. Marks Place he ran upstairs—to prove he could still do five flights, two stairs at a time—and then, pausing at the top to catch his breath like the old women with bags of groceries he'd always smiled at sympathetically, he went in, changed his clothes, and was stopped on his way out by a man calling his sublet, leaving a message on his machine.

It was the same happy, ironic, kidding banter with which he and his friends had spoken twenty years ago—nicknames, plans, the name of the restaurant where they would be that night, hoping the sublet would join them—and when the line went dead, he sat down and thought, I'm the one who's depressed, not them. New York is still parties, drag, Rollerblading in the park, and plans for the weekend, for some people. And he sat there for an hour, under the severe light of a naked bulb in the ceiling fixture, and looked at his sublet's scrapbooks (a trip to Egypt, a drag wedding) and then he looked at his clothes—the thick, beautiful sweaters, the stacks of jeans, the sports coats and silk scarves—and then he went out.

The sidewalks were more crowded than they'd been when he lived here, the crowds as strange to him as he had been, no doubt, to the old Ukrainian men who had stood outside the building every evening in coats and hats, talking, the autumn he moved into the apartment. He didn't know any of these people now; the three Ukrainian men were dead, as he picked his way among the blankets covered with old magazines and records people were selling, to the pay phone on the corner, where he called the nursing home in Gainesville to check on his mother. That night she was sitting near the nurses' desk, where they could watch her; they put the phone to her lips and he heard

the barely audible voice—so tiny, hoarse, tired, and crushed—
that said, "Is it cold?"

"Yes!" he shouted. "It's supposed to snow!"

"Oh, how wonderful!" she said. "I'd love to see snow again,
before I die! Are you having fun?"

"Yes!" he said, laughing to hide an emotion that had nothing
to do with humor.

Finally, after asking when he was coming back, she said,
"Have a good vacation!" Then he hung up and walked straight
to a porn theater—the Jewel.

The little red doorway, the grizzled Jamaican at the box office,
took him in—and he went to a dark hallway that ran between
the theater and the street and brushed his body against other
bodies lining the hall, hoping a spark would, like dry wood,
ignite them. But it did not. The men twisting each other's nipples looked to him like scientists in a hut at the Arctic Circle
trying to tune in a radio frequency. So he went up onstage and
stood behind the screen on which the images were flickering,
looking down at the people in the audience, their figures coated
with silver light. ("Why are gay men so promiscuous?" his
cousin had asked him one evening as they sat watching a segment about AIDS on the evening news. "Because," he said—
thinking, Because sex is wonderful, and who wouldn't want to
do it as much as possible? Because sex is ecstasy, and there's
no ecstasy left in this civilization anymore. Because we thought
penicillin could cure everything. Because people are looking for
Love. Because in this society we can't find support for stable
partnerships. Because we're ashamed, and seek out sex with
strangers we don't have to say hello to in the street the next
day, much less mention at our funerals. Because, because, because, he thought, and then he turned to her and said, "Why
do you smoke?")

Then he walked down the steps beside the stage, left the
Jewel, and began walking south to Astor Place, and then to

Broadway, where, just before he reached city hall, it started to snow—lightly at first, and then so thickly, he walked up onto the Brooklyn Bridge to watch it fall—this snow that always turned the city, when it was falling, into a Steichen photograph, a canvas by Childe Hassam, an earlier New York that would always seem to later generations better, more elegant, more romantic. This city Sutcliffe had loved. Oh, bless this city, he thought as the snow fell past him in a dense, heavy, drifting cloud; soothe, heal, obliterate, transform it. Cleanse us all, he prayed as the snow brushed his face, fell upon the graves of an entire generation wiped out, subtracted, gone. This snow his mother could not feel or see, nor Sutcliffe either, falling on a city that could no longer see him, even when he walked back off the bridge and started home, searching in the light of store windows for that face, that glance, that would justify his existence; till finally, at Chambers Street, he fled into the subway, a fragile, tentative stranger who no longer felt he could handle whatever happened on the IRT. Which is why he is relieved now when the police car turns off at Twenty-third Avenue and leaves him alone.

Animal Happiness

~~~~~~

The police have already stopped people at the boat ramp; one night a brusque blond woman in uniform jumped out of her police car seconds after he parked in his usual spot, asked for his driver's license, and made him stand in the beams of her headlights while she ran his license through a check. Then she told him he should not be in the park after dark, though there are fishermen who go out on the lake at night. He drives by without turning in now. We're like roaches, he thinks; we're a problem in pest control. We find a place to gather, we gather, they notice us, they eradicate. Gather, eradicate; gather, eradicate. The next day he wakes up and thinks, I have no choice. I'll go. And he sets out on Highway 26 toward Jacksonville.

Twelve miles out of town he stops at a small state park—in the hope that this will make a longer trip unnecessary, that a hike will calm him down. The park has two features: a sinkhole filled with trees that grow unusually tall to reach the sunlight, and a small lake with a beach. On weekdays the park is always empty. Once he met two lesbians here, sitting on a bench by the old mill. They had moved up from Miami to escape their husbands and live together in Gainesville. He never saw them again. He wishes men would come here to meet other men— it's quiet and wooded—but he's never met anyone that way. He takes the walk along the ravine by himself, then branches out along another path that leads through a fragrant forest of pine, circles back to the little lake, takes a seat at one of the picnic tables on the slope, and watches the breeze move across the water. Then he goes into the men's room to take a leak and ends up standing there, looking through the screen window, at the beach and the picnic tables below.

The men's room, like the changing room adjacent, the covered breezeway, the picnic tables, the pavilion at the top of the slope, has that clean vacant air of a summer camp, in a state park anywhere; there's something impersonal, neutral, benign about the white-painted wood, the exposed beams, the plain and rustic architecture. He stands there with his face near the screen as he waits for the urine to flow from his penis, conscious of the cleanliness, the emptiness, the innocence of the place—redolent of childhood, summer afternoons, a voice calling you in for dinner. He wishes he could have sex in this room. But there is never anyone else here; it's too perfect, he thinks; even gay people have no taste. When he finishes peeing he goes to the window and looks at the lake, the line of floats that demarcates the swimming area, the small gray lake that stands for all the lakes in this part of Florida, the quiet, drab, unspectacular beauty of the sand-hill scrub.

People pass their lives in the chain of being, he thinks as he watches a young father and mother, with a child, walk down the sand to the water's edge this Monday afternoon. There's a buzz of fertility, like bees on a hive, linked through cellular multiplication and blood. They're never alone. Once when he asked the postmistress to hold his mail because he was going away to New York for ten days, she looked at him and said, "I've not been away from home since the birth of my youngest son."

"How old is he?" Lark asked.

"Twelve," she said.

She's never been alone, he thought as he walked out of the post office, in twelve years.

Now he watches the family wade into the still silver water

and thinks, There is no wealth but life. The most important space in the universe is not that from here to Mars or Jupiter, but from you to another human being; it is that space we are always trying to conquer, that space that must be bridged. The magazines and psychologists, the dispensers of popular culture, call this Intimacy. I call it Animal Happiness. The blur, the buzz, the commotion, the smells and sounds and touch of living in a pod. Becker has a daughter, his parents, and whatever his daughter attracts, or acquires, in the future. (Will her husband accept a gay father-in-law? Will Becker get respect, or will he always be tolerated, even by his own, like an uncle with a drinking problem? Is that the most one can expect heterosexuals to grant homosexuality—the status of a human handicap, like alcoholism or diabetes? Is that what *I* think of it? he wonders as he watches from the vacant men's room up the slope.)

As he watches, more families appear on the beach. A couple take a canoe out. A pair of brothers take a rowboat and tease a third boy by rowing away from him as he tries to cling to the boat. The horrors of childhood—the cruelty of the Fifth Ape— are all in the terrified shrieks of the boy whose older brothers are trying to row away from him in deep water. The same instincts, the same human nature, B. F. Skinner complained, are repeated in every generation. Another family wades into the clear gray water. It's a pond in the African veld, he thinks, where animals gather to drink at twilight. They are all here in this small state park, this obscure retreat in central Florida, on a late August afternoon, far, far, far from the madding crowd, the mobs that have ruined the national parks. The room in which he sits down now on the toilet—the painted wooden door of the stall he has opened so he can look through the screen window at the scene below—was built in the Depression by the Civilian Conservation Corps: an earlier, better America, even if much poorer. We have finished building the country, he thinks, and now everyone sits around squabbling over who gets what.

A tall man in mirrored sunglasses, baseball cap, white T-shirt, and green bathing trunks walks down the beach with a teen-age girl with a huge mass of black curls, one of those absurd hairstyles that come out of Hollywood, a mega-permanent in which every strand of hair has been made into a curlicue, a sort of beehive of hair; and as they lay their towels down on the sand, and the man takes off his T-shirt, Lark lifts his buttocks off the toilet seat, leans forward, lips parted, and realizes, It's Becker and his daughter.

They do things together, he thinks, standing up to be even closer to the screen. He took her to the beach last spring—not the gay one at South Ponte Vedra, the one at Crescent Beach. He's off work, she's out of school; they've come here to relax and swim together. Becker lights a cigarette. His daughter walks down to the water's edge. All is still. All is peaceful. A breeze blows through the screen. The third brother has stopped shriek-ing; he has reached a little strip of sand between two sections of weeds farther down the shore. The pale sliver of a moon hangs in the soft blue sky.

Becker's body is nut-brown from the sun. He has worked outdoors all summer at the construction site, and his chest and arms are so red-brown they're the color of the earth in parts of Georgia. Not very wise, thinks Lark, who has not gone out into the sun in ten years, since his last skin cancers were removed by a dermatologist in Gainesville. Becker gets sunburned, he thinks, and he smokes; both contraindicated. But that's why I love him: He takes care of the important things (he's told his parents and daughter he is homosexual) and slips up in the minor things: his own health. Whereas I slavishly follow dictates of the magazine culture—I don't smoke, drink, or go into the sun—but mess up on the big things, like refusing to tell my mother I'm homosexual when she asks. I don't smoke and I don't go into the sun and I don't tell her I'm homosexual, he thinks; so here I sit, pale as a ghost, white as a corpse, perfectly skinny, eating my broccoli, flossing my teeth, avoiding fat, tar nicotine, booze, and ultraviolet light; a pale specter, a white worm, staring at Becker from its lair.

"You're only as sick as your secrets," an openly gay Hollywood tycoon said in an article Lark read recently. That means Becker is as healthy as can be, and I'm deeply ill, he thinks. I'm a *piñata* of secrets. A small grenade. In the toilet, while Becker lies on the beach in the late-afternoon sun watching his offspring wade into the water.

The breeze corrugates the surface of the lake, runs up the beach and through the screen window of the men's room. Becker stubs his cigarette out in the sand and turns over on his stomach. He has no ass. People with big dicks often have no ass, Lark thinks; as if the flesh can be concentrated only on one side, not both. He has learned such strange things in his life, his education wasted. Years ago he studied Schopenhauer; now he thinks the bumper sticker that says LIFE IS A BITCH, AND THEN YOU DIE more succinct. What a world.

The boy stranded on the narrow strip of sand between two segments of weeds, probably full of water moccasins, calls to his brothers in the rowboat to come get him. They shout back something Lark cannot understand, and row on. The family in the canoe turns around in the middle of the lake. A hawk appears above the oak trees on the western shore, circling on a current of air. He thinks, I'll just walk down the beach and say hello to Becker. I'll sit down beside him on the sand to be introduced to his daughter; I'll see how bright she is and offer her tutorial lessons in some subject—French or piano. Then I'll be invited to their home. I'll ingratiate myself into their private life. I'll encourage her in extracurricular activities. Then one evening she'll come home from school, late after band practice, and she'll come out of the house into the backyard, asking where her father is, and I'll say, dabbing my lips with a handkerchief, I've eaten him. But don't be alarmed—I'll explain later; just go back into the house and work on that Chopin nocturne.

Instead the daughter wades into the lake all the way to the line of white plastic floats that demarcates the swimming area; the lake, due to the last fifteen years of drought, is so low the water there comes up only to her shoulders, and her head rests now, like the Bernini bust of the Sun King, on the surface of the lake.

Her father lies there, his ankles crossed, his elbows propping him up so that he can watch her through the mirrored sunglasses. The position stretches his narrow chest and accentuates the ridges of his stomach. Is this pornography or real life? Lark wonders. I can no longer distinguish the two. Becker's that odd thing, a porn star on a beach in one of the most obscure state parks in the state of Florida. All my life, thinks Lark, I've been trying get People and Place together, and it's been very hard, if not impossible. All my life I've tried to integrate sex with domestic happiness. The task of man, said Hannah Arendt, is to make himself a home on earth. How hard that is to do. What excesses, what mistakes—the things we put up with! I have the emotional life of a dog, he thinks. But here is Becker, this perfect beacon of erotic pleasure, this grave, handsome, courteous, subdued, grown-up man, not far away in some city, but right here. On the shore of this little lake, lighting up a cigarette—even as his daughter, watching him from the lake, makes a motion meaning "No!" with her index finger—that cigarette that has always stood in Lark's mind as an indication of someone addicted to oral sex, but that here may mean nothing more than a certain repressed nervous energy that finds no outlet in this godforsaken place. If only he would see me as that outlet, Lark thinks.

But Becker is younger than I am by thirteen years, still handsome, very handsome, in the prime of life—and knows it. Is rich, in Beauty and Time; can pick and choose. Has a daughter whose upbringing is the most important thing in the world to him. Has a lover, equally handsome I'm sure, four years younger than himself, from the same background—a small, dull town— a person Becker pursued even when the boyfriend said, "Don't fall in love with me." (Becker went ahead, and now says, "I love him but I'm not in love." *In love* is all that counts, thinks Lark.) Becker does not read books, did not go to school, has never asked Lark a question about himself, does not hide in men's rooms at beaches in state parks wondering if he should walk down and speak to someone. Becker is: self-centered, tightly controlled, disciplined, autocratic, and willing to be by himself for long periods of time—watching constellations through his telescope, keeping the house clean, watering flowers. He has not called in a year. This means something, Lark thinks. This means he can get along without me. This means: No.

On the other hand, he thinks, Becker has stayed behind in this godforsaken town, for the same reason Lark is staying there: Family. They are both here for the same reason in fact—a single instant that had consequences: Becker's orgasm (inside the womb of a woman he now holds in contempt and claims has married nine times), Lark's mother's getting up in the night to go to the bathroom and tripping on a rug. Single moments that have lasted forever. I preside over a woman dying, he over a woman growing.

And then there's Becker himself. "I like to talk to people first," Becker said at the boat ramp the night they met. Oh God, thought Lark, a human being. Talking to people first was, of course, a risk. Sometimes it made them more attractive. Sometimes less. With Becker it was more. The knowledge that this was a seduction, at that late hour, as the town lay sleeping around them and Becker slowly smoked his cigarettes, informed the whole pleasure of their conversation, its disclosures, candor, intimacy. When they got to Lark's house, they talked for hours. They talked about Becker's daughter and his boyfriend and his old black Nissan—"New cars are worth shit!"—and his job, working on the construction of a new residential development near Palatka: a World Golf Village. He talked about the boredom of driving a forklift till Lark got bored himself, and then it dawned on him: This was finally the man in the pickup truck. The man he'd been driving behind the past ten years, on all those highways—shirtless in summer, in a denim jacket when it was cold, always with a dog beside him on the seat, or his girlfriend and his dog. A man, a truck, a woman, a dog: Southern Man. That was it. The normal package. A man who could understand. A friend to cling to in a hostile environment—just like Them, but gay. The only other gay man at the South Pole. The reward for all his efforts, the relief of all his loneliness.

"Stand up," Lark said that night finally. And Becker stood up immediately, as quick as a soldier; Lark crossed the floor and they embraced and the words stopped and the still, cool air, and the lateness of the hour, all came to rest, and he felt a deep strength, a deep peace, like Antaeus touching his mother, the Earth. That was the best moment: the feel of Becker's lean, muscular back, two bodies finally joined. Becker smelled like fresh laundry.

After that, he thinks now as he adjusts his buttocks on the toilet seat and looks out at Becker's daughter—her head just above the water, resting on the surface, more like the head of John the Baptist now, or even the Medusa—everything seemed to happen quickly. After leaving Becker in the bedroom for a moment to lock the door, he returned to find Becker already undressed, stealing that glance at himself in the mirror, then facing Lark with that submissive, humble, apologetic expression on his face—as if ashamed of his beauty and the responsibility, or the expectations, it might give rise to; and Lark reverted to the feeling he often had now when having sex—the feeling that he was pulling off a bank job, plundering a museum, robbing a church.

He felt this way because he was old now and he felt guilty for being old. He knew there were young men who desired only older men: There was a handsome bookstore clerk in Gainesville Lark could not interest because Lark wasn't old enough; the clerk's previous lover looked like Santa Claus—but it didn't matter. Lark was like those people in the nursing home whose photographs of themselves when young and comely hung on a bulletin board in the Hall of Memory. He was, that night, two people: the man whose lips were grazing Becker's white body and the man who, thirteen years ago (when Becker was the father of a three-year-old, now swimming in the lake as a teen-ager), was Becker's age. In other words: He was forty-seven, and Becker was thirty-four. And that made all the difference in the world.

"It's very heavy," Becker said as he took his own penis in his hand, a long penis bent, at an angle, halfway along the shaft; Lark approached it, wondering what reply that remark called for, wondering if people in small towns liked to talk dirty, with the standard vocabulary of porn, or if it was really true. That was the trouble with sex: It was always an audition. You were always trying to figure out what the other person wanted—while you were doing it. ("It's like traveling," said Sutcliffe. "By the time you've a figured a new place out—where to stay, where to eat, what to see and what not to—you're leaving. And you start all over again in some other town.") Lark wanted to do the right things to Becker that night, but not so right that it seemed knowing; he wanted to be skilled but not professional. Each one of them had done this before with other people. He wanted to let Becker know this time it meant something.

It meant so much he couldn't really enjoy it. He wanted simply to bury his face in Becker's scrotum, the way a person praying bows his head, the way a cat plants its forehead against your forearm when it purrs; and when finally Lark did do that, when he at last surrendered to his desire to say a prayer in the smooth crevice between Becker's thigh and scrotal sac, Becker produced an orgasm immediately. And lay there for a moment afterward, looking down at Lark with a grave, sad expression as Lark, expelled from his pew in the darkest corner of the church by a Spanish verger telling the parishioners the church was closing until evening, began licking his way up Becker's groin, causing Becker to flinch and shudder each time he touched his skin; while Lark recalled a dead friend telling him one day, as they passed a man sitting in the harbor of the Pines, that drug addicts are more sensitive to touch than ordinary people.

Becker was not a drug addict, but he was more sensitive than ordinary people; he was a very sexual person. So sexual a person, so handsome, so grave, that Lark felt—as he stood before the shower moments later, knocking on the glass door so that Becker would open it for him—like a tourist trying to summon the sacristan who would let him reenter the church. Inside the shower, the same shower in which Lark bathed his mother on Sunday afternoons on an aluminum folding lawn chair, he picked up a bar of soap and began washing Becker's back— irrelevant, he realized, to Becker's ablutions; already a part of the past. Then Becker was outside, toweling himself dry. Then Becker was dressed, going back down the hallway to the bedroom to find his lighter. And then, after listening to Lark say, "Call me anytime," he was gone; and Lark lay awake till dawn, in that state of grace that ensues when the world gives us a present we had no idea we deserved.

"He was all to pieces," Rick, the sculptor, said when Lark, still suffering, finally told him about his night with Becker. "He thought his boyfriend was moving to Atlanta when you met him. His boyfriend wanted to move to a city where he could change planes more easily. Becker told me when I saw him at the bar. Now the boyfriend has changed his mind, he's staying; he's going to buy a house in Orlando, in fact. When you met him,

Becker thought his friend was leaving him. That's why he went to the boat ramp. He was probably depressed. No, he isn't a mean person," he added, when Lark protested, "he's very sweet. But he's not a saint. You don't know what Becker used to be like. The first time he cruised me, he'd just come from oral surgery, from the dentist, and his mouth was still full of those cotton pads they put in to soak up the blood. And he still wanted to go home with me! Believe me, Becker was just demented— you couldn't go to the john at Shoney's on Thirteenth Street without finding him standing at the urinal next to yours when you looked up."

That Becker does have this compulsive, promiscuous past is part of the attraction, Lark thinks now as he sees Becker raise himself on his elbows to watch his daughter swim along the line of little white floats. Because he's past that now; he's thirty-four—not old, but not young anymore, either; disillusioned with the craziness that makes you take a booth near the men's room at Shoney's and pop in every time someone handsome goes inside. That dreadful, ecstatic, reckless, compulsive eroticism is all behind him now. At thirty-four a certain melancholy sets in, a small doubt about the future. No wonder Becker decided to stay in town, ostensibly to raise his daughter in a better atmosphere. He wanted some order and calm in his life, as we all do eventually. He's home now, in town, biting the bullet, taking care of her, explaining menstruation, cooking dinner. He *used* to go to bars and proposition people with bloody wads of cotton in his mouth. But now he doesn't, thinks Lark. AIDS and age have ruled that out. Even twentysomethings can't do that anymore. Which is why we're so right for each other. He's much more disciplined. He's much more grounded. He's a father whose daughter is doing the Australian crawl at this moment. He's organized. He's mature.

And he has no interest in me. In fact, the only way I could acquire a connection to Becker, he thinks as Becker's daughter leaves the lake, would be to marry Becker's daughter. Then Becker would be my father-in-law. And my son would be his grandson. And my mother would be happy because I'd finally have a child. That's it, he thinks, I'll marry Becker's daughter. Becker will give me away—my father-in-law *and* lover. And we'll finally be joined by blood. I'll marry his daughter, he thinks as she walks up the beach, shaking her head, throwing off droplets of water like a dog.

Now is the time, he thinks as his heartbeat accelerates—walk out, go down to Becker, speak to him while his daughter is toweling her hair dry. Find out your fate, one way or the other. Force the issue. What did that female deejay on WBLS in New York say every time she signed off in the early seventies? "You get only half of what you try for, but you get nothing of what you don't." Lark used this pep talk to put on a fresh T-shirt and go out to the bars. He stood in the Eagle's Nest for hours on summer nights because of the undeniable logic of Va Higginson's little *aperçu*. Then there's the whole tradition of this theme in literature—from Marvell to Thoreau to Henry James. He's read them all. The grave's a fine and private place / But none, I think, do there embrace. Lark's brain floods with adrenaline; it buzzes like a beehive; he feels as if wasps are circling him. "Whatever you're going to do, do it *now*," his mother said to him one day before her accident as he lay reading. Reading. Reading his life away. That was all he did when he came home to visit: read. She, waiting, like any parent, to see what this work of hers, her child, would do in the world, could have no idea—because he didn't tell her—that he'd been trying to get married. To a man. And now everything had crystallized in Becker. All the tears and fears and years had come to this single moment, this one person. Do it *now*, he thought. *Do it now.*

The sky above the wooded hill opposite, the dried-up remains of what used to be another, bigger lake, is a dark plum-purple— the most spectacular sight in this part of Florida: the sky before a thunderstorm. It looks now like a giant cloud of ash, turning darker and darker gray, as bolts of lightning streak to the ground, with their curious pale brevity, so harmless looking, so murderous in fact. The brothers paddle in to the shore in their rowboat; the family follows in its canoe; a gust of wind blows fallen oak leaves up the hill. Becker and his daughter gather up their blanket, Walkman, cigarettes, flipflops, and sunglasses; and then, before Lark can even get up the nerve to walk down and propose, they dash toward the trees, where a man with a crew cut and handlebar moustache who has been sitting on a picnic table jumps off, takes the blanket and the folded umbrella Becker has been carrying awkwardly under one arm, and walks with them to a small black Nissan at the top of the slope.

Becker's boyfriend. The tableau is now complete. The salesman who told Becker not to fall in love with him, the man who brought Becker back issues of *Details* to read while recuperating from his hernia operation, had been watching Becker and his daughter swim too; only he had been watching while sitting on the picnic table in the deep shade of the live oaks, thinks Lark, and I was squatting on a toilet. Ah, well. The privileges of Love! I who am nothing salute you. I who am trapped inside the rest room, smelling the fragrance of the rain on old, dried paint, wondering if there is any point in going to the baths, since Becker will obviously not be there. No, Becker is driving home, through the rain, with his daughter and his boyfriend, the very image of the brave new world of modern homosexuals I am too retrograde to be a part of, he thinks, the three of them about to stop at Hardee's or, more probably, cook dinner at home. Home, where he moved to raise his daughter, and which I always have to leave, thinks Lark—as the door to the rest room suddenly swings open and in walks Becker. He stops in the middle of the floor and says to Lark, as frightened and as paralyzed as a rabbit when you come upon it in the garden, "You've been staring at me all afternoon. I've seen you drive by my house. I've about had it. You've got to leave me alone." And Lark, too stunned to move, can scarcely join the pleasure of hearing that deep, rich, melancholy voice with the horror of the words just spoken to him, until Becker walks out of the room, and Lark slips off the toilet seat, onto the damp cement floor, wondering how his sorrow can increase now.

Il Paradiso

~~~~~~

He takes a locker when he gets to the baths—after driving faster than usual to put sixty miles between himself and Becker quickly—though he knows this disappoints; mature men, he suspects, are expected to bring money—take a room—while the young need merely a five-dollar locker, their beauty being their contribution. He doesn't care. The minute the door closes behind him, he feels a sense of relief, as if this is where he can obliterate the memory of that embarassing scene more quickly than anyplace else. The foolishness of his obsession, the inappropriate quality of his courtship, the lunacy of even imagining for a moment that Becker was his soulmate, are clearer with each step he takes down the corridor to the locker room. I was a fool, he thinks, a vain, deluded, old queen. Only here, he thinks, as he passes a clump of men at the vending machine, everyone is even older than I am. In the afternoon there are always men older than himself, retired, on disability, or taking a long lunch; men who have come here by bus, who have to be home at night with their families, or who don't want to stay out late. He is younger than they, at least. This is the Hour of the Manatees, and it will be till shortly before five o'clock; till then he's young—a beneficiary of this ruthless system in which men who refused to consider older gentlemen when they were young now have to use the same standards on themselves. He who lives by the sword, he thinks as he walks down the hall, dies by the sword. The baths in the afternoon are like the games in the Colosseum; only here the gladiators cry, "We who are about to die want you!"

The television used to be downstairs; one could watch reruns of *Laverne & Shirley* while appraising the men entering and leaving the steam room through the glass doors beyond. Now the television is upstairs, in a sort of theater; the ground floor contains only gym equipment and lockers. On Friday afternoon they set up a table with free pizza. On Tuesdays once a month they administer tests for HIV. It's such a clean, well-run, civilized place; he's always been, and always will be, grateful for its refuge. Even now when his face still burns with the memory of Becker at the urinal. I used to go to the baths, he thinks as he opens his locker and unties his shoes, because it was a refuge from the bars; you didn't have to speak, or play games, or pretend you were interested in whatever topic you dreamed up to start a conversation with the man you wanted. I used to go to the baths because it was the most honest form of communication there is: My body wants your body. Does yours want mine? Like his mother, he values honesty. ("How are you?" people would say to her, on long distance, as he held the telephone to her ear. "I'm paralyzed," she would say. "How are you?") He used to go to the baths because it cut through all the games and affectations, the pretense, the tedious peregrinations of seduction. Now he goes because he has no place else to go. Now he goes because Time is passing, Becker's told him to get lost, and in two months he will have even less hair than he does now. The indignities of loss, he thinks as he removes his pants and puts them into the locker. Indignities Becker will not have to deal with for some time. Life is an Indian giver that takes back everything it gives you. I am approaching that peculiar time, that psychological stalemate, he thinks as he pauses for a moment in his underwear (a look he feels turns people on), when a man is too old to be pursued, but too proud to pursue. The trap of Vanity. The tomb of Pride. Lined with mirrors like the one at the end of this locker room—a mirror he used to check his appearance in but that he now ignores, because he's worried the sight of his reflection would cause him to dress and go home, if not lose consciousness.

Going to the baths has become almost as difficult as walking down the sidewalk in New York. But he goes anyway, because the baths are always a throw of the dice. No matter what happened the last time, he thinks, the next will be different. Even Becker cannot deny him that. As at the boat ramp, there is no predicting, no pattern. How could there be, for something as irrational as sex? *Abandon logic, all ye who enter here* should be written above the doorway. He no longer even understands it himself. Or knows what is expected of him by the men who are now drifting through the locker room (on the pretext of visiting the vending machine) to examine the new body. That's the mantra of gay life, he thinks: *Show us your meat.* Like the Sodomites demanding that Lot show them his houseguests. Instead, waiting till the locker room is empty, he removes his underpants with the celerity of a quick-change artist, then wraps a big blue towel around his loins, makes sure the knot will hold, and walks away as a man with a white handlebar moustache passes and stares at him.

The stare is comforting, even if it's not Becker's, and even if he has no idea what it means. Each person who walks into a bar or baths, he thinks, is an enigma—a complex accretion of longing, disappointment, desire—a personal history that cannot be narrowed into anything so tiny as a look, or even a sexual gesture. Yet that is what we do when we come to these places, he thinks—reduce ourselves to body parts. Only now my outside no longer resembles my inside. Outside I am somewhere between what Sutcliffe used to call a Dried Arrangement and an Unwrapped Mummy. Outside I look like a retired marine drill sergeant—a man who has just spent six months training drug agents at a jungle camp in Ecuador. People with rings in their nipples and shaved heads stare at me.

He has no idea what Becker saw when they met. Perhaps Becker slept with him that night simply because he was there. He cannot be sure. That's why he's come to the baths; although even here he's lost his ability to discern his role. At the baths, because he no longer looks in mirrors, all he has to go on is the mirror of men's eyes, so often averted these days. He's left that time of life when one person looks at another and each knows immediately, clearly, wholeheartedly: *Yes.* There's a certain defensiveness, a craven apology, in offering himself now. He hates it. Driving to the baths in 1983 was like going to Valhalla, he thinks as he walks down the hall. Going to the baths in 1995 is like driving in to have his tires rotated and oil changed.

In other words, he thinks, I've become my father. That's what he did his last decade of life, when the only reason for an excursion away from the house seemed to be car care. The day the oil needed changing, or the tires rotated, was a day of purpose, action, excitement. The others were spent on the porch, turning cards over in a game of solitaire: a man in prison, the prison of retirement. Ernie is right to keep going to the boat ramp, he thinks as he walks toward the stairs. You have to stay interested in something. You have to keep going out, no matter what. Look at my friends left in New York, plunged in depression, hunkering down in their tiny apartments till the plague is over, which it won't be before they die. Better to be cheerful, to live. My own mind is a septic tank, he thinks as he climbs the stairs. I can't hope to be happy here in this black mood. Empty your mind of its misery and shit, he thinks as he enters the lounge upstairs. Flush your mind, like a toilet, and smile!

This he does, but the four men watching *Oprah* in the lounge are too busy arguing about whether or not Michael Jackson will beat the sex rap to notice. Oh, Becker, Becker, he thinks, throwing himself down in a chair. A moment later he gets up and walks down the hall of rooms, which lately have begun more and more to resemble the halls of his mother's nursing home; only through these open doors, he sees men lying in towels upon narrow beds—in the nursing home, he sees odd shapes of both sexes, connected or not connected to a call button, propped up or not propped up in hospital beds, often calling, "Nurse!" But one thing the occupants of both sets of rooms seem to have in common, in his present state of depression: They all need help.

Every two months Lark reads in the newspaper another article about our need to be touched; that's all he wants. He no longer knows what others want from him. "After forty," Ernie told him, "all men are looked on as daddies. Your trouble is you don't want to be a daddy." Right, thinks Lark as he walks downstairs. The sight of a real child walking hand in hand with a real father makes me melt—but to impersonate a marine sergeant, a football coach, the pop they never had—forget it! I'd rather pretend I'm a German shepherd.

He doesn't really want the young anyway; and in point of fact all he gets is men his age or older who have let their figures go. Manatees. The young man with black hair and tattoo, a leather cord around his neck, who wakes up from his debauch the night before and leaves his room to dunk himself in the pool, can live without him. The two old men he steps between in the showers both say "Hello," however.

There are four of them, in various shades of silver: men with rounded shoulders and white hair, standing motionless in the showers, like elephants beneath a waterfall in some Cambodian forest—bull elephants, ancient and wrinkled. He would no more consider sleeping with them than he would with the patients in the nursing home. Even though the man with white hair on his left has, he can plainly see, bone structure that made him gorgeous when young. Which means the man on his left also ignored older men in his youth, received his share of admiration, of being desired (though the share is never enough), and endured the gradual disappearance of interest on the part of others, the gradual spread of invisibility, limb by limb, feature by feature, till now—even though he stands beside Lark, letting the warm water course down his shoulders—he has no corporeal value whatsoever. He is a ghost. One of many. Since, in the afternoons, men like him, in various shades of gray and white, with bodies obese or trim, with small cocks or big cocks, all come—for warmth; not just the warmth of the steam room, but the warmth of other human beings; including one handsome hoar-frosted Father Time who stands naked in the middle of the wet area, an enormous sausage hanging between his legs, staring at Lark as if to say, This has always got me what I wanted before, why not now? (Because, thinks Lark, repeating his cruising mantra, it's not the penis, it's what the penis is connected to.)

The point is, thinks Lark as he washes what's left of his hair, one does not so much reject the old when one goes out as ignore them—which is the most complete form of ostracism—the way whites make blacks invisible. Sometimes the old can't be ignored. In the seventies, he often found himself on the steps of the St. Marks Baths, in the red-lighted darkness, waiting impatiently for some old man to put his foot carefully on the next step down, afraid to fall; and Lark would wonder how he dared hold everyone else up, when that cute blond with the moustache had just gone downstairs and was probably lying in his rooom with the door open. Hurry up, hurry up, he shouted at the old man silently. Why do you come here at all? What on earth are you doing in this place?

Now he knew: company. The sight of other men's bodies. The off chance that something might happen. The sounds of lovemaking that sometimes carry through the walls of a cubicle upstairs. Even Lark stops to listen to these five minutes later, in a cluster of other men who stand there enthralled by the gasping "Yes! Yes! Yes!" they hear repeated over and over again, as two bodies collide with the wall; and Lark is reminded that even now, in the age of the virus, people are still Doing It.

He is too proud to linger long at such concerts and too crushed by Becker—he pauses for only a second, a wry smile on his lips, refusing to look at the old man who smiles at him on the basis of this auditory bond and grabs Lark's genitals, hoping to take advantage of the reflected radiance of the two men grunting, groaning, and hissing beyond the slender wooden wall. Lark instead disengages and keeps walking, as if he is above all that—until, on a dimmer, darker hallway, when no one else is around, he becomes stock-still listening to another set of faint hisses, gasps, and garbled murmers: proof that, if he is too afraid, too disillusioned, too hopeless to engage in such a surrender, others aren't. Nobody knows now what bargain someone else has made with the situation. And the moment he hears one of them rise up and put his hand on the doorknob, he springs like a gazelle around the corner, as if the sounds are not, at his point, the sweetest in the world—thinking, as he moves on, I am now one of Them. One of those men who linger in the hall, listening to other people screwing.

And so he walks past other doors, thinking, Nice stomach. The Hour of the Manatees is never exclusively that; a few young men taking the day off lie patiently in their rooms, waiting for the opportunity to cash in on their beauty. He used to want to climb such a stomach with his tongue, scale it the way rock climbers ascend cliffs, but now he thinks, What is the point? What is the point of any of this? My God, he thinks, I am finally, more than twenty years late, arriving where I knew I should have been in 1972: I can no longer have sex with strangers. (I have to be introduced.) I no longer want to have sex with someone if it doesn't mean anything.

And then an old man rounds the corner. This man is tall, skinny; he has a caved-in chest and protruding belly, like someone with malnutrition. His ribs show beneath the skin. His head is birdlike, gaunt, with a beak of a nose, silver hair across a balding scalp. It is astonishing that he should come here and actually hope to have sex. He looks the way Lark's father looked when he was eighty-nine. He looks the way Lark will look if he ever reaches that age. He is, this bony, tall, cadaverous man with sagging flesh, so pitiful that Lark thinks, That's right! Push the envelope! See how old you can be and still go to the baths! Set new frontiers for the rest of us to come!

Let's face it, he thinks, we are all packages. An assemblage of elements. The traditional three are youth, beauty, cock. When you have all three, you are a god. When you have two of the three, you still do okay. But when you have none, you are in trouble. Perhaps I should think in terms of export, he thinks. Perhaps I should go to Japan. The baths in Kyoto, after my mother dies, a room with one piece of her furniture to remember her by—a vase, a figurine—my hair completely hennaed. The children of Nippon will shriek when they see me.

Or just quit, he thinks. Admit defeat. Like an opera singer who knows she can no longer perform certain roles. I am approaching entropy. I now get only the ones the ads say *need not respond:* fatties, fems, drug addicts. Thank God for all three. Thank God for the ones who still look, who still say, "Good evening." Thank God for Compromise Sex! Hell is the inability to love, said Dostoevski. Hell is the inability to touch Beauty, thinks Lark. Beauty is out of my reach. I'll take *willing.* Though I am less and less willing myself. Which is the better reason not to have sex, he wants to ask the attendant putting clean sheets on a mattress in a room he passes, HIV or meaninglessness? Maybe HIV provides meaning—that's what Roy said when he got it, at any rate: "Now my life has some structure."

Whatever the reason, Lark can no longer predict what happens to him here—he's lost a sense of himself. So he sits down on a bench in the locker room, a wraith, a wreck, and waits for someone else to tell him what his problem is. "What do you see when you look at me?" he wants to say to one of the Manatees.

Instead he gets up, when the Hour of the Manatees comes to a close and several of the white-haired old men open their lockers to dress, and walks down the hall, past the room of a tall, skinny young man with a crew cut and crucifix around his neck and a bottle of poppers on the table. For a second Lark's eyes meet his; for a half second Lark pauses and holds the glance; then the youth averts his eyes while a sneer deforms his lips— a sneer that carries the caption: Don't even *think* of parking here! Lark blushes as if he'd just been slapped on the face. I must be careful, he thinks; I must remember my place. An aged man is but a paltry thing, a tattered coat upon a stick. The supercilious shit!

He falls in behind a short, beautiful Cuban with curly hair and an aquiline nose who walks on the balls of his feet, as if trying to increase his height, and follows him upstairs, far from the sneering beanpole, and sits down to watch Deborah Gianoulis and Tom Wills deliver the same news they are reciting to the patients in the nursing home seventy miles to the west—a universal ritual, he thinks, like the mass.

The beautiful Cuban slumps in a chair in the front row, while a man older than Lark, pink-faced and porcine, stands against the wall masturbating under his towel as he watches the young man. Sleeping Beauty, thinks Lark. The Cuban is not really sleeping, only closing his eyes to eliminate the embarrassment of his admirer, who refuses to recognize the deportment, the expression, of all these young men who know older men are looking at them—young men who simply endure it, the way travelers avoid flies when going through a marketplace in Sierra Leone; something they have to put up with, but don't like. I know how you feel, Lark thinks, how you regard and edit us out, the silent onlookers, the Greek chorus to your search for Love, because I too once wore that expression. I too endured and ignored the looks of older men. I too once was annoyed to find only the old when I checked in. I too knew I had what they wanted—Youth and Beauty, the self-sufficient oxygen pack that enables you to traverse this cold and lonely planet; whereas we, the old, with only a dwindling supply, must eventually suffocate and die, while the young continue to explore.

The Cuban suddenly stands up and leaves the room. The old man against the wall, still fiddling with himself, glances over at Lark, as if to say, Will you be my valentine instead? But Lark stands up and exits the lounge too.

That particular man is always obnoxious, thinks Lark, as he walks down a dark, cool hallway—the other Manatees are all models of rectitude, restraint, reserve. So much so that when he goes downstairs, he realizes that most of them are gone. The Hour of the Manatees is over. The lull between it and the Invasion of the Virile has begun—a strange, unpredictable period when anything can walk through the door: people who want to get an early start on their evening, men just off work, or the Regulars.

The Regulars are people who seem to live here. One in particular is never not here when Lark comes; he's decided the man must have an arrangement with the owner, a secret room upstairs. Lark calls him Coach, a potbellied, bald man with a fat penis, who rents only a locker, and then goes around choreographing group sex in the steam room or bathrooms as if he were running around a large gym supervising basketball games. The other Regulars include the Bartender, a lean man in his thirties with an enormous dick, who brings with him an overnight bag containing hair care products and stands in front of a mirror in the locker room spraying his hair—once long, now worn in a Dorothy Hamill cut—and then goes to the steam room, where he shaves his groin on a tiled ledge while the others there gape; the Telephone Lineman, a big, beefy man with thick black hair all over his body and tits so big it looks as if he could give milk; the Mean Cold Queen, a gaunt man with a shaved head and expression of discontent so deep Lark cannot imagine what would please him; the Kid, a slender, white youth of indeterminate age, who has black hair so thick it forms a sort of cloud around his head and a voice Lark has heard only once—when the Kid asked in a nasal, clogged whine if he could change the television channel; and the Hippie, a frankly effeminate man with a ponytail and bleached-blond moustache who seems to move around the halls without touching the floor—who glides, slides, floats, zooms, cigarette in hand, making wisecracks and being friendly to people. "Cute bottom," he says of a man dressing at his locker, as Lark sits there waiting. "Nice feet."

All of these people are at the baths almost every time Lark goes; and because they are, he refuses even to nod at them. Only the Kid was an exception to this rule. He looked so skittish, frightened, timid, nerdlike, Lark thought him anything but a Regular the first time he saw him; but when he paused one evening before the room in which the Kid lay, the Kid shook his head ever so slightly, and Lark, stung, moved on. So Lark pretends to ignore him now; devastated by the Kid's superiority, he watches the boy come in, go to the steam room, select whom he wants, and disappear. (The functional disappear at the baths almost immediately: They are having sex. The dysfunctional remain in view, sitting in the TV lounge or on a bench in the locker room, like Lark—a penitent in the street before Santiago de Compostela, asking only the pity of the passersby.)

After an hour, the Kid emerges, returns to his locker, and dresses—while Lark sits there still, thinking the Kid must be wondering why Lark never seems to meet anyone or have sex. Lark wonders the same thing; or rather, he expected that one day he would envy the young their smooth skin, their beauty, but what he never thought he would envy was their ability to find all this significant—to feel desire. I can no longer access Lust, he thinks, as the Kid checks out. I can no longer pretend that brief ecstasy is adequate. Because I grow old, I grow old, he thinks, I shall wear the bottoms of my trousers rolled. I do not dare to eat a peach, much less beg to suck the Kid's fat cock.

He sits there instead like a man who has stumbled into a suburban racquetball club, watching Coach scamper past with yet another trio he has put together in the steam room. He sits there watching them walk by, go into rooms with one another, talk among themselves, laugh, nod, and sometimes smile at him. He thinks: Sex *is* like racquetball. Especially when you've divorced it from the procreative function. It *is* like going to the gym—you may not feel like working out beforehand, but you always feel better afterward. Because the skin needs to be touched. Esalen says this is good. The Church says it is bad. Tennessee Williams said, "Each time I pick someone up on the street, I leave a piece of my heart in the gutter." It's true, he thinks. There is a cost to this. There is a constant, cumulative cost. Slutty is as slutty does. Then why, he wonders, is this man smiling? Coach trundles past with an overweight, sexy young man who looks like a football player and has obviously begged Coach to let him suck his dick. And Lark watches them go into the toilet opposite the weight room on the first floor.

Wittgenstein told us not to ask certain questions, thinks Lark as he listens to them lock the door—metaphysical questions, questions of angst—because they have no meaning. I am doing the same thing with sex, he thinks as he sits there on the bench in the locker room; I am trying to freight it with meaning. I am trying to make a connection with another man that will justify my life, will make all that has gone before and is going on now worthwhile. And I cannot. I can only collide with their bodies; I can only lick a stomach, suck a dick, and maybe—this I would really like—embrace, if I am lucky. Though the way I want to embrace, he thinks, I cannot. I want to embrace the way a father enfolds a son.

Except these are not my sons, he thinks. These are my family, perhaps; the band of men on whose embrace I have relied the past two decades. Only that embrace is now becoming harder to obtain: a scary prospect. And it's all my fault. I'm not what you think, he wants to tell the black youth with an earring who stares at him as he goes by: I'm a self-loathing queen who carries an image of a younger self within him. Like the men in San Francisco John met at parties for PWAs, who would show him photos of themselves when healthy—photos that made John weep when he told Lark about them afterward. John, who is now almost certainly dead, though Lark cannot bring himself to call his family in Massachusetts to find out. Why remind them? Why bring the subject up again? They lived with it for six horrifying years.

Maybe that's it, he thinks—having sex with these men here would be like spitting on his friends' graves. Too many have died, too many have suffered, for sex to be casual again or what it used to be. "The first time you heard the Tomb Scene from *Aida* is not the five-hundredth time," Sutcliffe said one evening. "It's different."

It's more than different, thinks Lark. It's sacrilegious. Though none of the dead—the ones who lived the Tomb Scene—would agree with that; they'd want to have sex. Certainly Eddie. His favorite line was Auntie Mame's: "Life's a banquet, and most poor fools are starving to death." "I'm so glad I was born in America with a big, fat dick," Eddie said one night, as Lark sat in his bedroom happily watching him dress for Flamingo, "and not on some garbage mound in Egypt!" But you were, Eddie, you were, thinks Lark. Or you might as well have been, toward the end. The virus made us all third world. And changed absolutely nothing otherwise. Even though the moment it began, everyone thought, Everything will change now. Change utterly.

At first he thought it meant the end of the sex, and with that, the end of gay life; then he thought gay life would be humanized somehow, that all this suffering would make gay men nicer to one another. It didn't. If Joshua were to come back from the dead right now, he thinks, all I could tell him would be "They've got fat-free ice cream now, Joshua. Totally fat-free!" (And that would not be enough for Joshua, who used to sit there, guiltily spooning Häagen-Dazs right from the carton after his gym work-out, and saying in the dreamy voice of Katharine Hepburn in *Stage Door*, "If only eating ice cream made your penis bigger." Well now, he thinks, there's penile enlargement surgery; that doctor in Los Angeles is opening franchises.) Otherwise, things are pretty much the same, as far as human nature goes, except the fact that a lot of people have been depressed on some sub-conscious level. (Would Prozac have saved Joshua? he wonders. Odd, how all the drugs people took illicitly in the sixties are now prescribed.) With total strangers, it's still the hunt, the hunger, the horrendous haughtiness of queens. Because, as Dr. Johnson said, no man is a hypocrite in his pleasures. We don't sleep with people to be nice, he thinks. AIDS changed nothing in that respect—the rest is just the same. What else could it be, he wonders as he watches Coach and the young football player emerge from the toilet, smiling.

The Regulars he will not sleep with, and the men who want him—the Manatees—he does not want, so he sits on the bench in the locker room, smiling at Coach when he goes by, watching people go up and down the hallways of rooms without meeting their eyes. Look at the eyes, one of his lovers told him years ago when Lark asked him how he assessed people, the eyes. He cannot. Now it's the eyes that tell you if someone has AIDS, he thinks, remembering Eddie, in 1983, before many people even knew what it was. "It's a look in the eyes," Eddie said, and Lark heard those words, thinking, The same visual acuity that enables him to design rooms, furniture, clothes, now lets him ferret out PWAs at Studio 54. Different uses for the eyes. At the baths, he never looks at anyone's. He's afraid of what they will see in his. He looks at their stomachs, their chests. When he is seated on the bench, that is just what passes in front of his eyes; it's perfect. He should leave, but he doesn't; he stays for the Invasion of the Virile.

The Invasion of the Virile begins not long after the departure of the Manatees. He sits there and watches the young come around the corner of the locker room, at the very start of what will be a long night for them. It's so odd, he thinks, when not only the doctors but the men at the baths are younger than you. They run to the wet area like puppies, shaking the water from their hair as they come back from the steam room and shower. This foreign race—the clientele the baths manager desires—the ones the attendants give free passes to when they go out to the bars on fishing expeditions. He watches them all come in: the shy, the downcast, the merry and bright, even a short-haired man in black shorts, black tank top, black baseball cap, and black shoes—a young clone, a fashion victim, an Act-Up trickle-down he watches undress. His chest is hairy and black, Lark thinks, while mine is hairy and gray. The man slams the locker shut with a bang, looks back at Lark with a smoldering, mean expression that withers him on the bench, and walks down the hallway to the steam room. Lark stands up, pricked by the man's contempt, and goes up the hallway to see what the young man passes up.

What the young man passes up is something Lark thinks will do very nicely: a man he has seen here before, who walks down the hallway now, fully dressed, towel and key in hand, and weaves groggily toward Room 186. He is drunk; Lark sits down on the rowing machine in a corner of the gym and watches.

Sometimes this man is bombed when he gets here, and sometimes sober—when sober, he is prim, cold, intellectual; he sits in his room smoking with one leg drawn up against his chest, exposing a large thigh Lark finds intimidating. When he is drunk, lying naked on his pallet, he turns into a Christ lying on the sepulcher by Mantegna. The man is now in transition. He has just come from the bar. Through the open door, Lark watches him undress, lie down on the bed, and fall asleep with the door still ajar. Moments pass. Then, like a vulture that can feed only on dead things, Lark enters the room carefully, and quietly closes the door behind him so the Food will not awaken—just as he sat by the telephone after lunch as a child, guarding the nap his father took when he came home from work. He stands there, making sure the man is truly slumbering, and then, ever so gently, begins to lick his thigh.

This is much easier than the reality of another man, fully awake, with his needs, idiosyncrasies, tastes, and snobberies, the dreadful competition of sex, the fact that they have both done this little dance many, many times before and it has not freed them. The failure of another man to meet Lark's dreams is so great, what he wants from another person is so incommunicable at this point, only someone asleep will do. A man who looks, as this one does, like a farmer, or a coal miner in a sepia photograph taken years ago: long, lean, Scotch-Irish, altogether beautiful. A ghost. Because a real person could not possibly understand, he thinks, what is in my heart, the large accumulation of grief. Fifty-seven miles and one hour and twenty minutes from home, all depression vanishes in three licks of a tongue, and Lark is thinking, as his lips graze on the surface of the flat white stomach, I bring you gray skies, a light rain-soaked breeze, the sound of wind in the trees, the translucent panels on either side of Becker's door late at night, the care with which he raises his daughter, and the gazebo he's building out back. I bring you his long, lean torso, not unlike yours, and the thunderstorm that drove him, his daughter, and his boyfriend from the beach back to a town I cannot find Love in but that I live in anyway.

I bring you all the desire for Love that town engenders in me, including the young high-school student who bought cigarettes

in the Jiffy as I was filling out my Lotto card just yesterday—
about five feet eight, brown curly hair, a thin moustache, a perfect butt, an upper body that was a slab of milk-white muscle.
I bring you his faded blue jeans, and the butt beneath his white
football jersey as he walked away across the parking lot and I
glanced through the glass doors, compelled to look at him. I
bring you the woman who sold me my Lotto card as she asked
the young man with the thin moustache whose upper body was
a slab of milk-white muscle, "How do you think we'll do?" and
his reply, "Okay, I hope," and I wondered if she, in her twenties,
desired him, in his teens, and whether sex did not make everyone in this town as bananas as myself, and no doubt Becker. I
bring you all the handsome men in that town besides Becker,
including the two policemen standing in uniform by the road as
I returned from the convenience store, and the mother and the
small boy who stopped at the bin at the public beach to put in
their newspapers to be recycled. I bring you the tall, skinny,
black-haired young man who works at Publix, and his colleague
with straight brown bangs across his forehead, in camouflage T-
shirt and faded jeans, as he talked to the supervisor with an
earnest, supplicatory expression.

I bring you Becker in his jeans and black T-shirt the time I
saw him standing in Produce with the cabbage held like a basketball in his right hand. I bring you his enormous hands; the
way he smokes a cigarette; his grave, leaden, melancholy voice;
the fact that he too must admire the stocky, cheerful bag boy
who scooped up a small blond toddler running amok and returned her to her mother before beginning to bag my groceries.
I bring you the beefy, blond father getting out of his car outside
in the parking lot, with a blond son on his arm, saying, "You'll
be all right, you'll be all right," with the majestic calm of someone who is no longer afraid himself of what frightens three-year-
olds.

I bring you the young man mowing the lawn of the electrical

cooperative as I drove by. I bring you the long, soft luxury and peace of a summer afternoon in an American town where goods and services are distributed efficiently among the populace, and extremes of wealth and poverty are not noticeable. I bring you all the bag boys, the football players whose pictures are already taped on the window of the drugstore in preparation for that most priapic of seasons, and Becker, who lends his beauty only once to mortals, myself included.

I bring all this to you, the soft gray afternoon in town, sixty miles to the east, through neon and strip mall, gas station and supermarket, an ocean of moving metal; to you, the soft flesh beneath my lips—*not* the stomach of the boy at the Jiffy buying cigarettes, *not* the desire the older woman felt when she inquired about the chances of the football team, *not* my hopeless, humiliated love for Becker, but something close to it—yes, even the love of my parents, the deaths of my friends, and what still survives, my love of summer afternoons, the whole erotic force that makes me come here to discharge my desire, like something ricocheting off someone else, so stupid, so pointless, so neurotic, but all I've got. I bring you this, he thinks, and takes the penis into his mouth.

And the man lifts his head gently and says, "Do you have poppers?" as Lark feels the penis he has enclosed in his mouth begin, miraculously, to swell. And all sadness and regret fall away.

Eventually even this must end, however; and, when his ministrations have brought the corpse to life, when a marmoreal hand reaches out to grab Lark's own penis, he separates himself from the ghost, rises, wraps his towel about him, and, holding the tainted saliva in his mouth, leaves. Then he rinses his mouth out with the red mouthwash in the bathroom and decides to go home. Time is running out. This is not the solution. He goes upstairs anyway and watches a rerun of *Roseanne* beside a handsome, talkative Jamaican with a shaved head and earring. Then a movie about a suburban killer on USA. In America, he thinks, Love means having someone to watch television with; but when the Jamaican gets up, says, "I'm going to do one more cycle," and leaves, Lark realizes the friendliness was after all just that and nothing more. Nothing more, nothing more. What I'm facing, thinks Lark, is the Void.

The Void means I believe in none of this anymore. I'm ashamed of being gay, of being old, of being ashamed of being gay and old. How stupid. I resent the men at the baths for no fault of their own—I resent them because they're not my friends, because they're men in Jacksonville. Hardly their fault, he thinks, yet on some level I hate them for it. What a recipe for mental health. And he gets up and walks into the dark maze of hallways that is the only place he feels safe these days, safe and still and peaceful.

It's so peaceful that when he sees, down one of the most obscure, least traveled hallways, a young man lying on his bed smoking a cigarette in bright light, he stops, like a traveler coming to a hut in the forest, and the young man waves him inside. He is not particularly good-looking: The curly hair of a permanent is receding already from his forehead; his lips are thin, he wears glasses, he starts talking the moment Lark enters the room and does not stop. But Lark is grateful to be taken in, out of the storm, and happy to listen, with a detached, avuncular air, to the young man's explanation of why he's here—a bartender he is in love with, six years younger than himself, who comes here sometimes before work and sometimes after, and won't return his phone calls. He's obsessed. In fact the young man himself—managing a Hardee's on Blanding Boulevard—is about to be fired from his job. "I'm missing work because of him, and you know what? I don't really give a damn."

At this point Lark sits down on the edge of his bed, and then, when the man moves to his side, he accepts the invitation to stretch out beside him. There they lie for several minutes while

Lark, psychiatrist *manqué*, asks his companion questions about the bartender that lance the boil of obsession and Lark listens patiently, happy to be hearing about somebody else's unrequited love, even smiling at the more painful details. Misery loves company, he thinks, as he rolls over on top of the manager of a fast-food franchise, lays his head on the mattress next to his companion's, and slips his arms underneath his back.

Oh God, he thinks, I could lie here forever, this feels so good! It's always felt so good, this connection, this embrace. It's like finally plunging into the water after a long, hot car ride to the ocean as a kid. It's like finally rushing into the waves, naked, free, joyous at last. It's all the thoughts I cannot express, and all the things I cannot say, and all the feelings I cannot act upon, and all the sadness, all the failure, all the grim reality wiped out in a single electrical spark—my body's warmth against his body's warmth, raising each a few degrees. It may be only temporary comfort, the current may be cut off in a few minutes, the sea may dry up, but for now—even if it has no meaning—I am happy, he thinks; and the common woe of heart-sickness, the solid grace of this man's body, his embrace, weld their torsos together in a sticky, sweaty glue, till Lark stops listening to the actual words being slipped into the air between puffs on the man's cigarette, and does not even care when he stops talking altogether.

Then there is a silence, during which Lark sighs, and begins ever so gently to stroke with his thumb the backside of the man's right ear; at which point, the man says to Lark, "Honey, you need a pet."

Lark lifts his head like a man awakened from a deep sleep and says, "What do you mean?"

"I mean you need a pet," the man says. "I mean, you're holding on to me like I'm the puppy you just got for Christmas."

Lark leaps up. He laughs. He knots his towel. He says, "Well, I've got to get home and feed my real dog. Good luck with your friend," and leaves the room, pausing to adjust the open door—enough to let passersby know the man is Receiving, but not a quarter inch more, which would mean Slut—and takes the stairs two at a time. I'm needy, he thinks, as he dashes to the locker room. They can smell it. Like Richard Friel, toward the end. "Richard is a very needy person," Sutcliffe warned Lark. Not good to be needy. An open wound. Got to get out of here, he thinks, as two men his age round the corner with cardboard cups of coffee from the vending machine, talking loudly.

Old friends who lived in Washington, D.C., in the seventies but now live in different cities, the two men sit down on the bench while Lark opens his locker. They reminisce about a party one gave at which Roberta Flack was hired to sing. The tall man asks the short one, as Lark takes his clothes out, where a friend at that party is now. "Boyd lives in Kentucky, on a farm," says the other man. "Every day around five o'clock he buys a six-pack, gets in the Jeep, and starts driving the back roads, hoping he'll meet some fourteen-year-old." (Oh God, thinks Lark, that's it! That's simply all there is!)

"Does he still have his hair?" asks the tall man.

"Yes," says his friend, "but it's all on his back." And they burst out laughing.

It's all about hair. And cock, Lark thinks, when the two men glance at his genitals as they walk past him into the hall, suddenly silent with the seriousness of this chance to view the sacred item.

"Good night," says the youth when he checks out.

"Good night," says Lark, as the boy buzzes him through and he finds himself in the warm parking lot.

The Dying Fig Tree

It's not wise to leave the baths without having had an orgasm, he realizes, or an embrace of any real duration; it's like going to a grocery store and coming home with empty paper bags. It's a consumer failure. A wasted trip. He often argues that, given what's out there, in all its mutating varieties, it's better not to have sex (AIDS's comfort to the sexually deprived), but that doesn't work now. Because he knows that, having failed tonight to find the Magic Touch he needs at the baths, he will still have to find it somewhere else. In other words, the whole world now becomes the baths—if he can't get it on Hendricks Avenue, he has to get it elsewhere.

There are two bars just down the road—the Eagle and the Phoenix—but he doesn't feel like stopping at either one before heading home. He'd like to go into a bar and meet a man who will, the moment they meet, have already been in a relationship with him for six years. There is no time to start from scratch. The clock is ticking. He needs to meet someone who's been his lover for six years already; and since that can't happen, he sees no point in going to the Eagle or the Phoenix.

He sees no point in going anywhere at the moment, except home. Home is the place that makes more and more sense: his own monastic cell. I'll spend the rest of my life watching television, he thinks as he proceeds down San José Boulevard. They've made it so entertaining, it's what they want me to do, so why not give in? Why not just stay home and watch television for the rest of my life, and not have to go out?

Why does anyone have to go out? Lark wonders as he passes a man in black shorts jogging in the humid night. Because, Sutcliffe would say, we have to lay our eggs! "Because," he said on many occasions, pushing a gob of saliva to the edge of his lower lip, "I want to merge my Unity with your Oneness." Because no matter how *gemütlich* the dinner party, the lighted candles, the tasteful flower arrangement, the minute the door closed behind you, any reasonably sensitive soul had to run, not walk, to the bar or baths to assuage that psychic wound resulting from failure to bond with Dad. In fact, the nicer the dinner, the faster you raced to the Everard afterward. Oh God, thinks Lark as he passes yet another glistening shirtless runner, do you never acquire the object? Do you never get to rest? Do you have to keep going till your knees start to lock, like Ernie's, and you ask them to help you afterward, or you get punched in the nose by your dance partner because you tried to kiss him, or you end up at Tea Dance sobbing when old friends come up to you because there are so many gone or on their way out?

No. "It was the apartment of a man dying," said a friend who went with Lark one day to pick up Sutcliffe for lunch. "The minute I walked in, I saw that there wasn't a single personal touch in the whole place. He had either given it all away or it was all stored someplace, and he didn't care. And that ficus tree! That dying fig tree! It was all I could do to keep from asking if I could give it water. You blocked it out," he said to Lark, who could not remember the tree at all. "You refused the information. But I could tell the minute we walked through the door—this man was dying."

A fact I never like to face, thinks Lark. Except now he's dead, and I am driving down San José Boulevard at eleven o'clock at night, after yet one more stillborn attempt to Only Connect, and I ask myself, What would Sutcliffe do? Funny, the dead don't always leave a legacy; sometimes you have to discern one, for your own purposes. But nobody leaves a Letter-to-Be-Opened-After-My-Death evaluating your mistakes and telling you just what you have to do to live happily ever after. You have to write the letter yourself. Because I *am* faced with a problem, he thinks. I'm still alive. Which means: I have more Time than they did. I have Time that they did not. The problem is, I don't know quite what to do with it. "I just don't see the future," he said to Sutcliffe one day as they sat beside the invisible dying ficus tree, the tree he never could remember, the tree their friend had seen the significance of the moment he walked in the door. "I just don't see the future."

"That's because you're a pessimist, dear," said Sutcliffe, as he leaned forward to brush the ash from his cigarette against the plate of Brie. "You think the future is provided by kids, and we didn't have any. No kids, no future. For you it's that simple."

"But then—what am I supposed to do? Cruise for the rest of my life?"

"Yes," he said. "That's *exactly* what you have to do. Cruise for the rest of your life."

"But—"

"No buts, dear. Just do it!"

"I can't," said Lark.

"You have to," said Sutcliffe.

"But—"

"No, no!" he said, his voice rising.

"What?"

"You're going to wallow. I can feel it coming on," he said. "And, whatever you do with the rest of your life, that's the one thing you can't do. *Don't wallow!*" he said.

But I am, thinks Lark as he drives past the old du Pont estate, now condos for yuppies. I'm wallowing. I've been wallowing for years. I'm wallowing in death. ("One should strike a balance," said the priest who came each Saturday to give his mother communion. "One should try for, here as everywhere, a golden mean. To be ignorant of Death, to ignore it altogether, would be foolish. But to despair over it, to lose heart, to be paralyzed, is equally wrong. Death gives Life its meaning. Always remember: Christ rose from the dead. To triumph over death. In Him, we live forever." But we don't, thinks Lark, we don't at all, unless you believe Christ is the Son of God. That's why He had to rise from the dead. Would people have believed in Him otherwise? No. He had to be able to guarantee the big miracle, against the big terror: He who believes in Me will have life everlasting.) Well, here I am, believing basically in zilch, on Route 13 in Jacksonville. Because I see no future, and the present is never enough. I'm wallowing! he thinks as he pulls into an Exxon station.

The last man is always the handsomest—the attendant at the Exxon station just before the turnoff to 295. Around eleven they change shifts, and he has to wait while they count the money in the cash register. It's the young who get the graveyard shift. The slender youth taking the money from the older man wears a uniform of brown pants and striped shirt, with sleeves rolled up; he has dark bushy hair, a very thin moustache; his thick fingers are already stained with grease as he counts change in the palm of his hand. The handsomest is always the last, he thinks watching him, the last one you see before you're free of the neon, the strip malls, the plastic shit of expanding Jacksonville.

His father, on the trips his family made out west during the summer, was always friendly to the men working the gas pumps; it annoyed Lark as a ten-year-old to see the affection and good humor lavished on strangers he'd never see again. Why isn't he that way with us? he wondered in the back of the car as his father traded pleasantries and jokes with the man filling the tank with gas. Now, years later, Lark understands perfectly: The friendship, the goodwill, the bond you feel with people who run gas stations in the dead of night, are felt because you never *will* see them again. They stand outside your life, know nothing of you, nor you of them, and so—perfect strangers shorn of all that make us little, dull, and selfish; two lives meeting that will otherwise never mesh—you feel the same bond you feel sexually with a man you have no intention of exchanging a single word with. That's my problem with Becker, thinks Lark: Becker wanted me to be a gas station on 301; I wanted him to be Home. How on earth do people stay married?

Once he leaves the Exxon station and crosses the Buckman Bridge, there is a great sense of relief, out on the dark, broad river; Jacksonville glows in the distance, like the planet earth seen from the space shuttle, a small bright cloud of light, and he is startled that he is so far south of it already. Then, across the St. Johns, off the freeway, he plunges into the tangerine radiance of Blanding Boulevard, which at this hour, with little traffic, looks like a giant bowling alley. He glances into each car he pulls up beside at every stoplight, as if once someone will look back and understand, and they will pull off the road together. But they never do. He should tape a cardboard sign on his window: WILL SUCK COCK FOR FOOD. But he doesn't. Instead he keeps hoping for a hitchhiker all the way to Middleburg, where the highway divides (Starke to the right) and darkness engulfs everything. There are a few cars on the road; it's slightly cool, even in August.

The next thing he comes to, half an hour later, is the stoplight at Highway 16. The light is red; he stops and falls into a deep pool of silence—on all four sides of the intersection there is nothing but pinewoods and darkness. The family that sells watermelons, peaches, and tomatoes at the southwest corner has folded its tent and gone away. The walls of pine at Camp Blanding are twenty feet high on all sides. At midnight, at the empty intersection, there is for one instant while the light glows red a perfect peace, a perfect solitude, and a perfect moonlight.

But it lasts only a moment. With a soft clunk the light changes color, and he depresses the gas pedal, thinking, as he crosses Highway 16, that he is now entering the zone in which lies Becker. Between the stoplight and the town in which Becker lies in bed is a farm with haystacks in the field and, across from it, along the highway, gigantic spools of wire and the cement pillars that the electric company is erecting all the way down to his town—a *fait accompli* citizens, alarmed by the rumor that power lines cause brain cancer, can only protest. After the farm is the junction with County Road 305, a fire tower, a few fields in which wisps of fog lie, a church with a portable sign that says YOU STAND TALL WHEN YOU KNEEL FOR JESUS.

Then everything changes: the convenience stores, used-car dealer, real-estate office, aerobics club, mobile home lot, lumberyard, hardware store, and Sears warehouse that have made the west side of town a miniature version of Blanding Boulevard. He turns left at a pet store, passes the sign that says CAUTION: SENIOR CITIZENS AHEAD, and stops at the post office—his last chance for any form of contact with another human being at this hour—and, after finding six solicitations from nonprofit corporations in his mailbox, he pauses in the lobby to read the "Most Wanted" FBI page with the photograph of a criminal, a description that includes "Known to frequent discotheques." I used to frequent them myself, thinks Lark, and he leaves the post office, its empty, lighted lobby the final seal of solitude.

A week ago he would have driven by Becker's house just to see if the windows were lighted, but it is late now, and a week later. The main street of the town is lighted and empty. It's lovely, like a person sleeping. As the radio plays Lully's music for the entrance of the Sun King into Notre Dame, he considers driving right through the town all the way to the boat ramp to make an entrance of his own. But the chance of finding someone there at that hour is slim, and he slows down instead to turn onto the dirt road that leads to his house, repeating in a low monotone Shakespeare's description of Lust: "The expense of spirit in a waste of shame."

When his father was alive, even though he usually went to bed at seven or eight o'clock, Lark would come home from the baths at four in the morning to find him sitting up and eating ice cream and watching a movie on TV. Lark never said a word, nor did his father; his father merely waved his hand, Lark waved back and went down the hall to his bedroom—like two ghosts meeting in a haunted house, or two soldiers who are held over after their platoons ship out and live in an otherwise deserted barracks.

Now his father consists of a small white jar of ashes on a shelf in the living room. Lark picked him up at the post office a week after he was cremated. He found one of those yellow slips in the mailbox that mean you have a package, went to the desk, and received, from one of the pleasant gray-haired women to whom his father had always given a box of Fannie May candy at Christmas, his father in a cardboard box. He opened the small white jar in the car and thought, For years my father came here every day to get the mail; today he *is* the mail. And Lark drove home with him on the seat of the car and put him on the shelf. So now when Lark returns home from the baths—at a much earlier hour, years deeper into middle age and more attached to a good night's sleep—there is no one sitting up watching TV, no one to wave to in silence before going to bed. His father is gone, and he went in so quick, so decisive, a way, it is hard even to feel sad about the event; to feel sad would be to question a decision his father had made, and *that* Lark has never done. His father died in a calm and businesslike fashion, because he had made a decision to proceed to the inevitable. Lark and his mother are superstitious in comparison, afraid of many things, including Death. His father was not. His father had taken care of everything in advance—summoned his son to his bedside; had the papers drawn up, the power of attorney signed; and then proceeded to turn his face to the wall and die.

"What did your father die of?" someone asked him later. "Boredom," he replied, "and those welfare mothers they used to put on the evening news just to upset viewers. Well, they gave my father a stroke." Actually it was while doing his taxes; he had long since given up on everything else—what his taxes were used for, that is—in a country that he and his generation had helped to reach its current incredible prosperity; it was too much to ask him to watch it fall apart. The day he had his stroke, he was using his calculator on the porch; Lark was reading in his room, thought he heard a voice, went out onto the porch, and saw his father sitting calmly in his chair in his red bathrobe. He said, "I think I've had a stroke. I can't lift my arm."

Lark crossed the room; he saw the arm his father could not lift from the table, and the small piece of Kleenex he'd put on a cut received when he had fallen against the window. Lark helped him hobble into his bed, and then went searching for the name of the doctor his father refused to divulge, knowing exactly what it would lead to; finally he found it, the ambulance was summoned, and two stout lesbians bore his father from the house upon a stretcher—two lesbians whose ambulance he followed to Gainesville, city of hospitals, city of Death, in an eerie silence—no siren, no sound, just the red light flashing as his father was borne across the flat green countryside by two daughters of Bilitis, as in a myth from ancient Greece; and then, after a brief cha-cha-cha between hospital and nursing home, Lark found himself one evening staring at the penis whose catheter his father was trying to pull out, and thought, So this is where I started—so small I issued through that aperture, and now so large, my cells having divided billions of times, I stand here a Gulliver beside my entrance hole into this world. And then his progenitor perished.

His father is still gone when he gets home from the baths years after this event, and going to bed in an empty house, Lark has come to realize, is not an experience to be taken lightly. He considers it evidence of some profound failure, in fact, and each time he comes home he scans the door as if there might be a message taped to it from some visitor who came while he was away.

The only visitor he finds this night, however, when he walks around the house to look at the moonlight before turning in, has a big, bushy tail, delicate ears, and a pointed head, in silhouette on the bright expanse of grass surrounding his father's favorite oak tree by the lake. In a novel of magic realism, this would be his father's ghost—no longer watching television at four in the morning, hunting instead for rodents and birds—but Lark thinks magic realism is dumb. In real life, it's only a fox. They stare at each other for several minutes. He gets down on his haunches, the fox lies on the grass, and they continue to regard one another, while the twinkling lights of a passenger jet cross the sky above them. Finally someone is cruising him: The only other nocturnal hunter in the neighborhood. It's so satisfying to be stared at, he crouches there until the animal rises, five minutes later, and walks away. And with that, the spell is broken. The fox disappears into the sweet myrtle, and he goes into the dark house.

The Middle of the Night

~~~~~~

To his complete surprise, Lark finds himself drowsy when his head touches the pillow—usually he's still driving the car at sixty miles an hour, punishing himself for having made that foolish trip, for thinking that any of his failures can be obliterated in the embrace of another human being—and the next thing he knows, he's wide awake, although it's still pitch-black outside. He has no idea what time it is—probably three. He lies there fully alert, as if he has to be up on deck for the invasion of France. Across the hall, no one is sleeping. He used to love lying here years ago, on his visits home, listening to the sound of his parents' breathing in their beds—the three of them embarked on some ship, sailing through the dead of night, together. The only sweeter sound was rain on the roof. Tonight it isn't raining. It's dead quiet, still, and dark.

He gets up and, keeping his eyes closed, uses his hands to feel the corner of the wall as he goes out, makes a left, and enters the bathroom—thinking of his blind uncle, who got around his house in Chicago that way for ten years after his wife died. Where is Joe? he wonders as he stands above the toilet. With God? And: Where's God? God is not in heaven, or in the sea, or in the clouds or sky, or in the tabernacle or the cathedral in which mass is being celebrated. He's in the bathroom at three in the morning. That's where He is. In the middle of the night. When you stand above the toilet bowl, face-to-face with Reality.

That's where my roommate was, he thinks after he returns to

bed and lies there wide awake in the warm darkness. Except that Joshua didn't kill himself in the bathroom—he did it in the kitchen. He did it at the big round table in the kitchen of their apartment in New York, presumably while watching television: took the pills in the middle of the afternoon, probably, lost consciousness, and eventually fell off the chair onto the floor, where he lay for a few days until the friend who was supposed to go with him to the theater on Friday night came down after getting a disconnect message when he telephoned—Joshua had taken care of everything—knocked on the door, and called the police. Poor Eric, thinks Lark now, having to discover Joshua. Oh, the mess of death. Unappetizing, to say the least. Joshua lay on the linoleum floor, leaking, and eventually the couple across the hall, who were just about to call the police when Eric arrived, began to detect an odor. (That's how I'm going to die, thinks Lark. The Odor Method. I'll be living alone somewhere, and the only way anybody will learn I'm dead is the odor of my decomposing flesh.) When he went up to New York after receiving the news of Joshua's suicide, Lark found nothing but a stain on the kitchen floor. He got a mop, a bucket, and a can of Comet and scrubbed the stain. That's how he said good-bye to Joshua.

Joshua always believed he'd get AIDS: Joshua told him so as early as 1983, just before Lark left the apartment building one day to go uptown to see Eddie at Lenox Hill Hospital. Joshua's friends at the gym were getting it; his best friend, Robert, went home to West Virginia and died without even telling Joshua he had it; and Joshua got scared. And lonely. All those attempts to distract himself—the sign language lessons, the new circle of deaf queens, the macrobiotic cooking school—didn't work. Instead, he got depressed. When people get depressed, they lose their personalities, they lose all the qualities that made you love them—the wit, vitality, sense of humor, smarts. They just become Sad. Sadness is uniform; it excludes all other qualities.

Coming back to the apartment on his visits to New York, Lark found Joshua sitting by himself in the kitchen, watching Tom Brokaw, with a bowl of baked squash and brown rice in front of him; Lark knew there was nothing to say to him that would break through the gloom. Joshua was smart. Joshua saw what was happening, what was to come, and Joshua was scared. So he became earnest and good. He kept all his macrobiotic meals in Tupperware in the refrigerator and Lark was no longer allowed to touch those; Joshua was keeping kosher. He came back one day telling Lark rapturously about a woman at the school who cooked for cancer patients. Oh boy, thought Lark, the Florence Nightingale Era begins. The Alternative Medicine Epoch.

One night Lark read the macrobiotic bible—a bald Japanese man, who seemed to be the founder of the concept, believed we should eat only locally grown foods, and that the nuclear family was ideal. Lark dared not crack a joke about it—till one day he realized, Joshua doesn't exist anymore. The Joshua I knew. The Joshua who could break me up by singing "Don't Leave Me This Way" in the prim, sharp voice of Julie Andrews as he stood at the sink, washing dishes. The Joshua who used to hang his muscular body over the windowsill of the Sheridan Square Gym and give Anna Magnani's speeches from *The Fugitive Kind* for the passersby. That Joshua died before he killed himself. AIDS killed laughter too.

Even Eddie lost his sunny disposition for a while. "How are you?" said a friend from Seventh Avenue one day when he got on the elevator and found Eddie, Lark, and Clovis between floors.

"I have the new gay cancer," Eddie said.

"Oh," said the man, crestfallen and silent till he got out at the next floor. Clovis turned to Eddie and, assessing his gaunt appearance, hissed, "Couldn't you have said you've been swimming *laps*?" (Four years later Clovis, his right leg amputated, died in a hospice near Times Square.)

So when Lark went up to see Eddie in Lenox Hill, he may

have felt, as he entered the hospital, as if he were walking into a hotel in Miami Beach; but despite the sunny cheer of the lobby and the woman who asked whom he wished to visit—Eddie was limited to ten minutes of visitors twice a day—his heart sank when he saw Eddie's nearly closed door plastered with signs bearing skulls and crossbones, advising visitors to don a gown and mask. I haven't worn a gown since graduation, thought Lark, as he peeked around the edge of the door.

Eddie lay in bed with tubes in his nostrils supplying oxygen, far skinnier than he had been the day Clovis advised him to explain his appearance by saying he was exercising excessively in the pool, his face reduced to a pair of burning, angry, big, dark eyes, looking like a very old man who had been mugged. Lark went in. And Eddie, to his credit, entertained him—Lark's first lesson in the paradox of visiting the sick: It's often the sick who put the well at ease—and when he rose to say good-bye, Eddie took a folded towel from the table, laid it across his forehead, and said, "Well?" Lark, at the door, stared. "Don't you think I look just like Mother Teresa?" said Eddie.

And Lark, at the door, said, "Yes," and, after saying good-bye, walked down the corridor thinking, He just did drag, that was a joke. Only I can't laugh anymore, it's too horrible, I just can't laugh.

Laughter was one of those joys the plague eliminated, the way it eliminated everything else. There was just one affect now: Sad. When he entered the apartment for the first time after Joshua's death, he was frightened—he pushed the door open just an inch or two, as if the accumulated sadness of Joshua's last year was still pent up in the room, like some monster in a cursed tomb; but when he finally stepped inside and gently closed the door behind him, there was nothing to be afraid of. It was just sad. An empty, sunny set of rooms, covered with dust, the cat gone, and the silence that was the best feature of the place still intact. Across the fire escape, a woman was putting laundry on a line, while her radio played softly; the neighborhood was as quiet and gentle as an Italian hill town at two in the afternoon. He alone was here remembering Joshua. He alone was aware that the gentle sunlight and silence in the apartment was compounded with the exhaustion of a particular life, its struggle spent and finally resolved.

Slowly Lark began to look around and, gaining courage, notice things. The first thing he noticed was a photograph, the sort you find in *Playboy* or *Penthouse,* of a naked, big-breasted blond woman, tucked into the lower left-hand corner of the medicine cabinet—the sort of thing a young straight college student might put there to make shaving more entertaining. The next thing he noticed was a framed photograph he had never seen before, on the bookshelf: a handsome, bearded man smiling at the camera as he held a tiny infant, presumably his own, in the air above his chest. A friend, Lark surmised, from the macrobiotic cooking school. The third thing he noticed was a quotation from Saint John, attached to the refrigerator door on one of those magnetic plastic plaques, that said, "In the twilight of Life, there is only Love." And the last thing he noticed was in a drawer he opened, a piece of paper on which Joshua had written in big letters: I DON'T LOOK IN YOUR DRAWERS, DO I?—as if he'd foreseen this moment, as if he knew Lark would come back and go through his things for an explanation.

At that moment Lark stepped back, as if Joshua himself had reached out and slapped him; then he sat down in the kitchen to collect himself, in the vacant, sad stillness of the empty apartment, and thought, Maybe Joshua was crazy, but he was crazy for a reason nobody gives much credence to anymore— he was dying, like some heroine in Henry James, for lack of love.

"Look," he said to Sutcliffe that evening, when Lark took him into the bathroom to show him the photograph of the big-breasted blonde tucked into the corner of the medicine cabinet mirror. "And look," he said, showing him the framed photograph of the bearded man with a baby on his chest. "And look," he said, showing him the quotation from Saint John on the refrigerator.

"Joshua was trying to go straight," said Sutcliffe.

"That's what I think," said Lark, as they sat down at the big round table in the kitchen—the table where they all had carefully placed the pills they would take when they went dancing, and wrapped them in little packets of aluminum foil (some to get high, some to come down)—and Sutcliffe removed his scarf, and the wind rattled the windowpanes, and Lark remembered the old excitement of winter nights deep in February when they would all set out from this kitchen to the clubs. "He saw no future in homosexuality," said Lark. "He thought, Maybe if I shave every day with a picture of a naked woman on the mirror, I can have a son too, like my friend at the macrobiotic cooking school. He ended up in a no-man's-land. He wasn't straight, and he didn't want to be gay anymore. He was in neither camp, he belonged to neither tribe, and he got lonely," he said, handing Sutcliffe the note he'd found in the drawer that afternoon. "He knew we would be doing this," said Lark. "He knew we would be going through his drawers."

"Joshua wasn't stupid," said Sutcliffe.

"He was brilliant," said Lark. "He could have been a brain surgeon—instead he chose to copy-edit Candlelight Romances like *Shalom, My Love.* Was that homosexuality too? I don't know. I do know he could never accept promiscuity, though. He was genuinely baffled when men with lovers slept with other men. He used to come back from the gym or baths and tell me all the gossip, but I think on some level it really shocked him, he deeply disapproved. He was a romantic, and that's what happens to romantics," he said, looking at the stain on the linoleum. "Of course, you can never know, with suicides, why they really did it. But it's funny. He used to say the only way he would ever leave this apartment was on a stretcher—and he was right. Because I deserted him," said Lark.

"You deserted him?" said Sutcliffe, getting up and opening the refrigerator with the quotation from Saint John.

"Yes," said Lark. "By going to Florida. He always asked me when I came back how my mother was—as if she was getting any better. Which was nice of him. But I still think he felt I had abandoned him. And I wasn't the only one. Robert got sick, went back to West Virginia, and died, without even telling Joshua. His best friend! Joshua's own family hadn't spoken to him in years, since they kicked him out when he told then he was gay."

"It's still done, dear," said Sutcliffe, "in darkest Brooklyn today. Is that where they are?"

"Queens," said Lark. "He always pretended his mother was a lesbian living in La Défense with a lover, but it was all made up: a fabrication, like so much that he told me. She's really a house-wife in Queens who couldn't accept her son's homosexuality. Somewhere I got the impression she told Joshua she didn't want to tell his father because he had a heart condition. The rest Joshua made up. I once asked him why he did that. He said, 'Because real life is so drab.' It certainly turned out that way," he said, looking around the room in the light of the ceiling fixture. "Life was wonderful for him for a moment, for several years, and then— crash."

"Joshua was high-strung," said Sutcliffe, pouring two glasses of wine. "Neurotic. He could have been a neurosurgeon, yes. Instead he made homosexuality his career. Instead he went to the gym three hours a day. Does it bother you to eat the tomato and mozzarella here on the table where he took the pills?" he said, looking at Lark. "Because if it does, let's go to Spaghet-teria."

"No, no," murmured Lark, thinking, We must be sensible.

And he sat there watching Sutcliffe arrange alternate slices of cheese and tomato on the bias, and then sprinkle it all with olive oil and sprigs of basil. *"Ecco,"* said Sutcliffe, sitting down. "It's important to make a nice plate," he said, as the wind shook the windows in their frames. "That's what I learned in Rome. That's what this country—where Beauty is not listed on the stock exchange—is just beginning to admit. That it matters how the tomato and the mozzarella are presented on the plate."

"Just beginning to admit?" said Lark. "This country is nothing *but* making pretty. We invented advertising! That's what our culture consists of—making products pretty!"

"Now, now," said Sutcliffe.

"That's what gay life was too, before this happened—only it wasn't tomato and mozzarella, it was tits and ass!"

"And purple dick," said Sutcliffe, raising his glass for a toast. "Here's to Joshua, wherever he may be."

"Why do *you* think he did it?" said Lark.

"She was nuts," said Sutcliffe calmly, cutting a tomato slice in half. "She was completely nuts."

"You don't think it was because he was terribly alone—me in Florida, so many friends dead? You don't think he had just reached an impasse, where he decided homosexuality didn't work and he couldn't be straight either, where all avenues of affection were cut off to him? You don't think he simply saw the bone that lies beneath the flesh?"

"We're *all* alone, we *all* have lost friends, we're *all* scared of dying," said Sutcliffe. "We *all* see the bone beneath the flesh, we *all* know we're getting older and our breasts have fallen," he said, "straight and gay. She was nuts."

"Nuts?" said Lark. "Or more intelligent than the rest of us?"

"Nuts," said Sutcliffe, slicing his mozzarella. He leaned forward and said, "It's very hard to remember, it's very hard not to get a little crazy over all of this, but try to repeat—it's just a germ. It's *not* God's judgment on us, it's *not* what we deserve, it's *not* what everyone thinks it is—divine justice—it's a germ that used to live in a green monkey in Africa, and decided to come to New York. Why not? New York is fun. Or it used to be. I was in Chicago last week for a conference—'Can Man Plan?'—and when I got back to La Guardia, I was so glad to be home—"

"Because New York is the only city that—"

"Stop," he said. "New York is the only city. This is the only city, and now it's a cemetery," he said, "because of a stupid germ."

"You don't think—"

"No! Don't moralize!" he said. "You're always trying to find the moral! You were like this before the plague! Your parents want you to be happy—they told you so—but you won't believe them! Because you're a Calvinist! A puritan! You don't think the tomato and the mozzarella matter at all!"

"I do, I do," said Lark, "it's just that—"

"You want to dwell on the imperfection. The Jesuits call it morose delectation. That's why you and Joshua got on so well— he was a rabbi, and you are a priest! More wine?"

"No, thanks," said Lark. "I think Joshua was just—trapped. He looked for a Hot Daddy all those years, and when the Daddies all died, he decided *he* should be a real one. Have a child. But he couldn't. So he got lonely."

"Everyone's lonely," said Sutcliffe. "She was nuts." He looked down at the spot on the floor. "More Comet," he said, "and some bleach." And with that, they scrubbed the stain once more, washed the dishes, and went to the Jewel.

The Divine Pollen

~~~~~~

Children, Lark thinks when he finally gets up before dawn, and walks out to get the newspaper on the dirt road behind the house, are what give meaning to most people's lives: the creation of the next generation. As Gore Vidal said, the solution to the problem of Life is more Life. No solution at all, of course, but it keeps everything going till one is found. Like interferon and all the other medicines Eddie took.

On the road to Gainesville that afternoon, Lark finds himself behind the school bus, wondering if Becker's daughter will get off. The sky is soft gray, the dust raised on the dirt roads white. Years ago, when he first had to drive, he did not even know one was obligated to stop for the school bus; driving down a road in the suburbs of Chicago, he saw the red lights flashing and, at the very last moment, the alarmed face of the driver, as Lark sped nearer and the little red stop sign popped out from the side of the bus; and it dawned on him that he must stop.

He regards the school bus now with a certain awe—even if he knows it's filled with bullies and brats trying to inflict pain on gentler children—as he watches them get off the bus at the dirt road that leads into a pod of trailers among the pine trees on the shores of Lake Sampson. Nothing has changed: Some kids get off by themselves, walk over to a mailbox, open the lid, then flip it back in disgust. (They need mail too, he thinks. Perhaps I can spend the rest of my life writing children letters.)

Others get off in clusters, laughing, sparring with each other. The whole moment of getting out of school is unchanged—the vacancy, the loneliness, the question "Will Mother be drunk or sober?," the problem of what to do back home before dinner: where to go, whom to play with, how to avoid chores. Problems that *still* plague me, he thinks.

Just past a small nursing home—A COUNTRY VILLA, the sign says—whose six residents are sitting on metal chairs on the driveway on this sunny afternoon, the bus stops again and a solitary youth descends with his blue plaid shirt unbuttoned in the heat, a bookbag slung over his shoulder, and a torso that reminds Lark of the Elgin Marbles: the problem of Beauty. He watches the young man take off his blue plaid shirt and walk down the dirt road, the youth obviously aware that everyone in the cars stopped behind the bus can see him—as if they've stopped, thinks Lark, not to ensure his safe passage but to pay homage to his beauty; and he thinks of all the years he has expended in pursuit of this quality distributed so randomly among the populace, as likely to be found at two-thirty in the afternoon on a dirt road in Florida as in some bar in New York. You can't keep track of it, he thinks.

So he passes the car in front of him after the bus turns off, as if the sooner he gets to the nursing home, the more quickly he can wipe out, cancel, refute the hopelessness of his own obsession, the years wasted with nothing to show for them; as if, with one act of kindness, one corporeal act of love, one single line ("I'm so glad to see you; you have no idea how much I have to tell you; quick, get me out of here!"), he can refute the last twenty-four hours of his meaningless life. He has no time to stop at the boat ramp. Let the others sit and wait—and wait and wait—for someone to drive in. He hasn't the patience.

He drives on past the abandoned pecan farm whose fifty acres of trees were ruined when the owner sprayed them with treated sewage and accidentally killed them; past the next farm, which still survives, though five of its trees were tainted with the fecal mist; past the line of forest that whoever owns it recently enclosed in a fence; the open field of a ranch confiscated years ago as part of a drug bust; the feed store at the turnoff to Earleton; and finally the long stretch to Highway 301, whose trees have moved the past ten years from one side of the road to the other, like the forest in *Macbeth,* as the timber owners harvest one stand of pines and reseed another. At 301 he comes to a stop and watches the big trucks and the station wagons whose roofs are covered with luggage under flapping tarpaulins drive by—hell-bent for Disney World. Then the light changes and he drives through Orange Heights, past the big white house where a young man from Boston, who used to go to the boat ramp but now lectures high-school students on the dangers of HIV, lives; past the white Baptist church where, every Saturday morning, a handsome man mows the lawn with his son; past woods that are now being cut down for a reason he does not know but that worries him; past the turnoff to Windsor, where two men are selling collard greens from the back of their truck; past the blueberry farm he visits when the berries are ripe; past the juvenile detention center, the home for unwed teen-age mothers, the Lamplight Trailer Park, the airport, and finally the stoplight at Waldo Road.

He's in Gainesville now. He's in a smart, expanding, booming university town that he should want to live in but doesn't, he's not sure why; he turns left on Sixth Street and drives down to Eighth Avenue and then crosses town to the nursing home.

That evening a paramedic passes his mother's doorway while they are watching *Wheel of Fortune.* Five eight, stocky, V-shaped torso with noticeable tits beneath a powder-blue T-shirt, massive biceps, a perfect butt in dark blue slacks, black boots—the paramedic causes Lark to stand up and wheel his mother into the hall the moment the game show pauses for a commercial. There a stretcher sits in the corridor, waiting to bear someone away; he walks two doors down, peers in, and finds a cluster of men kneeling over a patient he cannot see.

"Mrs. Renaldi," says one of the aides.

"No!" Lark and his mother say together. One of their favorites. A woman with a sense of humor who has been deteriorating lately, pestering the nurses about her medicine, stopping Lark in the hall to say she is looking for her daughter and cannot find her. All these women look for their children! Earlier that week, he had to assure another lady, standing in her doorway, that her son did not have to go to the hospital, that he has returned to work, that she could go to bed and not worry. "Is that true?" she said over and over again.

"Yes, it's true," he said.

Now Mrs. Renaldi. They all crack eventually; if you have your mind when you enter, you won't for very long. What other response is there to the fact that there is no hope, that you will never leave the place?

His mother has been saying lately, "I have a proposition. I'm eighty-four, I only have a couple years more, I'll pay for the nurses: I want to go home, where I belong." Unassailable words. She wants to die at home—like men in prison. She does belong at home. Everybody does, thinks Lark. The idea that she can come home only when she's dying—when there is a fixed limit on the visit—is ironic, but it's true. He can't imagine bringing her home for good. Whatever freedom he has now would be gone. Freedom to sit in his car at the boat ramp, hoping someone wonderful will drive in; freedom to walk the hallways of the baths; freedom to waste the freedom he has and she does not— but freedom nevertheless. He listens to her make her proposition and lowers his eyes. It's heartbreaking. But so is everything at the nursing home. The original Heartbreak Hotel.

And here is Mrs. Renaldi, 102, on the floor, surrounded by paramedics, handsome as archangels about to bear her off to Heaven. Outside, through the glass door, he sees the red lights at the rear of the ambulance. They wait, he and his mother, to see them put her on the stretcher, thinking it might help her to see friends; but nobody comes out.

"She fell, she's been dizzy," says the aide. "She fell and cut her head and it's bleeding quite a bit." Get out of my way, thinks Lark, I'm waiting to see the paramedic in the blue T-shirt, the one with the perfect butt, massive biceps, and beautiful, silken dark hair. Who gets to sleep with him? he wonders. The lucky soul, whoever it is.

They wait and wait. No one comes out. He suggests they return to his mother's room, but she says, "No." She adds, "I want to wish her luck." But nobody comes out. Finally, he takes his mother back to her room to see the Bonus Round; when he comes out again, a Chinese-American doctor from Newport Beach has won $37,567, and the hallway is empty. The stretcher and the ambulance are gone, and in the doorway of the room sit a washbucket and a mop, to clean up the blood. Mrs. Renaldi's wheelchair, her name written on a piece of masking tape stuck to the back, sits empty in the hallway, like a horse without its rider, or an abandoned ship, adrift. My God, he thinks, that's all it took—one Bonus Round—for her to disappear. She's gone. Someone, he thinks, will have to call her son and tell him that his mother has fallen and cut her head and has been taken to the hospital. Someone will have to call and tell him he's about to be an orphan.

After *Wheel of Fortune*, they watch *Crossfire*, a debate about Bosnia; then *Murder, She Wrote*, an episode about a cursed jewel he has seen nine times; and then, as *Larry King Live* begins an interview with Carl Reiner, he puts his mother to bed. "Think about my proposition," she says as he turns out the light and makes ready to leave. "I'm eighty-four, I've only a couple more years. I should be home where I belong." What a genius she has, he thinks as he kisses her good night, for the killing phrase. He picks up his copy of *The New York Times*, tucks it under his arm. "Do you still miss New York?" she says. He doesn't know what to say. "I'd go with you, if you want to move back," she says.

"And leave your house?" he says. "And the neighbors? What about the neighbors?"

"So what?" she says. "I can make new friends."

That's more than I can do, he thinks as he bends down once more to pantomime a kiss, three times, on alternate cheeks. I can't stand new people.

"I want to tell you something," she says. "Everyone should have a son like you." He doesn't know if this is something an aide or nurse told her, or if she means it; and he can't tell her what he really feels—that he admires *her* for enduring her loss without complaining—because he's afraid that telling her he thinks her situation is horrible will make her more conscious of that; he does not know, he cannot guess, what delicate form of acceptance, what profound stoicism, has allowed her to get through an experience like this. Her last on earth. No one should have the last part of life a horror, which includes everyone he's known who died of AIDS. People should go out on a grace note, with a good memory. Instead, life saves the worst for the end. His mother had a good life, but she's ending it with this: a precursor of purgatory. You've more than paid for your sins by now, he thinks as he looks down at her; you're working on other people's at this point. He wishes that somehow she could become unparalyzed—while she is still alive—so that they could look back on the past and talk about it. But no, she's never going to walk, never going to stand, never going to dress herself or go out the door of her own free will. She's going to end this way. Here. "It's true," she says again. "Everyone should have a son like you."

"Oh, Mother," he says, and bends down once more and kisses the air beside her cheek. "Sleep well. I'll see you on Saturday morning." And he walks out of the room, while she begs him to move her arm, just one more time, she's stuck this way all night—requests he has learned to ignore in order to make this exit. Oh, Mother, he thinks as he walks down the hall hoping he will run into nobody, the angels will stand with their trumpets when you arrive in heaven, and God will tell you it is all right now, your ordeal is over, your body is restored, and you can walk. And you will join all the people you loved, your mother, your father, your sisters and brothers, your husband, in the strength and beauty that were yours when I was a child and you took care of me, and you will be upright, and you will walk on, young again and beautiful, rewarded for all your patience and compassion and fair-mindedness while you were alive; and the shit you have had to eat these past twelve years, when you have been on the lowest rung of the ladder, at the mercy of even a fly, will not matter. Oh, Mother, he thinks as he rounds the corner by the nurses' desk and goes out the door into the hot night, you'll never know how much I admire you.

And with that he blinks his eyes and sees, out under the orange radiance of the lamppost, its light making thick the moisture in the air, a woman in her nightgown looking back at him. It's Mrs. Rowe. "Come back, come back!" he calls, and he rushes out, takes her by the arm, and leads her to the nursing home—the last time she made it all the way to the Red Lobster—where an aide takes her arm and thanks him.

My mother really would move to New York, Lark thinks as he walks to the car. Because she's bored, she wants something better than this. *She's* willing to start all over someplace else and make new friends. I'm the one who can't. I'm the one that's paralyzed, he thinks, getting in and opening two windows to let out the overheated air that has not cooled, three hours after sundown. And he drives away, wondering where in the United States he would go if he could—dragging his mother with him, like a Chinese man with his ancestor on his back. Los Angeles? New York? Boulder, Colorado? Easier instead to drive to the gay bar, where he finds a parking space opposite the entrance, turns off the engine to watch people enter and leave, hears the alcoholic regulars cackling inside, turns the engine back on, and drives off.

At the red light at Waldo Road he comes to a stop, thinking, Let's face it, life has not been normal since 1983. You have not had a shred of normal life in all that time, he thinks. You have seen many people suffer who did not deserve it. If anyone deserves to suffer. You left New York one evening in 1983 thinking you'd be gone twelve days, and twelve years later you're still gone. You and your mother have clung to each other. You've tried in some peculiar way to maintain a status quo that is, deep down, begging to move on. You've tried to arrest Time. Instead Time arrested you. Charged you with all its crimes, including the chief one: growing old. Your mother could start over, she really could, but you can't, he thinks, so lost in thought he does not even see the old white Oldsmobile that pulls up beside him or the girl in the front seat closest to him, who leans out of the window and, with her mouth a foot from his ear, shrieks at the top of her lungs. He jumps, startled. The other teen-agers in the car laugh; the girl who frightened him with her scream laughs loudest. It's a trick teen-agers play in Gainesville; it's happened to him once before.

Something in the girl's laugh—her youth, her ignorance of all that he is suffering and she will suffer if she lives long enough, the smug complacent wealth of American life, the mindless prosperity of driving around town on a joyride, the whole smugness of the county itself, adolescence and its dumb oblivion—makes him turn and say, "That was very funny. Do you have other things you do that are funny? Do you think you will find new ones before you grow up?" The girl who scared him leans out of the window and laughs again in his face. "Perhaps when you grow up," he says, "you'll think of even funnier things to do. I've just been with a quadriplegic, and I didn't find it funny at all."

The light changes; the teen-agers accelerate; he keeps pace beside them, screaming through the window as they speed down Thirty-ninth Avenue toward the point at which the two lanes merge, just past the drug rehabilitation center. My God, he thinks as he drives, that laugh, that hideous, stupid, callous, full-of-herself laugh! Just before the two lanes became one, aware they have a maniac at their side, the teen-agers floor the Oldsmobile so that it pulls ahead of Lark, whose Buick falls in close behind them and continues on their tail, faster and faster, past the Lamplight Trailer Park, till the stop sign at Highway 26, where they come to a squealing halt, and a boy in the backseat leans forward and flashes a peace sign with his right hand out of the window at Lark—who goes in the opposite direction, toward home, after the teen-agers turn south on 26. Touched by the peace sign the boy in the backseat extended to him, triply depressed for having behaved in this way, he thinks, It's just sleep, I need sleep, I'll feel better tomorrow, at Tara.

Good-bye

~~~~~~

Lark gets a flat the next day at the Shell station while he is filling the tank. A car sits on the other side of the divider, a big, old, rusted beige Oldsmobile filled with three small children, barefoot, in shorts and suntans, three small white-trash children, who look at him with the still, shy politeness of frightened monkeys, while their mother sits in the front seat in Levi's cutoffs and a soiled halter top, smoking a cigarette and waiting for her husband to return. "Do you know you have a flat tire?" she says.

He looks. "Thanks," he says.

A young man with a dark beard puts on the spare, as Lark wonders why auto mechanics all look like young men in Civil War photographs: and the next day he drives into Gainesville several hours before he has to appear at the nursing home and goes to Sears to get new tires. At Sears the young man who fills out the forms also looks like a handsome soldier at the Battle of Shiloh, and after everything has been arranged, Lark wanders off to kill the hour and a half it will take to put on the new tires and align them—an hour and a half he spends partly in a chair in the furniture section watching other handsome young men walk by with their families in tow, and partly looking for earplugs, in an aisle where he meets three kids who not only know where the earplugs are but have spent the entire day in that aisle playing with toys they have no money to buy, like water sprites who live in a sacred spring, and then he goes back to the auto repair counter and learns he forgot to leave the car keys behind. So now he must go across University Avenue with a new time assigned for his car pickup, the hour and a half wasted.

He doesn't even get angry with himself; he shows up at the nursing home in a calm mood. His mother, however, is agitated. He can't explain the cause. She won't stop making requests as he wheels her around: to be put to bed, then to get up again, to make sure the nurse knows she gets two extra-strength Tylenols at bedtime. Nothing seems to calm her; she won't stop talking. He puts her to bed after dinner and says, "I'm going to Sears to pick up the car, I'll be right back, I won't be five minutes," and he leaves her there lying in her brown pants and brown shirt, the outfit an aide selected for her earlier that day, and goes to Sears. He leaves her there with the curtain drawn across the window that looks out onto the courtyard because the light now hurts her eyes—and when he returns she seems to be asleep, till he approaches the bed and sees her eyes rolled back in her head, and a small stream of blood running from her lower lip as she makes a low sound caused by the scraping of her teeth. He runs down to the nurses' desk in a panic. A nurse comes back with him; they cannot rouse her; they bring oxygen and call the doctor. He says, "No hospital," because she didn't want to go the last time, and thus begins the moment they have been postponing for over a decade.

He sits there watching her breathe with the same feeling he had during his friends' memorial services: This isn't really happening. He cannot believe this is happening because he is so used to solving all the problems that have come up, the urinary tract infections, the bedsores, the broken arm, the muscle spasms, the skin irritation, the loss of weight, the depressions; her doctor has used her in lectures as an example of how to avoid bladder problems. The small obstacles have all been conquered. They have survived the loss of roommates, changed rooms, gotten used to new bed partners, new nurses; they have outlasted everyone in the place, except two or three people. Everyone has died, except her.

Even now, the oxygen revives her. In two days, she gets better. He drives her home. His mother has clearly had some sort of stroke, though the doctor calls it a seizure and explains the difference—but she is improved enough to be taken off the oxygen, and the next day they resume the routine they have maintained for twelve years now. On Sunday at home he gives her a bath; he puts her on a chair in the big shower, the shower in which he stood behind Becker, to soap his back. Instead he soaps his mother now. She shuts her eyes like a child in the stream of water, and he spreads the soapsuds all over her emaciated frame, this body she has surrendered all claims of modesty to. He washes her hair, her face, her feet, her toes. He lifts her into the towel-covered wheelchair and gently pats her dry, thinking how odd her silence is. For twelve years she has always fought with him at this moment—claimed, "You haven't rinsed me thoroughly, there's still soap in my eyes!" And he has said that this was impossible, she was utterly rinsed. This time she does not argue. He dries her, and sprinkles talcum powder on her body, and dresses her, and sets her up again on the pillows; then, as he is arranging the pillows, she asks him if they are paying him enough at his summer job at Brown's (the five-and-dime uptown). He says, "Yes," and then he lies down on the bed next to hers, the one his father retreated to when he had his stroke. He lies there, thinking, she is dying, and worried about my having a job. She thinks I have a job uptown at the five-and-dime. She wants me to work at Brown's, he thinks. And all the things he has not told her make his throat ache. She doesn't understand what is happening to her, he thinks, or she knows she is losing her grip on life; something is pulling her away—from earth, this room, these lamps and tables, me—and she is trying to stay here; the way she's furious when she awakes from a nap if I tell her she's been sleeping. She doesn't want to concede she is falling asleep now, he thinks, in a much deeper way.

At midnight, when she opens her eyes, he brings her ice cream; but she shakes her head after one bite. Ice cream was the last thing my father ate, he thinks—when they stop eating ice cream, that's it. Not even ice cream will keep her on earth. And he goes to bed with an old magazine, determined to sit up all night.

But like the apostles he fails. The lamp is still on when he awakes in the morning. He goes to his mother, touches her forehead, and feels a film of cold sweat, like dew on the hedge outside the window. Then he moves her to another room to have breakfast, and the seizures begin again.

The seizures are so bad he calls the nursing home and drives her there one last time, giving up all sentimental ideals of her dying at home. When he reaches Gainesville, a policeman who goes to his gym stops him for speeding on Thirty-ninth Avenue, but when Lark says his mother is sick and the policeman looks in the backseat, he lets him go with a grudging remark. At each stoplight Lark turns to look back. Her face is being twisted and contracted as if the folds of her flesh were attached to strings someone is pulling this way and that, in spasms that draw back her lips, her eyelids, her cheeks. The last cruelty, he thinks, as the arches of McDonald's come into view—the last insult to her body, a game someone is playing with it one last time, before it is discarded entirely, every drop of suffering and degradation wrung from it: Full Value.

The nurse on duty is not one they know well, but she is kind, gives his mother a shot of morphine, draws the curtain around the bed, and leaves them alone. Mrs. Klein, his mother's roommate, is in the Activities Room, playing bingo; a picture of Jesus on which someone has hung a rosary watches his mother, as it has followed and watched her in every room she has occupied in this place; it is quiet and cool, and the oxygen machine makes a soft whooshing sound. He sits in a chair beside the bed and strokes her silver hair, the hair that is so much thicker than his own now; he smooths it back against her temple over and over, as if he can smooth whatever it is inside her flooded brain that is causing the seizures. He pushes her hair back from her forehead, that beautiful wavy hair, and thinks, All deaths until now have been bearable. None of them counted, somehow, till this one. And now, they will all count. At midnight he kisses her good night and leaves.

The next day he drives back to the nursing home later than he might, because he is now like those people who never came to see her because it was too painful—even their favorite nurse, the one they have been with five years, has called in sick—and when he turns the corner, he sees a sign on the door of his mother's room that reads DO NOT ENTER, SEE NURSES' DESK, and he knows: It is over.

She looks, when he finally enters and walks around the curtain, as she has many afternoons when he arrived and found her sleeping—only this time she does not open her blue eyes, smile, and say, "Oh, I'm so happy you've come, I'm so happy." This time she lies there on the bed, eyes closed, her nightgown without a wrinkle, her skin cool to the touch. She might be napping on an ordinary afternoon. But now the oxygen machine has been turned off, and though the picture of Jesus continues to look at them, nobody comes to the room to give her medicine or food. He sits with her the rest of the afternoon, waiting for the undertaker.

And sitting there, he finally sees that Death has robbed him of all his artificial power—Death has made them equal again; Death has cured her paralysis, has taken away the awful advantage he had over her, has made her once more a "normal" person, equal to everyone else. And he sits there thinking, This woman who grew up in a pleasant suburb of Chicago during the twenties, so shy she would sit at the top of the stairs at the age of fourteen and refuse to come down to join people visiting in the living room, and then so beautiful she turned heads when she worked in the city, and still so beautiful when she went overseas with her husband, and then moved back to this country to a town she never found enough in to amuse her, and then this. This long punishment for imagined sins. All gone now. Along with the twenties, and Oak Park, and the big family that produced her and the America she grew up in: all gone. And he marvels at the length of her long humiliation, leans close, kisses her cheek, and says the last thing he will ever say to her, just as the undertaker knocks on the door: "I'm sorry for keeping you alive so long."

For that is how everything he has done seems to him now: an act of egotism on his part. He takes a yellow sweater, an eye-shade, the paperback life of Katharine Hepburn they never finished, the rosary, and the picture of Jesus, and walks out of the room. The administrator is in the hallway—even his thick black hair has begun to gray—and Lark starts to go toward him to talk, but the administrator says something that indicates that is all he wishes to say, so Lark changes course ever so subtly and walks to the nurses' desk, where he tells them to give the television and the wheelchair, which still has his mother's name on a piece of torn adhesive tape across the back, to someone who needs them. Then he walks out the front door into the warm afternoon, starts the car, drives out of the parking lot and on up the hill, even though this time, he realizes, he has no place to go; while three young women, students no doubt at the university, jog down the hill, their long shining hair bouncing in the sunlight—finished with classes for the day.

Good-bye for Real

~~~~~~

And now he begins to miss her. Now he begins to blame himself for all the nights he woke and screamed at her for awakening him—ranting at her across the space between their beds: How could he? All the mornings he awakes and goes to the porch to eat the same dull breakfast become all the mornings she awoke in her same room to have the same dull bowl of oatmeal. All the moments he lies on a sofa, staring out the window, turn into the moments she lay quietly on Saturdays, waiting for him to pick her up: How could he have made her wait? All the cruelties, the fatigue, the impatient way he shifted her from wheelchair to bed, come back to haunt him now. And, worst of all, the fact that he never went in on a Tuesday that whole summer, because, he thought, he needed to recuperate from the sleep-deprived weekend. "Surprise me," she said, more than once, about those Tuesdays. Why hadn't he surprised her? What else did she have to look forward to? All of that comes back, and he sees the depths of her helplessness, greater than he had allowed himself to think at the time.

That time is now completely gone, and all the things he did not say to her—that he admired her for her stoicism, good nature, never complaining—now make his face burn; and finally when he drives past the five-and-dime uptown, the store she imagined he had a summer job in, the depths of his failure, and her disappointment, crash down on him.

Then he drives to the ocean late one afternoon, and stops at a filling station near I-95, and discovers, when he gets to the beach, that he has left the cap off the gas tank. And he remembers all the times she said, each Saturday morning after he stopped at a gas station before leaving Gainesville, "Did you put the cap back on?" And he drives back and searches for it in vain.

Each Saturday morning he gets up and, instead of getting into the car and driving to Gainesville to pick her up, to free her from the nursing home, he goes nowhere; he takes books out of the town library and makes sure he has three or four to read, so that he won't have to think. But he does think. He thinks, We never foresee the real disasters—that's why they're disasters. We worry about one thing, but it's something else entirely that destroys us. The things we worry about don't get us, because we are on the alert. The things we've never bothered about get us instead. And that includes the way you've spent your life. There comes a time when you finally see what you've done with it. Whether or not God exists, there is a Day of Judgment: our own.

At least that is what he thinks when he wakes in the middle of the night now, and goes to the bathroom with his eyes closed so he won't awaken any more than he has to, feeling the wall with his hands. All other perceptions are simply the false product of daylight. The truth is in the middle of the night, he thinks, going next to a chest of drawers to find a set of earplugs to stifle the sound of the tree frogs rasping in the flower bed. Instead he finds in the top drawer a heap of unused condoms, still in their wrappers—the rubbers he has been collecting each time he's gone to the baths and the bar the past twelve years—and a photograph of Sutcliffe when he was younger. And he thinks of what Sutcliffe said one day before he died: "Life is madness. Madness." (And that was caused merely by his doorman's forgetting to tell him a package had arrived downstairs.) Lark looks back on his obsession with Becker as a symptom of his loneliness. Now he is lonely in a new way—a sense that the rest of his life will simply consist of killing time. That's all he has now: time—more time to kill, in his case. He has the freedom of failure. Nothing is required, because nothing seems to matter as much anymore; the people he cared for he has failed in some way—Sutcliffe crying at Tea Dance, his mother calling his name when he was not there. There is no way now to make reparations.

One night in Gainesville, leaving the mall, he sees Roy at a pay phone in the colonnade, dressed in his aide's uniform; and he stares in disbelief—as if the whole nursing home should have crumbled into dust, or shut down, the day his mother left. It has not; and he remembers instead the nights he would drive there after the gym, walk across the lawn behind the building to peer into his mother's room, and see her lying there, taking her five o'clock medicine from a nurse, unable to turn to the window when he began to tap on it, but still excited because she knew it was her son. Then he drives home.

At the stop sign near the post office, he sees Rick—scowling behind the wheel of his leopard-skin truck, waiting for a break in the traffic, squinting in the sun, worried about his credit card debt, his sculptures, his own family. His worries, and Lark's desire to be his friend, seem a million miles away now as Lark lifts his forefinger from the wheel; by the time Rick recognizes him, he's gone by, and neither of them turns around and drives back to talk.

Our sexual lives are utterly solitary after all, he thinks; sometimes they cause other people to adhere to us for brief moments, or even lifetimes, especially those created by our flesh. Sometimes they do not. He will meet new people, he supposes, but they will always remind him of someone he has known already, someone gone. Eventually life can offer only a recycling of former happiness; or so he thinks, puttering around the house, waiting for dark before he goes out to the grocery store.

That night he goes to the grocery store at nine o'clock to get Fig Newtons. It is quiet inside. There is hardly anyone there. A very skinny old woman with glasses and bony hands, clutching her shopping list, stands behind her shopping cart in front of the broccoli next to a young woman; the old woman says, "You're sure they'll let me get two of these with coupons?" and the younger one replies, "Yes," and the old woman says again, holding her shopping list so taut between her bony hands he expects it to rip, "You're sure, with these coupons, they'll let me get two?" and her companion says, "Yes," and Lark walks by thinking, Eventually you end up with a volunteer from the Senior Citizens' Center to take you shopping, and the store policy on coupons assumes the terribleness of God. He wheels his cart to the long, low, open freezer to look for frozen yogurt. He is standing there, comparing the price of nonfat yogurt to that of nonfat ice cream, when he notices a tall, skinny, handsome man in faded jeans and a white T-shirt, standing at the end of the aisle, examining the frozen pizzas. He looks at the man and thinks, He's very handsome, but that's not Becker.

His hair is shorter for one thing, it does not spray up from his head like peacock feathers, and it isn't the same dark color—it's a plainer brown. He does have a big nose and a thick moustache, and he is burnished by the sun, but the chin seems smaller, and Lark does not even try to catch the man's eye; he goes to the checkout counter instead, and waits behind a drunken couple buying cheese and pretzels with food stamps, and a twelve-pack of beer with a ten-dollar bill. The cashier is weary. So is he. He looks up and sees his reflection in a small round mirror above the shelves of jellies and jams, and realizes it's the first time he has seen his face in a mirror in years—his hair bright silver, his white face gaunt. I look like Death. And he realizes his nightmare has come true, when he sees the man in the white T-shirt go by and disappear down the aisle of condiments: He has run into Becker again, a year later. Only Becker is still handsome, sun-burnished, thick-haired, skinny, and striking—and he is old, gray, and eccentric. He thanks the tired cashier, goes out into the parking lot, and sits there in the car, waiting for the man in the white T-shirt to emerge. He is sure it is Becker now, not because of his appearance so much as the nimble, nervous way the man moved about in the grocery store, with the same alert intensity Becker showed when looking for his lighter the night he went back to the bedroom of Lark's house before leaving for good.

And he thinks, The look in that man's face is also Becker's— the guarded, serious, absorbed-in-the-task-at-hand look of a mole burrowing through the earth, his big sensitive nose leading him to the store brand of mustard on sale for nine cents with Shoppers' Cash, sniffing, searching for the right items, both sex- ual and alimentary, as he darted about the store. That's Becker. Let's face it, he thinks as he watches the rain run down the windshield and waits for the man in the white T-shirt to come out of the store, Becker is more like than not that most common, garden variety of trick—the one who has sex but doesn't even say hello when he sees you in the bar the next night. One of my least favorite types, thinks Lark. A type I could not imagine existing here in this town, because it is so small. The very mis- take one makes at the boat ramp—the assumption that geo- graphical isolation induces intimacy. It doesn't.

He reduced me to a trick, Lark thinks, sitting there in the cold car. He reduced me to a trick. He waits tills the man in the white T-shirt comes outside, and when he puts his bag of groceries into the backseat of a pale-green Taurus at the curb, something about the way he does it—with an air of hurry, a concentrated effort to perform this task quickly—makes him certain it is Becker. So, he thinks, he got a new car after all. The black Nissan is gone—even if "New cars are worth shit!" Lark starts his car; to his amazement, Becker's car falls into place behind his, as they leave the parking lot of the shopping center, its lights in the rearview mirror, and for a mile and a half back to town he relives that wonderful moment three years before when Becker followed him back from the boat ramp like an eager dog. Now Becker has a new car. And there is no relationship between them whatsoever.

Just before the stoplight, he sees Becker's turn signal flicker, and Becker turns right, down a side street that leads to the house Lark ascertained is his. The two of them alone, in the same town, on this rainy night, going back to separate houses, not even talking to each other.

The next day he awakes and goes outside to get the *Gainesville Sun* and notices the sky has changed. It's autumn. The heat is indistinguishable from the previous day's, but as he drives the light is different, falls at a different angle on the high grass, the pinewoods, the pastel-colored shacks outside Green Cove Springs where a few black people have introduced—with the big red Coke machine, the banana trees, the people sitting in the doorstep of a lime-green house with purple window trim— a note of the Bahamas. There's goldenrod along the road too, and purple beauty-berries, so lustrous and bright they look as if they're made of wax, and as he drives past the cemetery in Green Cove Springs where a friend who died of AIDS is buried, even that seems peaceful for the first time and not a place so hot you expect the pine trees to explode, and there is the sense that the earth is heading, thank God, away from the sun—which means that it is not too hot to sit with Ernie at the boat ramp anymore, Ernie tells him, when they go to pick grapes together the next day at a vineyard near Grandin. But Lark has no desire to go. He listens to Ernie tell him, as they move down the quiet rows of grapes under a threatening sky, who's been stopping in and which ones he's got with. It sounds to Lark like the customs of a distant tribe in the forest of Sumatra. He has no reason to go there anymore. He no longer has any reason to go anywhere, really. He no longer has to worry when the phone rings that it's a nurse saying his mother has broken her arm, or had a skin tear, because she's dead. That fear, with which he lived for twelve years, is vanished. In its place is an indescribable emptiness, a lightness that is very heavy, a long, golden autumn in north Florida he has no idea what to do with. Forbidden pleasures no longer forbidden now, nothing proscribed. He has no one to disappoint or lie to or feel guilty about. He's like a limb that falls off a tree in a storm and lies there, the leaves green, for several days, as if alive—till finally the leaves turn brown.

He stays home and reads all day and night. He forgets his mother's death when he is reading. The boat ramp, Becker, the paved roads connecting all the little towns around him, he no longer thinks about—he just reads.

Then one evening the phone rings and it's Ernie asking him if he would like to hear "The Letter Song" from *La Périchole.* He goes over and Ernie plays it several times for him, with different singers; and then he tells Lark about the security guard from the prison north of Starke who is very handsome and has started coming to the boat ramp in the early afternoon.

A week later Lark has his car windows tinted, and goes to the boat ramp, and sits there in his car till dark, without once getting out; while other people wonder who it is and finally drive off, tired of waiting.